A Modern Guide
to Demons
and Fallen Angels

A Modern Guide to Demons and Fallen Angels

Paradox Brown

For more information, write to:

PO Box 0794

Roswell, NM

88202-0794

ISBN-10: 1-893788-24-5

ISBN-13: 978-1-893788-24-4

The Scripture versions in this book are throughout the book, and include the NASB, NIV, KJV, NLT, RSV, unless otherwise identified. Copyright is held by the respective owners, and I thank them for their hard work in translation and publication of the Holy Scriptures.

Good Illustrations by Ken Bertin.

Pencil sketches by Paradox Brown

Pictures credited in respective chapter notes, thank you for all contributions. Copyright belonging to the respective owners, and I thank them.

Any official problems, questions, changes, please contact me. I'm new at this.

To my beautiful children :

Ian, Faith, and Grace,

I have loved you, I do love you,

and I will always love you.

Trust Jesus.

Contents

Acknowledgments:

Thank you God and Jesus for helping me understand these things and write about them, and for putting such loving and helpful people in my life.

Thank you to Guy Malone, Joe Jordan, and Pastor Chris Ward, Ken Bertin for all of his illustrations, help and encouragement. Thank you to Joe Palermo for sharing his ideas and perspective, Thank you to Joe Jordan, Mike and Jackie Slack, and Guy Malone for sharing their ideas towards changes in this later revision. Thank you to my Mom and Dad, my brother, and the rest of my family, And thank you to all the people who have been praying for me, and for my children, and for this work to be done. Prayer is powerful, and I thank you all for the blessing you have been to me by your prayer.

My special thanks to Guy, my hero, my husband, and my best friend.

Preface (Why this book?)

I have been a born-again Christian for about six years as of the time of the latest edition of this book. I came from a rather dark spiritual background prior to becoming Christian. As such my personal experiences led me to look for answers about the evil side of the supernatural. I have noticed that there is no concise complete guide for Christians on the subject of the evil side of the supernatural. It is my view that even the best books available are incomplete or inaccurate. Much good information is to be found on the Internet, but unfortunately it is scattered in bits and pieces here and there, and any one webpage will often contain many errors along with truth.

It is my belief that I have a good understanding of these subjects. I have done much research and brainstorming to try to understand my own past evil supernatural experiences, and to understand the history and origins of evil. I wish there had been a guide for me to read when I became Christian on these subjects, something that would explain both the history and powers of evil, as well as information on spiritual warfare methods. There was no such complete guide, which is why I am now writing one. This book takes a Young Earth perspective on Genesis, for reasons why see the appendix (basically I think that's what God wanted), and generally takes the position of inerrancy of the original God-breathed Holy Scriptures. I believe this book is something God wants me to do, for the sake of educating and helping the church.

All information presented herein I believe is true to the best of my knowledge at the time of this writing; I have tried my best. Still I encourage you, and ask you the reader, to prayerfully ask for discernment in reading, because we all make mistakes, and I know,

James 3:1 "Let not many {of you} become teachers, my brethren, knowing that as such we will incur a stricter judgment."

So please pray for discernment in reading, so I may be judged less severely for whatever might be my mistakes herein, and you will surely benefit more from your reading. For in James it also says,

"If any of you lack wisdom, let him ask of God, that giveth to all [men] liberally, and upbraideth not; and it shall be given him. But let him ask in faith, nothing wavering."

So, please pray and ask God to give you wisdom about this material as you read this book.

It is my hope that despite this book being full of such evil, dark, and hate-filled subject matter, that it will be used by you, the reader, as a tool to spread the Light, Good, and Love of the Lord Jesus the Christ.

This book is dedicated in the service of the Lord Jesus the Christ.

A Note on the Timeline Chapters:

What follows is a timeline of fallen angels, including Satan, and also demons, from a Young Earth Creationism perspective. Dates are approximated. I consulted both the Hebrew and the Greek versions of Genesis. There are some points I would like to make before continuing, and those are:

1. I tend to believe that the Greek is not inferior to the Hebrew, and the earliest date possible from combining the information in the two versions is the best date to use. I do not believe at this point it is possible to get the exact year of creation, or the flood, so all ancient years are approximations.

2. The earliest archeological evidence of written language dates back to about 6600 BC, from China. I believe those examples, found on tortoise shells, have been incorrectly dated as too early, or aren't writing at all, or are a deception. They are the exception to the rule. The next earliest record of writing dates to around 4000 BC, which would be within the time period after a Young Earth creation. The point is that there is no proof of humanity before proof of writing. As would be expected with a young Earth and literal reading of Genesis, the earliest found evidence of writing dates to after 5500 BC, which is about when the world was created. The majority of early writing generally dates to after 3500 BC, around the time of the Flood. Radiocarbon dating is not exact, and neither are the dates we can glean from scriptures. But they are close enough to fit in correctly with each other.

3. When God had Moses write the first 5 books of the Bible, and give those books to the people of Israel, God was honest with His people. He meant what He said. At the time, those books, especially Genesis, were all God's people had as the Holy Scriptures. God did not lie to his people. Gap theory is based off of books of the Bible, which were written later, and based off of making room for evolution, an incorrect theory that was invented much later. God made things clear to Israel, God did not lie, and God did not deceive. Genesis was the only book He gave them which dealt specifically with creation. As such, Genesis must stand alone in its interpretation. Using passages from later books of the Bible to add additional material to Genesis is the same thing as saying God lied to his people Israel. God made creation clear to them, and He makes it clear to us also. Genesis stands alone as the truth given about creation, and it must stand alone, and must be weighted

with primary importance in studies of creation. And that being said, all later pieces of scripture that seem to support Gap Theory can in fact be reconciled with a Young Earth interpretation of Genesis, as I will attempt to demonstrate in the following chapters.

Chapter One

First Enoch: Book of the Watchers

I reference to a few parts of the First book of Enoch Book of the Watchers in the first several Timeline chapters of this book. This chapter explains why.

There are 3 books of Enoch. The book of First Enoch is estimated to have on average to have been written between 250 BC and 50 AD. It is the First book of Enoch, which contains a verse that is quoted in Jude, in the Bible, and thus is of interest to us. The book of Second Enoch is estimated to have been written in the late first century AD, and the Third book of Enoch is estimated to have been written in the 5th or 6th century AD. There is no reason to think either the Second or Third book of Enoch might be quoted in inspired scripture, and so we aren't going to be studying them here.

The First Book of Enoch is divided into 5 sections, each of which were written at a different time. They are: The Book of Watchers (chapters 1-36) dated 3rd or early 2nd century BC, The Book of Parables (chapters 37-71) dated late 1st century BC, The Astronomical book (chapters 72-82) dated 3rd century BC, The Book of Dream Visions (chapters 83-90) dated 165-160 BC, The Epistle of Enoch (chapters 91-108) dated early 2nd century BC.

And since these were separate sections, written at separate times, by likely different authors, we are at first are going to focus on the first 36 chapters of First Enoch, which compose the Book of Watchers. This is where the quote in Jude is found. I will refer to this section as First Enoch BW, please understand I am just referring to the Book of the Watchers.

2 Tim 3:14-17 You, however, continue in the things you have learned and become convinced of, knowing from whom you have learned them, and that from childhood you have known the sacred writings which are able to give you the wisdom that leads to salvation through faith which is in Christ Jesus. All Scripture is inspired by God and profitable for teaching, for reproof, for correction, for training in righteousness; so that the man of God may be adequate, equipped for every good work.

With what we can glean from Peter and Jude's letters, and Jude quoting First Enoch, I think it is clear that some of what is taught in First Enoch BW was considered reliable and true by the disciples of Jesus and early church. This would mainly have to do with the Nephilim, the dead of whom are demons, their fallen angel fathers, and the imprisonment of those fallen angels in the Abyss. The applicable verses are:

2 Pet 2:4 "For if God did not spare angels when they sinned, but cast them into Tartarus and committed them to pits of darkness, reserved for judgment"

Jude 1:6 "And angels who did not keep their own domain, but abandoned their proper abode, He has kept in eternal bonds under darkness for the judgment of the great day."

Which line up with:

1 Enoch 10:11-15 And the Lord said unto Michael: Go, bind Semjaza and his associates who have united themselves with women so as to have defiled themselves with them in all their uncleanness. And when their sons have slain one another, and they have seen the destruction of their beloved ones, bind them fast for seventy generations in the valleys of the earth, till the day of their judgment and of their consummation, till the judgment that is for ever and ever is consummated. In those days they shall be led off to the abyss of fire: and to the torment and the prison in which they shall be confined for ever. And whosoever shall be condemned and destroyed will from thenceforth be bound together with them to the end of all generations.

Jude also directly quotes from the First Enoch Book of the Watchers:

Jude 1:14-15 And Enoch also, the seventh from Adam, prophesied of these, saying, Behold, the Lord cometh with ten thousands of his saints, To execute judgment upon all, and to convince all that are ungodly among them of all their ungodly deeds which they have ungodly committed, and of all their hard [speeches] which ungodly sinners have spoken against him.

Which matches

1 Enoch 1:9 And behold! He cometh with ten thousands of His holy ones, To execute judgment upon all, And to destroy all the ungodly: And to convict all flesh of all the works of their ungodliness which they have ungodly committed, And of all the hard things which ungodly sinners have spoken against Him.

Enoch lived 7 generations after Adam, and First Enoch BW was written in the time between Malachi and Matthew, estimated somewhere from about 2nd to 3rd century BC. Some questions arise. How could First Enoch BW authentic if it claims to be written by Enoch, yet the date it was written would show that to be impossible? Jude is the one who declares that it is Enoch, 7th from Adam, himself, who prophesied what Jude quotes from First Enoch.

The real issue here is not whether First Enoch BW was considered canon at some time in the past (which it was in the early Ethiopic Christian church), but the question is how the Christian church should view the book today? Should we accept First Enoch BW as canon in the present? As inspired? As historically reliable? As useful, or not? What do we do with it now?

Also, how can Jude be considered reliable when he quotes from First Enoch BW, saying Enoch wrote it, if Enoch did not in fact write First Enoch BW? If Jude is scripture inspired by God, then Jude could not make the mistake of saying First Enoch BW was written by Enoch if it in fact was not. But Jude has been accepted as Holy Scripture for a long time, and must not be discarded. It can't be. So what is the solution then?

There is actually a Biblically sound and possible solution for how First Enoch BW could have been written when it was written, and still have been words from Enoch himself.

We read in the gospels, of John the Baptist,

"And if you are willing to accept {it,} John himself is Elijah who was to come." Matt 11:14)

Also in Mal 4:5-6 we read, "Behold, I am going to send you Elijah the prophet before the coming of the great and terrible day of the LORD. And he will restore the hearts of the fathers to their children, and the hearts of the children to their fathers, lest I come and smite the land with a curse." In Luke 1:11-17 we read:

And an angel of the Lord appeared to him, standing to the right of the altar of incense. Zacharias was troubled when he saw the angel, and fear gripped him. But the angel said to him, "Do not be afraid, Zacharias, for your petition has been heard, and your wife Elizabeth will bear you a son, and you will give him the name John. "You will have joy and gladness, and many will rejoice at his birth. "For he will be great in the sight of the Lord; and he will drink no wine or liquor, and he will be filled with the Holy Spirit while yet in his mother's womb. "And he will turn many of the sons of Israel back to the Lord their God. "It is he who will go as a forerunner before Him in the spirit and power of Elijah, TO TURN THE HEARTS OF THE FATHERS BACK TO THE CHILDREN, and the disobedient to the attitude of the righteous, so as to make ready a people prepared for the Lord."

It is very interesting that John the Baptist was filled with the Holy Spirit while still in his mother's womb. John the Baptist was somehow "in the spirit and power": the prophet Elijah. Elijah is one of only two men mentioned in the Bible to have not died. We read in the Bible that each man is given one time to die, and then the judgment. Elijah was taken to God without dying, and there we see in some way that John the Baptist was Elijah come again. Therefore, We know Elijah was John the Baptist because Jesus tells us this. Please note, I am not saying reincarnation for any people or person is possible or true as some Eastern religions claim. I do not understand how this worked, that John the Baptist was Elijah, but Jesus said he was, so we know it is true that somehow he was. This was a special situation and circumstance. I do not know exactly what this means, but the only other person in the Bible to not have died, and thus able to be another possible candidate for whatever This was, is Enoch. Both Elijah and Enoch did not die, because God took them up into the sky, still alive.

Therefore, I propose that Enoch also was somehow another person of a new name, 'in the spirit and power of Enoch', who lived from the time between the 2nd and 3rd century BC, in the same way that Elijah was also John the Baptist. God inspired this person, who in this indescribable way was Enoch, to write the line of scripture quoted by Jude out of First Enoch BW. Perhaps this person recorded down what Enoch actually said and did back in the time before the Flood of Noah's days. This person was Enoch in the same way that John the Baptist was Elijah (however it worked and I don't claim to understand how it worked- just that Jesus Himself said it was true that John the Baptist was Elijah. And if you are willing to accept {it,} John himself is Elijah who was to come." (Matt 11:14))

In this, the Holy inspiration of the book of Jude is no longer in question, as well as Peter and Jude's references and beliefs based on information in First Enoch are shown to be valid. In a way, Enoch himself actually did give the words of (at least some of) First Enoch BW. In this there is no conflict. This is a possibility, however it is not provable. But what is absolutely certain is that some parts of First Enoch directly correspond to what both Jude and Peter taught, and things that Jesus seemed aware of, things demons referenced to, and also 1 verse in First Enoch BW is directly quoted by Jude.

If nothing else First Enoch BW seems to clearly contain information that the apostles considered reliable, and as such I think some parts should be taken as historically reliable, if nothing else.

The question that next must be answered is if First Enoch the Book of the Watchers is reliable to any extent, then how much of it, and which parts of it?

I've read First Enoch BW, and erring on the side of caution, analyzed it.

So let's take it a piece at a time:

[Chapter 1] 1 The words of the blessing of Enoch, wherewith he blessed the elect and righteous, who will be 2 living in the day of tribulation, when all the wicked and godless are to be removed. And he took up his parable and said -Enoch a righteous man, whose eyes were opened by God, saw the vision of the Holy One in the heavens, which the angels showed me, and from them I heard everything, and from them I understood as I saw, but not for this generation, but for a remote one which is 3 for to come. Concerning the elect I said, and took up my parable concerning them:

The Holy Great One will come forth from His dwelling, 4 And the eternal God will tread upon the earth, (even) on Mount Sinai, [And appear from His camp] And appear in the strength of His might from the heaven of heavens.5 And all shall be smitten with fear And the Watchers shall quake, And great fear and trembling shall seize them unto the ends of the earth.6 And the high mountains shall be shaken, And the high hills shall be made low, And shall melt like wax before the flame7 And the earth shall be wholly rent in sunder, And all that is upon the earth shall perish, And there shall be a judgment upon all (men). 8 But with the righteous He will make peace. And will protect the elect, And mercy shall be upon them. And they shall all belong to God, And they shall be prospered, And they shall all be blessed. And He will help them all, And light shall appear unto them, And He will make peace with them'. 9 And behold! He cometh with ten thousands of His holy ones To execute judgment upon all, And to destroy all the ungodly: And to convict all flesh Of all the works of their ungodliness which they have ungodly committed, And of all the hard things which ungodly sinners have spoken against Him.

(These underlined verses are directly quoted in the book of Jude, Jude saying Enoch prophesied this himself. This first section of chapter one should all be taken as going together)

[Chapter 2] 1 Observe ye everything that takes place in the heaven, how they do not change their orbits, and the luminaries which are in the heaven, how they all rise and set in order each in its season, and 2 transgress not against their appointed order. Behold ye the earth, and give heed to the things which take place upon it from first to last, how steadfast they are, how none of the things upon earth 3 change, but all the works of God appear to you. Behold the summer and the winter, how the whole earth is filled with water, and clouds and dew and rain lie upon it.

[Chapter 3] Observe and see how (in the winter) all the trees seem as though they had withered and shed all their leaves, except fourteen trees, which do not lose their foliage but retain the old foliage from two to three years till the new comes.

[Chapter 4] And again, observe ye the days of summer how the sun is above the earth over against it. And you seek shade and shelter by reason of the heat of the sun, and the earth also burns with growing heat, and so you cannot tread on the earth, or on a rock by reason of its heat.

[Chapter 5] 1 Observe ye how the trees cover themselves with green leaves and bear fruit: wherefore give ye heed and know with regard to all His works, and recognize how He that liveth for ever hath made them so. 2 And all His works go on thus from year to year for ever, and all the tasks which they accomplish for Him, and their tasks change not, but according as God hath ordained so is it done. 3 And behold how the sea and the rivers in like manner accomplish and change not their tasks from His commandments'.4 But ye -ye have not been steadfast, nor done the commandments of the Lord, But ye have turned away and spoken proud and hard words With your impure mouths against His greatness. Oh, ye hard-hearted, ye shall find no peace. 5 Therefore shall ye execrate your days, And the years of your life shall perish, And the years of your destruction shall be multiplied in eternal execration, And ye shall find no mercy. 6a In those days ye shall make your names an eternal execration unto all the righteous, b And by you shall all who curse, curse, And all the sinners and godless shall imprecate by you, 7c And for you the godless there shall be a curse. 6d And all the . . . shall rejoice, e And there shall be forgiveness of sins, f And every mercy and peace and forbearance: g There shall be salvation unto them, a goodly light. I And for all of you sinners there shall be no salvation, j But on you all shall abide a curse. 7a But for the elect there shall be light and joy and peace, b And they shall inherit the earth. 8 And then there shall be bestowed upon the elect wisdom, And they shall all live and never again sin, Either through ungodliness or through pride: But they who are wise shall be humble. 9 And they shall not again transgress, Nor shall they sin all the days of their life, Nor shall they die of (the divine) anger or wrath, But they shall complete the number of the days of their life. And their lives shall be increased in peace, And the years of their joy shall be multiplied, In eternal gladness and peace, All the days of their life.

I think that chapters 2-5 should also be taken as reliable. They are in fact a continuation of chapter one. The term "elect" is used repeatedly throughout chapters 1-5, and the prophecy has a flow that runs together. Chapter 2 through the beginning of chapter 5 talks a lot about God's command over nature, which seems a break in the flow, but it all ties back in at the end of chapter 5 to match up with the sound of chapter 1. So I think Chapters 1-5 should all be taken as one section of First Enoch BW, and as historically reliable.

Martin McNamara M.S.C., Biblical Scholar, writes of the Book of the Watchers: "This section of 1 Enoch is itself a composite work. It begins with a Parable of Enoch on the lot of the wicked and of the righteous (1-5). Next comes The Book of the Watchers (i.e. the Angels) proper. This recounts the sin of the angels through their sexual union with earthly women, on which follows the demoralization of humankind. We are then told of the doom pronounced by God on the angels and of the joys in store for the just (6-11)..."(Intertestamental Literature, p. 55)

James VanderKam, Professor of Hebrew Scriptures at the University of Notre Dame, write on First Enoch:

"1. Chaps. 1-36 The Book of the Watchers may date from the third century BCE. Parts of its text have been identified on several copies from Qumran cave 4; the earliest fragmentary manuscript (4QEnocha) dates, according to the editor J.T. Milk, to between 200 and 150 BCE. All Qumran copies are in the Aramaic language. This section may be subdivided into several sections:

1-5 a theophany followed by an eschatological admonition

6-11 the angel story (stories)

12-16 Enoch and the failed petition of the angels who descended

17-19 Enoch's first journey

20-36 Enoch's second journey (chap. 20 is a list of angels who are connected with the journeys)"

So chapters 1-5 are considered to be one section, 6-11 a second section, etc.

We could stop here, after section 1-5 which Jude quotes from, but there is information about the fallen angels imprisoned in the Abyss that is given by Peter and Jude, which comes up in the very next section of First Enoch BW. Because Peter and Jude's understanding is in the Holy Bible, and thus basis for church doctrine, there is a major problem that the information they had is nowhere in the Old Testament, and cannot be drawn from the Old Testament. Gen 6 does not give details about the imprisonment of the fallen angels in the Abyss, but Jude and Peter accepted such as truth. There should be some written information that Peter and Jude accepted as solid teaching about the fallen angels and the Abyss, but this is missing from the Bible today. And that information is found in the very next section in First Enoch BW. Here it is:

[Chapter 6] 1 And it came to pass when the children of men had multiplied that in those days were born unto 2 them beautiful and comely daughters. And the angels, the children of the heaven, saw and lusted after them, and said to one another: 'Come, let us choose us wives from among the children of men 3 and beget us children.' And Semjaza, who was their leader, said unto them: 'I fear ye will not 4 indeed agree to do this deed, and I alone shall have to pay the penalty of a great sin.' And they all answered him and said: 'Let us all swear an oath, and all bind ourselves by mutual imprecations 5 not to abandon this plan but to do this thing.' Then sware they all together and bound themselves 6 by mutual imprecations upon it. And they were in all two hundred; who descended in the days of Jared on the summit of Mount Hermon, and they called it Mount Hermon, because they had sworn 7 and bound themselves by mutual imprecations upon it. And these are the names of their leaders: Samlazaz, their leader, Araklba, Rameel, Kokablel, Tamlel, Ramlel, Danel, Ezeqeel, Baraqijal, 8 Asael, Armaros, Batarel, Ananel, Zaq1el, Samsapeel, Satarel, Turel, Jomjael, Sariel. These are their chiefs of tens.

[Chapter 7] 1 And all the others together with them took unto themselves wives, and each chose for himself one, and they began to go in unto them and to defile themselves with them, and they taught them charms 2 and enchantments, and the cutting of roots, and made them acquainted with plants. And they 3 became pregnant, and they bare great giants, whose height was three thousand ells: Who consumed 4 all the acquisitions of men. And when men could no longer sustain them, the giants turned against 5 them and devoured mankind. And they began to sin against birds, and beasts, and reptiles, and 6 fish, and to devour one another's flesh, and drink the blood. Then the earth laid accusation against the lawless ones.

[Chapter 8] 1 And Azazel taught men to make swords, and knives, and shields, and breastplates, and made known to them the metals of the earth and the art of working them, and bracelets, and ornaments, and the use of antimony, and the beautifying of the eyelids, and all kinds of costly stones, and all 2 colouring tinctures. And there arose much godlessness, and they committed fornication, and they 3 were led astray, and became corrupt in all their ways. Semjaza taught enchantments, and root-cuttings, 'Armaros the resolving of enchantments, Baraqijal (taught) astrology, Kokabel the constellations, Ezeqeel the knowledge of the clouds, Araqiel the signs of the earth, Shamsiel the signs of the sun, and Sariel the course of the moon. And as men perished, they cried, and their cry went up to heaven . . .

[Chapter 9] 1 And then Michael, Uriel, Raphael, and Gabriel looked down from heaven and saw much blood being 2 shed upon the earth, and all lawlessness being wrought upon the earth. And they said one to another: 'The earth made without inhabitant cries the voice of their cryingst up to the gates of heaven. 3 And now to you, the holy ones of heaven, the souls of men make their suit, saying, "Bring our cause 4 before the Most High."' And they said to the Lord of the ages: 'Lord of lords, God of gods, King of kings, and God of the ages, the throne of Thy glory (standeth) unto all the generations of the 5 ages, and Thy name holy and glorious and blessed unto all the ages! Thou hast made all things, and power over all things hast Thou: and all things are naked and open in Thy sight, and Thou seest all 6 things, and nothing can hide itself from Thee. Thou seest what Azazel hath done, who hath taught all unrighteousness on earth and revealed the eternal secrets which were (preserved) in heaven, which 7 men were striving to learn: And Semjaza, to whom Thou hast given authority to bear rule over his associates. And they have gone to the daughters of men upon the earth, and have slept with the 9 women, and have defiled themselves, and revealed to them all kinds of sins. And the women have 10 borne giants, and the whole earth has thereby been filled with blood and unrighteousness. And now, behold, the souls of those who have died are crying and making their suit to the gates of heaven, and their lamentations have ascended: and cannot cease because of the lawless deeds which are 11 wrought on the earth. And Thou knowest all things before they come to pass, and Thou seest these things and Thou dost suffer them, and Thou dost not say to us what we are to do to them in regard to these.'

[Chapter 10] 1 Then said the Most High, the Holy and Great One spake, and sent Uriel to the son of Lamech, 2 and said to him: 'Go to Noah and tell him in my name "Hide thyself!" and reveal to him the end that is approaching: that the whole earth will be destroyed, and a deluge is about to come 3 upon the whole earth, and will destroy all that is on it. And now instruct him that he may escape 4 and his seed may be preserved for all the generations of the world.' And again the Lord said to Raphael: 'Bind Azazel hand and foot, and cast him into the darkness: and make an opening 5 in the desert, which is in Dudael, and cast him therein. And place upon him rough and jagged rocks, and cover him with darkness, and let him abide there for ever, and cover his face that he may 6,7 not see light. And on the day of the great judgment he shall be cast into the fire. And heal the earth which the angels have corrupted, and proclaim the healing of the earth, that they may heal the plague, and that all the children of men may not perish through all the secret things that the 8 Watchers have disclosed and have taught their sons. And the whole earth has been corrupted 9 through the works that were taught by Azazel: to him ascribe all sin.' And to Gabriel said the Lord: 'Proceed against the bastards and the reprobates, and against the children of fornication: and destroy [the children of fornication and] the children of the Watchers from amongst men [and cause them to go forth]: send them one against the other that they may destroy each other in 10 battle: for length of days shall they not have. And no request that they (i.e. their fathers) make of thee shall be granted unto their fathers on their behalf; for they hope to live an eternal life, and 11 that each one of them will live five hundred years.' And the Lord said unto Michael: 'Go, bind Semjaza and his associates who have united themselves with women so as to have defiled themselves 12 with them in all their uncleanness. And when their sons have slain one another, and they have seen the destruction of their beloved ones, bind them fast for seventy generations in the valleys of the earth, till the day of their judgment and of their consummation, till the judgment that is 13 for ever and ever is consummated. In those days they shall be led off to the abyss of fire: and 14 to the torment and the prison in which they shall be confined for ever. And whosoever shall be condemned and destroyed will from thenceforth be bound together with them to the end of all 15 generations. And destroy all the spirits of the reprobate and the children of the Watchers, because 16 they have wronged mankind. Destroy all wrong from the face of the earth and let every evil work come to an end: and let the plant of righteousness and truth appear: and it shall prove a blessing; the works of righteousness and truth' shall be planted in truth and joy for evermore.17 And then shall all the righteous escape, And shall live till they beget thousands of children, And all the days of their youth and their old age Shall they complete in peace.18 And then shall the whole earth be tilled in righteousness, and shall all be planted with trees and 19 be full of blessing. And all desirable trees shall be planted on it, and they shall plant vines on it: and the vine which they plant thereon shall yield wine in abundance, and as for all the seed which is sown thereon each measure (of it) shall bear a thousand, and each measure of olives shall yield 20 ten presses of oil. And cleanse thou the earth from all oppression, and from all unrighteousness, and from all sin, and from all godlessness: and all the uncleanness that is wrought upon the earth 21 destroy from off the earth. And all the children of men shall become righteous, and all nations 22 shall offer adoration and shall praise Me, and all shall worship Me. And the earth shall be cleansed from all defilement, and from all sin, and from all punishment, and from all torment, and I will never again send (them) upon it from generation to generation and for ever.

[Chapter 11] 1 And in those days I will open the store chambers of blessing which are in the heaven, so as to send 2 them down upon the earth over the work and labour of the children of men. And truth and peace shall be associated together throughout all the days of the world and throughout all the generations of men.'

In section 6-11 is found understanding of what Peter and Jude referenced to when they said:

2 Pet 2:4 "For if God did not spare angels when they sinned, but cast them into Tartarus and committed them to pits of darkness, reserved for judgment"

Jude 1:6 "And angels who did not keep their own domain, but abandoned their proper abode, He has kept in eternal bonds under darkness for the judgment of the great day."

I see nothing in this section which conflicts with the Bible, but rather it seems to be a work which is referenced to in the Bible for information by Peter and Jude, as being at least historically reliable.

However, this section 6-11 does not explain why demons are fearful and dread the Abyss place, as seen in Luke 8:31,

"Jesus asked him, "What is your name?" "Legion," he replied, because many demons had gone into him. And they begged him repeatedly not to order them to go into the Abyss."

An explanation for the familiarity of demons with the Abyss, and their dread of it, this is found in chapters 12-16.

[Chapter 12] 1 Before these things Enoch was hidden, and no one of the children of men knew where he was 2 hidden, and where he abode, and what had become of him. And his activities had to do with the Watchers, and his days were with the holy ones. 3 And I Enoch was blessing the Lord of majesty and the King of the ages, and lo! the Watchers 4 called me -Enoch the scribe- and said to me: 'Enoch, thou scribe of righteousness, go, declare to the Watchers of the heaven who have left the high heaven, the holy eternal place, and have defiled themselves with women, and have done as the children of earth do, and have taken unto themselves 5 wives: "Ye have wrought great destruction on the earth: And ye shall have no peace nor forgiveness 6 of sin: and inasmuch as they delight themselves in their children, The murder of their beloved ones shall they see, and over the destruction of their children shall they lament, and shall make supplication unto eternity, but mercy and peace shall ye not attain."'

[Chapter 13] 1 And Enoch went and said: 'Azazel, thou shalt have no peace: a severe sentence has gone forth 2 against thee to put thee in bonds: And thou shalt not have toleration nor request granted to thee, because of the unrighteousness which thou hast taught, and because of all the works of godlessness 3 and unrighteousness and sin which thou hast shown to men.' Then I went and spoke to them all 4 together, and they were all afraid, and fear and trembling seized them. And they besought me to draw up a petition for them that they might find forgiveness, and to read their petition in the presence 5 of the Lord of heaven. For from thenceforward they could not speak (with Him) nor lift up their 6 eyes to heaven for shame of their sins for which they had been condemned. Then I wrote out their petition, and the prayer in regard to their spirits and their deeds individually and in regard to their 7 requests that they should have forgiveness and length. And I went off and sat down at the waters of Dan, in the land of Dan, to the south of the west of Hermon: I read their petition till I fell 8 asleep. And behold a dream came to me, and visions fell down upon me, and I saw visions of chastisement, and a voice came bidding (me) I to tell it to the sons of heaven, and reprimand them. 9 And when I awaked, I came unto them, and they were all sitting gathered together, weeping in 10 'Abelsjail, which is between Lebanon and Seneser, with their faces covered. And I recounted before them all the visions which I had seen in sleep, and I began to speak the words of righteousness, and to reprimand the heavenly Watchers.

[Chapter 14] 1 The book of the words of righteousness, and of the reprimand of the eternal Watchers in accordance 2 with the command of the Holy Great One in that vision. I saw in my sleep what I will now say with a tongue of flesh and with the breath of my mouth: which the Great One has given to men to 3 converse therewith and understand with the heart. As He has created and given to man the power of understanding the word of wisdom, so hath He created me also and given me the power of reprimanding 4 the Watchers, the children of heaven. I wrote out your petition, and in my vision it appeared thus, that your petition will not be granted unto you throughout all the days of eternity, and that judgment 5 has been finally passed upon you: yea (your petition) will not be granted unto you. And from henceforth you shall not ascend into heaven unto all eternity, and in bonds of the earth the decree 6 has gone forth to bind you for all the days of the world. And (that) previously you shall have seen the destruction of your beloved sons and ye shall have no pleasure in them, but they shall fall before 7 you by the sword. And your petition on their behalf shall not be granted, nor yet on your own: even though you weep and pray and speak all the words contained in the writing which I have 8 written. And the vision was shown to me thus: Behold, in the vision clouds invited me and a mist summoned me, and the course of the stars and the lightnings sped and hastened me, and the winds in 9 the vision caused me to fly and lifted me upward, and bore me into heaven. And I went in till I drew nigh to a wall which is built of crystals and surrounded by tongues of fire: and it began to affright 10 me. And I went into the tongues of fire and drew nigh to a large house which was built of crystals: and the walls of the house were like a tesselated floor (made) of crystals, and its groundwork was 11 of crystal. Its ceiling was like the path of the stars and the lightnings, and between them were 12 fiery cherubim, and their heaven was (clear as) water. A flaming fire surrounded the walls, and its 13 portals blazed with fire. And I entered into that house, and it was hot as fire and cold as ice: there 14 were no delights of life therein: fear covered me, and trembling got hold upon me. And as I quaked 15 and trembled, I fell upon my face. And I beheld a vision, And lo! there was a second house, greater 16 than the former, and the entire portal stood open before me, and it was built of flames of fire. And in every respect it so excelled in splendour and magnificence and extent that I cannot describe to 17 you its splendour and its extent. And its floor was of fire, and above it were lightnings and the path 18 of the stars, and its ceiling also was flaming fire. And I looked and saw therein a lofty throne: its appearance was as crystal, and the wheels thereof as the shining sun, and there was the vision of 19 cherubim. And from underneath the throne came streams of flaming fire so that I could not look 20 thereon. And the Great Glory sat thereon, and His raiment shone more brightly than the sun and 21 was whiter than any snow. None of the angels could enter and could behold His face by reason 22 of the magnificence and glory and no flesh could behold Him. The flaming fire was round about Him, and a great fire stood before Him, and none around could draw nigh Him: ten thousand times 23 ten thousand (stood) before Him, yet He needed no counselor. And the most holy ones who were 24 nigh to Him did not leave by night nor depart from Him. And until then I had been prostrate on my face, trembling: and the Lord called me with His own mouth, and said to me: ' Come hither, 25 Enoch, and hear my word.' And one of the holy ones came to me and waked me, and He made me rise up and approach the door: and I bowed my face downwards.

[Chapter 15] 1 And He answered and said to me, and I heard His voice: 'Fear not, Enoch, thou righteous 2 man and scribe of righteousness: approach hither and hear my voice. And go, say to the Watchers of heaven, who have sent thee to intercede for them: "You should intercede" for men, and not men 3 for you: Wherefore have ye left the high, holy, and eternal heaven, and lain with women, and defiled yourselves with the daughters of men and taken to yourselves wives, and done like the children 4 of earth, and begotten giants (as your) sons? And though ye were holy, spiritual, living the eternal life, you have defiled yourselves with the blood of women, and have begotten (children) with the blood of flesh, and, as the children of men, have lusted after flesh and blood as those also do who die 5 and perish. Therefore have I given them wives also that they might impregnate them, and beget 6 children by them, that thus nothing might be wanting to them on earth. But you were formerly 7 spiritual, living the eternal life, and immortal for all generations of the world. And therefore I have not appointed wives for you; for as for the spiritual ones of the heaven, in heaven is their dwelling. 8 And now, the giants, who are produced from the spirits and flesh, shall be called evil spirits upon 9 the earth, and on the earth shall be their dwelling. Evil spirits have proceeded from their bodies; because they are born from men and from the holy Watchers is their beginning and primal origin; 10 they shall be evil spirits on earth, and evil spirits shall they be called. [As for the spirits of heaven, in heaven shall be their dwelling, but as for the spirits of the earth which were born upon the earth, on the earth shall be their dwelling.] And the spirits of the giants afflict, oppress, destroy, attack, do battle, and work destruction on the earth, and cause trouble: they take no food, but nevertheless 12 hunger and thirst, and cause offences. And these spirits shall rise up against the children of men and against the women, because they have proceeded from them.

[Chapter 16] 1 From the days of the slaughter and destruction and death of the giants, from the souls of whose flesh the spirits, having gone forth, shall destroy without incurring judgment -thus shall they destroy until the day of the consummation, the great judgment in which the age shall be 2 consummated, over the Watchers and the godless, yea, shall be wholly consummated." And now as to the watchers who have sent thee to intercede for them, who had been aforetime in heaven, (say 3 to them): "You have been in heaven, but all the mysteries had not yet been revealed to you, and you knew worthless ones, and these in the hardness of your hearts you have made known to the women, and through these mysteries women and men work much evil on earth." 4 Say to them therefore: " You have no peace."'

It is in section 12-16 that we can find the clarification that the Nephilim spirits, when their bodies dies, became evil spirits upon the earth, also known as demons. This would explain why the demons are afraid of being sent to the Abyss, a place rarely referenced in the Bible, for the demons remember a time when their fallen angel fathers were imprisoned in the Abyss.

Chapters 6-16 cover all the vital information about the fallen angels that we need in order to understand where Peter and Jude were getting their information, and this verse in Luke. I see nothing here that is in conflict with already accepted Holy Scriptures. I would accept chapters 6-16 as being historically reliable.

Moving on:

[Chapter 17] 1 And they took and brought me to a place in which those who were there were like flaming fire, 2 and, when they wished, they appeared as men. And they brought me to the place of darkness, and to a mountain the point of whose summit reached to heaven. And I saw the places of the luminaries and the treasuries of the stars and of the thunder and in the uttermost depths, where were 4 a fiery bow and arrows and their quiver, and a fiery sword and all the lightnings. And they took 5 me to the living waters, and to the fire of the west, which receives every setting of the sun. And I came to a river of fire in which the fire flows like water and discharges itself into the great sea towards 6 the west. I saw the great rivers and came to the great river and to the great darkness, and went 7 to the place where no flesh walks. I saw the mountains of the darkness of winter and the place 8 whence all the waters of the deep flow. I saw the mouths of all the rivers of the earth and the mouth of the deep.

[Chapter 18] 1 I saw the treasuries of all the winds: I saw how He had furnished with them the whole creation 2 and the firm foundations of the earth. And I saw the corner-stone of the earth: I saw the four 3 winds which bear [the earth and] the firmament of the heaven. And I saw how the winds stretch out the vaults of heaven, and have their station between heaven and earth: these are the pillars 4 of the heaven. I saw the winds of heaven which turn and bring the circumference of the sun and 5 all the stars to their setting. I saw the winds on the earth carrying the clouds: I saw the paths 6 of the angels. I saw at the end of the earth the firmament of the heaven above. And I proceeded and saw a place which burns day and night, where there are seven mountains of magnificent stones, 7 three towards the east, and three towards the south. And as for those towards the east, was of coloured stone, and one of pearl, and one of jacinth, and those towards the south of red stone. 8 But the middle one reached to heaven like the throne of God, of alabaster, and the summit of the 9,10 throne was of sapphire. And I saw a flaming fire. And beyond these mountains Is a region the end of the great earth: there the heavens were completed. And I saw a deep abyss, with columns of heavenly fire, and among them I saw columns of fire fall, which were beyond measure alike towards 12 the height and towards the depth. And beyond that abyss I saw a place which had no firmament of the heaven above, and no firmly founded earth beneath it: there was no water upon it, and no 13 birds, but it was a waste and horrible place. I saw there seven stars like great burning mountains, 14 and to me, when I inquired regarding them, The angel said: 'This place is the end of heaven and earth: this has become a prison for the stars and the host of heaven. And the stars which roll over the fire are they which have transgressed the commandment of the Lord in the beginning of 16 their rising, because they did not come forth at their appointed times. And He was wroth with them, and bound them till the time when their guilt should be consummated (even) for ten thousand years.'

[Chapter 19] 1 And Uriel said to me: 'Here shall stand the angels who have connected themselves with women, and their spirits assuming many different forms are defiling mankind and shall lead them astray into sacrificing to demons as gods, (here shall they stand,) till the day of the great judgment in 2 which they shall be judged till they are made an end of. And the women also of the angels who 3 went astray shall become sirens.' And I, Enoch, alone saw the vision, the ends of all things: and no man shall see as I have seen.

I consider chapters 17-19 to be questionable as to their reliability, because

28

they seem to be a separate section from chapters 6-16. I also am not sure how essential the information therein would be to Peter and Jude's understanding, which their letters show they possessed. And we are getting further and further away from that which is confirmed by Holy Scripture (chapter 1 verse 9). Apparently my view on this coincides with James C. Vanderkam (Professor of Hebrew Scriptures at the University of Notre Dame), who also places 17-19 as a section, and chapters 20-36 as another final section.

However, some interesting things are brought out in chapters 17-19. One is that though chapter 10:12 says the fallen angels are to bound in the valleys of the earth, also called the Abyss or Tartarus, chapter 17 says they are bound at the end of heaven and earth. 2 Pet 2 says the fallen angels are bound in chains of darkness, and Jude says in darkness as well. But in 2nd Peter is a reference to the chains in specific. Yet 1 Enoch 18:10-14 describes this prison as containing heavenly fire, and the place sounds luminous, not deep darkness. There seems to be a conflict here between chapters 17-19 and Jude on the issue of darkness of the Abyss. As to the location of the Abyss, it must both be in the valleys of the earth, and at the end of heaven and earth, if 17-19 are reliable, and this seems to conflict. One possibility, as fallen angels are higher-dimensional beings as I describe in another chapter, is that the scene described in chapters 17-19 is on a higher-dimensional plane, yet the location of this higher-dimensional prison is still in the valleys of the earth. The term Abyss can refer to deep oceans, and tends to imply the location is below the earth, below the lowest depths of the sea, under the ground, in the earth. If the prison of the fallen angels is on a higher-dimensional plane, then it of course is not going to be found by 4 dimensional instrumentation or searching for it, but might have a general location in the world in the 4 dimensional sense. Yet, in plain wording and straight-forward understanding, there is a direct conflict between a luminous place and a place of darkness.

Another interesting thing is that the "women also of the angels who went astray shall become sirens". I am not sure what a siren technically is, but it may be a term referring to a female demon. If that is the case, then this fits in very well with ideas I will present later, that the fallen angels sired Nephilim, which sired daughters, and those daughters when they died became disembodied evil spirits, a.k.a. demons. If these verses are interpreted that way, then it makes sense. However if these verses are taken to mean that the human women who mated with the fallen angels became female demons, or really Anything different than just a normal dead person when they died, then these verses must be taken as unreliable, definitely conflicting scripture, because that isn't true. Humans don't become demons.

The next section I will include is chapters 20-22. I do not believe these are reliable whatsoever.

[Chapter 20] 1,2 And these are the names of the holy angels who watch. Uriel, one of the holy angels, who is 3 over the world and over Tartarus. Raphael, one of the holy angels, who is over the spirits of men. 4,5 Raguel, one of the holy angels who takes vengeance on the world of the luminaries. Michael, one 6 of the holy angels, to wit, he that is set over the best part of mankind and over chaos. Saraqael, 7 one of the holy angels, who is set over the spirits, who sin in the spirit. Gabriel, one of the holy 8 angels, who is over Paradise and the serpents and the Cherubim. Remiel, one of the holy angels, whom God set over those who rise.

In chapter 20 it starts with a list of the names of angels and what they are in charge of. Nowhere in Holy scripture do we see God tell us these things. The names of the angels are typically things that it seems God discourages us from learning about. That is because people have been too inclined to develop a worshipful fascination with angels. The information and style here is very different from anything in established scripture. The list of fallen angels earlier in Enoch is irrelevant when it comes to interaction with those fallen angels because they are now imprisoned in the Abyss. Some Holy Angels are mentioned earlier in First Enoch, but only in passing. Nowhere else is the main point of the passage that we learn the names of angels and what they do. Nowhere in the Bible is this kind of information or list found either. This chapter just strikes me as entirely uninspired scripture, and contradictory to the Bible in its type of content.

[Chapter 21] 1,2 And I proceeded to where things were chaotic. And I saw there something horrible: I saw neither 3 a heaven above nor a firmly founded earth, but a place chaotic and horrible. And there I saw 4 seven stars of the heaven bound together in it, like great mountains and burning with fire. Then 5 I said: 'For what sin are they bound, and on what account have they been cast in hither?' Then said Uriel, one of the holy angels, who was with me, and was chief over them, and said: 'Enoch, why 6 dost thou ask, and why art thou eager for the truth? These are of the number of the stars of heaven, which have transgressed the commandment of the Lord, and are bound here till ten thousand years, 7 the time entailed by their sins, are consummated.' And from thence I went to another place, which was still more horrible than the former, and I saw a horrible thing: a great fire there which burnt and blazed, and the place was cleft as far as the abyss, being full of great descending columns of 8 fire: neither its extent or magnitude could I see, nor could I conjecture. Then I said: 'How 9 fearful is the place and how terrible to look upon!' Then Uriel answered me, one of the holy angels who was with me, and said unto me: 'Enoch, why hast thou such fear and affright?' And 10 I answered: 'Because of this fearful place, and because of the spectacle of the pain.' And he said unto me: 'This place is the prison of the angels, and here they will be imprisoned for ever.'

Here we see the same scene repeated, redundantly, that was mentioned earlier in chapters 17-19. One of the key differences here is that here the angels are said to be imprisoned for a concrete "ten thousand years" which is a very defined period of time. In earlier, likely reliable portions, we are told they will be imprisoned for "even for ten thousand years" which is a loose term that implies a very long time, even up to or past ten thousand years. And we were also told they will be imprisoned "for seventy generations" which is another loose term, an unspecified long time. This is more the style of inspired scripture. We do not know exactly when Jesus will return, thus marking the beginning of His 1000 year reign on this Earth. And thus we don't know exactly when that will end and the day of judgment will come, following the end of Jesus' blessed 1000 year reign on Earth. And it is on the day of judgment that the fallen angels in the Abyss will stand judgment. So the Bible leaves the date unspecified of their release and judgment. As such, in keeping with scripture, potentially inspired portions of First Enoch would not give us a specific amount of time. There is a big difference between "even for ten thousand years" and "for ten thousand years"; the first is vague and the second is not. And so chapter 21 I would not consider reliable historically nor prophetically.

[Chapter 22] 1 And thence I went to another place, and he mountain [and] of hard rock. 2 And there was in it four hollow places, deep and wide and very smooth. How smooth are the hollow places and deep and dark to look at. 3 Then Raphael answered, one of the holy angels who was with me, and said unto me: 'These hollow places have been created for this very purpose, that the spirits of the souls of the dead should 4 assemble therein, yea that all the souls of the children of men should assemble here. And these places have been made to receive them till the day of their judgment and till their appointed period [till the period appointed], till the great judgment (comes) upon them.' I saw (the spirit of) a dead man making suit, 5 and his voice went forth to heaven and made suit. And I asked Raphael the angel who was 6 with me, and I said unto him: 'This spirit which maketh suit, whose is it, whose voice goeth forth and maketh suit to heaven ?' 7 And he answered me saying: 'This is the spirit which went forth from Abel, whom his brother Cain slew, and he makes his suit against him till his seed is destroyed from the face of the earth, and his seed is annihilated from amongst the seed of men.' 8 The I asked regarding it, and regarding all the hollow places: 'Why is one separated from the other?' 9 And he answered me and said unto me: 'These three have been made that the spirits of the dead might be separated. And such a division has been make (for) the spirits of the righteous, in which there is the bright spring of 10 water. And such has been made for sinners when they die and are buried in the earth and judgment has not been executed on them in their 11 lifetime. Here their spirits shall be set apart in this great pain till the great day of judgment and punishment and torment of those who curse for ever and retribution for their spirits. There 12 He shall bind them for ever. And such a division has been made for the spirits of those who make their suit, who make disclosures concerning their destruction, when they were slain in the days 13 of the sinners. Such has been made for the spirits of men who were not righteous but sinners, who were complete in transgression, and of the transgressors they shall be companions: but their spirits shall not be slain in the day of judgment nor shall they be raised from thence.' 14 The I blessed the Lord of glory and said: 'Blessed be my Lord, the Lord of righteousness, who ruleth for ever.'

In Chapter 22 there are several problems. First is the idea that Sheol has chambers. There is nothing else in the Bible, when it's understood as it was written, that supports this idea that Sheol (the grave) has chambers. The Grave is better understood as a state of being rather than a place, in my opinion. In any case, the only place in which any place of the dead is mentioned to have sections would be Hades, mentioned in Luke as containing Abraham's Bosom and Hades. This was a parable based off of a commonly known and understood pagan fable found in the Gemara Babylonicum, which drew from pagan concepts of Hades and the afterlife. It was popular and known among the Pharisees and Sadducees which Jesus was talking to when Jesus said this parable. As such, being a parable drawn from a commonly-known fable of the time, it was never meant to overshadow the rest of the Bible (which never mentions Sheol having sections) and be used to teach doctrine in this way. The 2 sides of Hades in the parable are analogously representative of the 2 places one may go after the resurrection of the dead and the judgment. But to use this parable to teach that Sheol has compartments is like using the parable of the sheep and goats to say all Christians will be turned into literal sheep in Heaven. That is not the case, it is just a parable in that sense. And so because nowhere in the entire Bible is it taught that Sheol has sections, we can safely disregard this section of First Enoch as unreliable and uninspired.

There is an even more convincing point to be made that shows chapter 22 is unreliable historically, and uninspired. It states "but their spirits shall not be slain in the day of judgment nor shall they be raised from thence" (thence being Sheol). What this tries to say is that some of the dead will not be raised out of Sheol at the judgment. That contradicts the Bible very clearly. And so chapters 20 and 21 I feel I have shown somewhat convincingly are not reliable, and I hope it is glaringly obvious that chapter 22 is definitely not reliable nor inspired. So by this point, erring on the side of caution, the rest of First Enoch BW has to be thrown out as unreliable as well. There is simply no way to safely accept any of the rest of it as reliable, because the established historically reliable section is over and done with, with no connection to later portions.

So for that reason I'm not going to bother doing analysis on the rest of First Enoch BW.

It is my belief that the first 16 chapters of First Enoch, the Book of the Watchers, should be taken as mostly being historically reliable, as they were very likely accepted by the apostles as such. But I only think this about the first 16 chapters. This reliability I think should especially be said about the sections which the apostles clearly reference to in the Bible. There is nothing in the rest of First Enoch that I see as being possibly reliable or inspired scripture, nor do I know of any Biblical reason to consider examining it, so I am not. The rest doesn't tie into the Bible like First Enoch the Book of the Watchers 1-16.

However, I do not think that First Enoch Book of the Watchers 1-16 should be taken as inspired scripture, as the book exists today, because of the verse that reads "3000 ells" (300 ft.) for the height of the giant Nephilim. This is five times the height of the tallest dinosaur ever found (60 ft.), and it seems unlikely that any giant could reach this height. This verse seems to be corrupted, probably from "300 ells" (30 ft.) in some copying error, possibly. So the first 16 chapters can not be assumed to be uncorrupted from the original, in total, despite that certain key information referenced by the apostles seems historically reliable and drawn from by them.

So, I think heavy weight of historical reliability should be given to chapters 1-16 especially in the parts referenced to in the NT. This is information which is found nowhere else in the Bible, yet referenced in the Bible as historically reliable. I think these sections are in some ways historically reliable and were accepted by the apostles and early church. However, these sections could not be accepted in total with the same trustworthiness as inspired scripture.

Chapter Two

A Timeline of Demons and Fallen Angels (The Beginning to the Flood)

In the Beginning....

~5516 BC God created everything in 6 24-hour days

On the First Day God Created the Heavens, including their host. All the angels were created on the first day, as God "created the heavens".

Gen 1:1-5 "In the beginning God created the heavens and the earth. Now the earth was formless and empty, darkness was over the surface of the deep, and the Spirit of God was hovering over the waters. And God said, "Let there be light," and there was light. God saw that the light was good, and He separated the light from the darkness. God called the light "day," and the darkness he called "night." And there was evening, and there was morning, the first day."

Nowhere are we told the details of the creation of the angels, sons of God, morning stars, or whichever term that is used to refer to the host of heaven. We know they are the host of heaven, and as such it makes sense to think they were created with the Heaven. God created the heaven, and the earth. First God created the heaven, and then second the earth, that is the order told in Genesis. This understanding is reflected in Job.

Job 38: 4-7 [God says to Job] "Where were you when I laid the earth's foundation? Tell me, if you understand. Who marked off its dimensions? Surely you know! Who stretched a measuring line across it? On what were its footings set, or who laid its cornerstone- while the morning stars sang together and all the angels shouted for joy?"

This shows the angels, including Satan, were present before the foundations of the Earth were laid- thus when God "created the heavens". In between when God "created the heavens" and "the earth" is when all the morning stars sang together and all the angels shouted for joy. And Satan was one of the singers and shouters.

It is important to note that the "earth" God made originally was made out of water, not land. Water was the original composition of the Earth. The Earth was originally made of water, as the word for "deep" in Hebrew, "thowm" (8415) means deep waters. This is further supported by:

2 Pet 3:3-7, "Know this first of all, that in the last days mockers will come with their mocking, following after their own lusts, and saying, "Where is the promise of His coming? For ever since the fathers fell asleep, all continues just as it was from the beginning of creation." For when they maintain this, it escapes their notice that by the word of God the heavens existed long ago and the earth was formed out of water and by water, through which the world at that time was destroyed, being flooded with water. But by His word the present heavens and earth are being reserved for fire, kept for the day of judgment and destruction of ungodly men."

Here we see the understanding that Peter had 2000 years ago, that the earth was formed out of water and by water. Originally the earth was water. When Genesis says darkness was upon the face of the deep (waters) it is because originally the earth was water when it was first made, formless, and void. There was no pre-adamic creation, or pre-adamic flood. The world was not in ruin from some pre-adamic civilization ruled by Satan. That is simply a lie. That lie is designed to make Satan out to seem more important than he ever really was. It is a lie that serves to bring renown and attention to Satan, and it simply isn't true.

People try to say that Jesus called Satan the "prince of this world" because he was here first, before Adam. That isn't true. Satan is prince of this world because power was handed over to him much later by other angels in power after they chose to rebel against God. (See Chapter 4 and other later chapters for more detail) But when Adam sinned, death came into the world, and then Satan gained some power, because he was the angel in charge of keeping people from the tree of life. Before Adam sinned, Satan did not hold that power. But Satan did receive that important anointing and ordination after the fall, as it says in Ezekiel:

Eze 28:11-14 "Then this further message came to me from the LORD: "Son of man, weep for the king of Tyre. Give him this message from the Sovereign LORD: You were the perfection of wisdom and beauty. You were in Eden, the garden of God. Your clothing was adorned with every precious stone-- red carnelian, chrysolite, white moonstone, beryl, onyx, jasper, sapphire, turquoise, and emerald--all beautifully crafted for you and set in the finest gold. They were given to you on the day you were created. I ordained and anointed you as the mighty angelic guardian. You had access to the holy mountain of God and walked among the stones of fire."

The King of Tyre here refers to the Spiritual ruler of Tyre at the time, who was Satan. On the first day Satan received special clothes made of precious stones, and later was in Eden. That means when God "created the heavens" on the first day, Satan at that time was created, and on that first day at some point he received special clothes, laden with precious jewels and stones. Later, after God made Eden, on the 6th day, Satan was in Eden. And Satan was ordained and anointed as the mighty angelic guardian, my guess would be a guardian over the tree of life, and thus the guardian over death. And what is death but the eventual result of not being able to sustain life?

I think the explanation is that Satan was the cherubim mentioned in:

Gen 3:24, "So He drove the man out; and at the east of the garden of Eden He stationed the cherubim and the flaming sword which turned every direction to guard the way to the tree of life."

This is the only "mighty angelic guardian" ordained and anointed, that is mentioned in reference to the time of Eden. In general, keeping people from the Tree of Life and thus immortality, resulted in focus on death, as well as authority over those that will die. Satan is the angel of death, insomuch as he is the angel responsible for keeping people from life by keeping them from the tree of life. More power was later given to him by other angels that subsequently fell, which is why by Jesus' time it was true for Jesus to call Satan the prince of this world. (See Chapter 4 for more detail) It is important to note that if this is the case, that Satan was not anointed as such until after Adam and Eve had already sinned, with the serpent (Satan's) full involvement. This anointing would not in any way have compelled Satan to be evil. If this is the case that Satan was the anointed cherub mentioned in Gen 3:24, by that point Satan had already shown he was evil, and Jesus' triumph over him had already been prophesied. Let's take a closer look:

On the sixth day God created Adam and Eve.

Gen 1: 26-27, 31 "Then God said, "Let us make man in our image, in our likeness, and let them rule over the fish of the sea and the birds of the air, over the livestock, over all the earth, and over all the creatures that move along the ground." God created man in His own image, in the image of God He created him; male and female He created them...God saw all that He had made, and behold, it was very good. And there was evening and there was morning, the sixth day."

All was very good as of the end of the sixth literal day from the beginning of creation. Thus Satan was not evil as of the end of sixth day, because all was good. The word for "all" here in Hebrew is 'kol' (3605) which means all, the whole all, the whole of any, each, every, anything, totality, everything. Satan had not become evil by the end of the sixth day of creation, the sixth day of Satan's existence.

Then, there was the first Sabbath day, the seventh day (7 evenings and mornings, approximately 24 hour periods) from the beginning. During these sevens days all the hosts (tsaba 6635 refers to angels) were completed including the angels and Satan.

Gen 2:1-4 "Thus the heavens and the earth were completed, and all their hosts. By the seventh day God completed His work which He had done, and He rested on the seventh day from all His work which He had done. Then God blessed the seventh day and sanctified it, because in it He rested from all His work which God had created and made. This is the account of the heavens and the earth when they were created, in the day that the LORD God made earth and heaven."

This is the entire account, folks. This is it. God made everything in 7 literal days, approximately 24 hour periods. Later in the book of Exodus, we learn the Sabbath day, which we are to keep Holy, is because of the original day of rest that God took in the first week of creation.

Exo 20:8-11 "Remember the Sabbath day by keeping it holy. Six days you shall labor and do all your work, but the seventh day is a Sabbath to the LORD your God. On it you shall not do any work, neither you, nor your son or daughter, nor your manservant or maidservant, nor your animals, nor the alien within your gates. For in six days the LORD made the heavens and the earth, the sea, and all that is in them, but he rested on the seventh day. Therefore the LORD blessed the Sabbath day and made it holy."

This is not symbolism devoid of meaning. Everything was made in a week, a literal week. And at the end of the sixth day, Satan was still good and hadn't done anything wrong yet that is recorded, because God saw all he made and it was all good.

Next, Satan convinces the serpent to tempt and deceive Eve, beguiling her. I know Satan was the brains, the serpent was the brawn. I don't know exactly how this worked, but somehow it worked. (Dr. Michael Heiser has some interesting ideas on this involving the word "Nachash") But that Satan was the serpent is confirmed in:

Rev 12:9 "And the great dragon was thrown down, the serpent of old who is called the devil and Satan, who deceives the whole world; he was thrown down to the earth, and his angels were thrown down with him."

Gen 3:1-5 "Now the serpent was more crafty than any beast of the field which the LORD God had made. And he said to the woman, "Indeed, has God said, 'You shall not eat from any tree of the garden'?" The woman said to the serpent, "From the fruit of the trees of the garden we may eat; but from the fruit of the tree which is in the middle of the garden, God has said, 'You shall not eat from it or touch it, or you will die.'" The serpent said to the woman, "You surely will not die! "For God knows that in the day you eat from it your eyes will be opened, and you will be like God, knowing good and evil."

The serpent is physically cursed and the serpent(s) made enemy with Eve's seed.

Gen 14-15 "The LORD God said to the serpent, Because you have done this, Cursed are you more than all cattle, And more than every beast of the field; On your belly you will go, And dust you will eat All the days of your life; And I will put enmity Between you and the woman, And between your seed and her seed;"

This speaks to the fact that humans and snakes have had enmity between them ever since.

Satan and his seed are made enemies of Christians, and Satan's eventual defeat by Jesus Christ is prophesied:

Gen 15-16 "And I will put enmity Between you and the woman, And between your seed and her seed; He shall bruise you on the head, And you shall bruise him on the heel."

The meaning of this ties into a couple other passages of scripture:

*John 8:42-44 "Jesus said to them, "If God were your Father, you would love Me, for I proceeded forth and have come from God, for I have not even come on My own initiative, but He sent Me. "Why do you not understand what I am saying? It is because you cannot hear My word. You are of your father the devil, and you want to do the desires of your father He was a murderer from the beginning, and does not stand in the truth because there is no truth in him Whenever he speaks a lie, he speaks from his own nature, for he is a liar and the father of lies."

One meaning is that when human beings reject Jesus, they are not children of God, but children of Satan, spiritually.

As Jesus also said in Matt 12:30 "He who is not with me is against me, and he who does not gather with me scatters." Another relevant verse is:

*Rev 12:13, 17 "And when the dragon saw that he was thrown down to the earth, he persecuted the woman who gave birth to the male child...So the dragon was enraged with the woman, and went off to make war with the rest of her children, who keep the commandments of God and hold to the testimony of Jesus."

Another way to look at this is that the church is made of the children of God. Eve, Sarah, the nation of Israel, Mary, and the church are all reflective of the woman, and her children are Christians, all Christians from the time of Jesus onwards to now, and Abraham's true children of Old Testament times, who were declared righteous by their faith.

Pre-Flood, before ~ 3284 BC

Some angels sired children with human women. In doing so these angels sinned and became fallen angels. These offspring were hybrids called Nephilim, who were very large giants, probably about 30 feet tall.

Gen 6:2,4 "That the sons of God saw that the daughters of men were beautiful; and they took wives for themselves, whomever they chose...The Nephilim were on the earth in those days, and also afterward, when the sons of God came in to the daughters of men, and they bore children to them. Those were the mighty men who were of old, men of renown."

1 Enoch 6:1-3 "And it came to pass when the children of men had multiplied that in those days were born unto them beautiful and comely daughters. And the angels, the children of the heaven, saw and lusted after them, and said to one another: 'Come, let us choose us wives from among the children of men and beget us children.'"

1 Enoch 7: 2-6 "And they became pregnant, and they bare great giants, whose height was three thousand ells: Who consumed all the acquisitions of men. And when men could no longer sustain them, the giants turned against them and devoured mankind. And they began to sin against birds, and beasts, and reptiles, and fish, and to devour one another's flesh, and drink the blood. Then the earth laid accusation against the lawless ones."

(Note: 3000 ells would equate to about 300 feet. My guess is that the numbers got confused somewhere, and the Nephilim were in fact about 300 ells, which would be about 30 feet in height. But I could be wrong. The Nephilim may have been comparable to the giants of Gulliver's Travels in size, 300 ft. I don't know.)

Now, on my use of 1 Enoch: Jude quotes from the book of 1 Enoch in the Bible: Jude 1:14-15 is a direct quote of 1 Enoch 1:9.

Jude 1:14-15 "Enoch, the seventh from Adam, prophesied about these men: "See, the Lord is coming with thousands upon thousands of his holy ones to judge everyone, and to convict all the ungodly of all the ungodly acts they have done in the ungodly way, and of all the harsh words ungodly sinners have spoken against him."

1 Enoch 1: 9 "And behold! He cometh with ten thousands of His holy ones To execute judgment upon all, And to destroy all the ungodly: And to convict all flesh, Of all the works of their ungodliness which they have ungodly committed, And of all the hard things which ungodly sinners have spoken against Him."

(If this section of 1 Enoch is good enough for Jude, Who was under the leadership of the twelve disciples/apostles, then it's good enough for me. As you can see below in the next scripture passage, Peter also considered some of what is taught in 1st Enoch to be correct. The First Book of Enoch also used to be official canon in the early church in Ethiopia, and was well used in the early church. While not considered Holy Scripture today, some of what is in First Enoch today seems to have been considered sound or historically reliable by the apostles and early church, to be quoted in the Bible. I only reference to sections that seem NT-referenced-to and apostle-approved in this chapter. See the previous chapter for more details.)

This breeding was a terrible perversion, and a sin against God. As such, these angels, now fallen angels because of their sin, were bound in chains in an unknown location, called Tartaros, or the "valleys of the Earth" until the Judgment Day. Tartaros is the same place mentioned as the Abyss in the book of Revelation.

2 Pet 2:4 "For if God did not spare angels when they sinned, but cast them into Tartaros and committed them to pits of darkness, reserved for judgment;"

Jude 1:6 "And angels who did not keep their own domain, but abandoned their proper abode, He has kept in eternal bonds under darkness for the judgment of the great day,"

1 Enoch 10:11-15 "And the Lord said unto Michael: Go, bind Semjaza and his associates who have united themselves with women so as to have defiled themselves with them in all their uncleanness. And when their sons have slain one another, and they have seen the destruction of their beloved ones, bind them fast for seventy generations in the valleys of the earth, till the day of their judgment and of their consummation, till the judgment that is for ever and ever is consummated. In those days they shall be led off to the abyss of fire: and to the torment and the prison in which they shall be confined for ever. And whosoever shall be condemned and destroyed will from thenceforth be bound together with them to the end of all generations."

As for the Nephilim hybrids, whose fathers were immortal angels, and whose mothers were mortal human women: when the Nephilim died their spirits were still immortal and active, but their bodies were dead like a pure human's would be. They became disembodied spirits. Like their fathers, they were bent towards evil in life, and also in death. These are "evil spirits" or "demons". The fallen angels who were their fathers were (before they became fallen) a type of angel originally known as a "watcher", or perhaps "guardian angels".

1 Enoch 15: 8-12, 16:1-2 "And now, the giants, who are produced from the spirits and flesh, shall be called evil spirits upon the earth, and on the earth shall be their dwelling. Evil spirits have proceeded from their bodies; because they are born from men and from the holy Watchers is their beginning and primal origin; they shall be evil spirits on earth, and evil spirits shall they be called. [As for the spirits of heaven, in heaven shall be their dwelling, but as for the spirits of the earth which were born upon the earth, on the earth shall be their dwelling.] And the spirits of the giants afflict, oppress, destroy, attack, do battle, and work destruction on the earth, and cause trouble: they take no food, but nevertheless hunger and thirst, and cause offences. And these spirits shall rise up against the children of men and against the women, because they have proceeded from them. From the days of the slaughter and destruction and death of the giants, from the souls of whose flesh the spirits, having gone forth, shall destroy without incurring judgment * -thus shall they destroy until the day of the consummation, the great judgment in which the age shall be consummated*, over the Watchers and the godless, yea, shall be wholly consummated."

(* See also Matt 8:28-9 for other mention of not judging demons till a set time: When he arrived at the other side in the region of the Gadarenes, two demon-possessed men coming from the tombs met him. They were so violent that no one could pass that way. What do you want with us, Son of God?" they shouted. "Have you come here to torture us before the appointed time?")

These are the demons mentioned so many times in the New Testament. Jesus cast these demons out of people. They were also called evil spirits. These demons do not have bodies of their own, but instead inhabit the bodies of humans and animals. (How this works is explained in another chapter on the physics of demons) Demons are the disembodied spirits of dead Nephilim. Demons are not the same thing as fallen angels. Fallen angels have bodies (of a sort), and demons used to have the bodies of giant men, but their bodies died, so now demons do not have bodies. Demons are evil spirits, and we know Jesus said spirits do not have flesh and bones.

Luke 24:37-39 "But they were startled and frightened and thought that they were seeing a spirit. And He said to them, "Why are you troubled, and why do doubts arise in your hearts? "See My hands and My feet, that it is I Myself; touch Me and see, for a spirit does not have flesh and bones as you see that I have."

Even the apostles were confused about this issue, as to what attributes a spirit has and does not have. The differences between demons and fallen angels and who does what and which has what abilities has been a matter of confusion for a long time. I'll go more into the differences in abilities and attributes in a later chapter.

[Note: The term "watcher" is used referring to angels in Daniel 4:13, 17, 23... as well as First Enoch. So the term is Biblical without a doubt.]

It is also interesting to note that demons in the New Testament which Jesus cast out were familiar with a place called the Abyss, mentioned in Revelation as the place where the "locusts" come out, which is likely the same place as Tartaros, and where Enoch, Peter, and Jude refer to the fallen angel fathers of the Nephilim (demons) being imprisoned. The demons are fearful and dread the Abyss place, in Luke 8:31, likely familiar that their fathers are imprisoned there. "Jesus asked him, "What is your name?" "Legion," he replied, because many demons had gone into him. And they begged him repeatedly not to order them to go into the Abyss."

With the interbreeding of fallen angels and humans, we see there is an additional meaning to the enmity between Satan's seed and Eve's seed. That is the enmity between the giant Nephilim, and human beings. The Nephilim while alive were terrible giants who "turned against and devoured mankind". So the Nephilim killed and ate humans. In death, the Nephilim became demons, which harass the "children of men" in every way they can. Thus there is enmity between the seed of fallen angels (under Satan in hierarchy), and the seed of humans.

However, it was not only the first generation of Nephilim that became demons. To the best of my understanding, the Nephilim themselves were not sterile. The Nephilim were all male, and virile. In Gen 6 we read of the Nephilim, I think this verse should read in modern English "There were giants in the earth in those days (and also after that) when the sons of God came in unto the daughters of men, and they bare children to them, the same became mighty men which were of old, men of renown." After looking at both the Greek and Hebrew, it is my interpretation that when the scripture says "and also after that" it means that there were giants on the Earth after the point at which fallen angels first sired giants with human women, but "Nephilim" after that only up until the Flood. (See next chapter for more detail on "and also after that".)

I do not think Gen 6:4 means that every giant is a hybrid Nephilim; far from it. I believe that the scriptures allow for another interpretation. I believe that the Nephilim, the hybrids, were firstly all male as the scriptures indicate, and secondly, virile and not sterile. As such, I believe the hybrid giants (Nephilim) also took human wives, and sired somewhat smaller giants. Here things start to get complicated.

It is important to understand: Lev 17:11 "For the life of the flesh is in the blood, and I have given it to you on the altar to make atonement for your souls; for it is the blood by reason of the life that makes atonement."

We know from modern science that the blood of a baby in the womb is produced from the combined genetics of the father through the sperm and the mother through the egg. We know that an egg by itself is incapable of developing a baby and the baby's blood. It is by the additional genetic information that comes from the sperm of the father that makes conception possible, and the resulting blood of the baby. Once the baby is conceived and life begins, and the baby's blood begins to form, it is kept separate from the mother's blood. This may seem counterintuitive because of the fact that the baby is in the mother's body, but it is true. The mother's blood never intermingles with the baby, nor does her blood go into the baby, but the placenta acts as a barrier between the mother's blood and the baby's blood, converting the mother's blood into the baby's blood. It was by this very mechanism that the Lord Jesus' blood was completely pure from sin, as his life and blood came from God the Father in his immaculate conception, and his blood was not in any way "contaminated" by the blood of his human mother Mary. The blood of all humans is contaminated with sin, but Jesus' blood was pure and clean from sin. It is from the contribution of the father of a child that life begins, without his contribution there would be no new life, no new baby.

We know from the Bible that the life of a being is in the blood, and there could be no life or blood for a baby without the father of the baby. We see that not only did Jesus' life and blood come God the Father, but we also know from the Bible that,

1 Cor 15:21-22 "For since death came through a man, the resurrection of the dead comes also through a man. For as in Adam all die, so in Christ all will be made alive."

Rom 5:12-14 "Therefore, just as sin entered the world through one man, and death through sin, and in this way death came to all men, because all sinned—for before the law was given, sin was in the world. But sin is not taken into account when there is no law. Nevertheless, death reigned from the time of Adam to the time of Moses, even over those who did not sin by breaking a command, as did Adam, who was a pattern of the one to come."

Here, it is shown that God counts that it was through Adam (not Eve) that death and sin were passed down to all of the rest of humanity. This demonstrates to us that the life (which is found in the blood) is counted through the paternal line. The life is determined by the father, not the mother. The life and blood is counted as being added by the father, because without the addition of the father's sperm, there would be no new life, no new blood, and no baby. The father is counted as essentially contributing the life and blood, the life being in the blood, the Bible shows that God considers the father to be the one who contributes the life-blood, not the mother. As such it makes sense that Jesus' life was the life of God, and his blood was pure and not tainted with any sin. (As a side note, I think it also is interesting to mention that though the traits of the baby are determined equally by the combination of the father and mother, the gender of the baby is determined by the father. So overall, the father's sperm has more "deciding power" over what the baby will be like than the mother's egg.)

That being said, let's resume our look at Nephilim, whose fathers were fallen angels. When the Nephilim hybrids sired children with human women, the children quarter-breed giants were also descended from the life-blood of fallen angels. As such, they were still Nephilim, and when they died, their spirits also were disembodied, and they became demons. And when the quarter-breeds sired children with human women, producing eighth-breed giants, and those giants were still Nephilim. When they died their spirits were disembodied and free to roam the earth as demons. These giants certainly became smaller and smaller as more of their genetics became human, with each generation. The life is in the blood, which God counts as running through the paternal line. Any giant whose paternal line traced back to a fallen angel was ultimately a Nephilim whose spirit became disembodied, and who became a demon, at death.

On the other hand, anyone whose paternal line traces back to a human being is a human being, because the life is in the blood, which is counted through the father. Although the first generation of hybrids are specified to have all been male, there is no reason I know of to think that subsequent generations of Nephilim-giants could not have been female, especially as more of their genetics became human with continued interbreeding. I think there were female Nephilim-giant descendents, whose paternity traced back to fallen angels.

And if a human man was to interbreed with the daughter of a Nephilim-giant, the resulting children would be giants, but they would also be Human giants. When these human giants died, their spirits would go to Sheol, because they were human, and they would not be demons on the earth. So human giants were also possible.

And so the world prior to the Flood was a mess of all sorts of interbreeding. There were Nephilim hybrids, and there were their descendents who were also Nephilim-giants. Then there were human beings, and Human-giants as well. When the Nephilim and their giant descendents died, their disembodied spirits harassed the human beings on the earth as demons. Of the Nephilim, and likely also their Nephilim-giant descendents it is written in Enoch: "Who consumed all the acquisitions of men. And when men could no longer sustain them, the giants turned against them and devoured mankind. And they began to sin against birds, and beasts, and reptiles, and fish, and to devour one another's flesh, and drink the blood."

And we also know, Gen 6:5-7 "Then the Lord saw that the wickedness of man was great on the earth, and that every intent of the thoughts of his heart was only evil continually. The Lord was sorry that He had made man on the earth, and He was grieved in His heart. The Lord said, "I will blot out man whom I have created from the face of the land, from man to animals to creeping things and to birds of the sky; for I am sorry that I have made them."

I think it's important to note that human-giants, whose maternal line traced back to fallen angels, were considered human, and God would have correctly called them "man". So the human-giants were included in the men that God was sorry He had made. It should also be noted that in Matt 24:38 Jesus says, "For in the days before the flood, people were eating and drinking, marrying and giving in marriage, up to the day Noah entered the ark". Part of the sin of humans before the flood was that both human men were choosing to marry female Nephilim descendents, and that human men were giving their human daughters away in marriage to male Nephilim giants. This was willing sin and perversion on the part of humanity, and surely part of why God was sorry He had made humanity.

Also, Gen 6:11-13 "Now the earth was corrupt in the sight of God, and the earth was filled with violence. God looked on the earth, and behold, it was corrupt; for all flesh had corrupted their way upon the earth. Then God said to Noah, "The end of all flesh has come before Me; for the earth is filled with violence because of them; and behold, I am about to destroy them with the earth."

And so God brought about a worldwide flood, to kill everything on the earth. But we also read, Gen 6:8-9 "But Noah found favor in the eyes of the Lord. These are the records of the generations of Noah. Noah was a righteous man, blameless in his time; Noah walked with God."

In the Greek Septuagint translation this reads:

Gen 6:9 "And these [are] the generations of Noe. Noe was a just man; being perfect in his generation, Noe was well-pleasing to God."

The word here for "generation" is "genea" (1074) which means "fathered, birth, nativity, that which has been begotten, men of the same stock, a family, the several ranks of natural descent, the successive members of a genealogy".

Noah was genealogically perfect. He was human, with his lineage tracing back to Adam, and his paternal line was perfect. In light of all this interbreeding between fallen angels and humans, it is important to note that Noah was perfect in his genealogy.

So Noah was chosen to build the ark and survive the flood, which was worldwide, and destroyed all animal and bird life, human life, and Nephilim-giant life on the earth, except for the life in the ark. However, before the flood, the first generation of the Nephilim killed each other off, as it says in 1 Enoch 10:

"And to Gabriel said the Lord: 'Proceed against the bastards and the reprobates, and against the children of fornication: and destroy [the children of fornication and] the children of the Watchers from amongst men [and cause them to go forth]: send them one against the other that they may destroy each other in battle: for length of days shall they not have. And no request that they (i.e. their fathers) make of thee shall be granted unto their fathers on their behalf; for they hope to live an eternal life, and that each one of them will live five hundred years."

So none of the first generation of Nephilim lived longer than 500 years. This was a great many years less than many people lived in those days, many times living to be over 900 years old. The fallen angels which sired the Nephilim were bound in Tartaros after they had seen their sons kill each other off. 1 Enoch 10:

"And the Lord said unto Michael: Go, bind Semjaza and his associates who have united themselves with women so as to have defiled themselves with them in all their uncleanness. And when their sons have slain one another, and they have seen the destruction of their beloved ones, bind them fast for seventy generations in the valleys of the earth, till the day of their judgment and of their consummation, till the judgment that is for ever and ever is consummated. In those days they shall be led off to the abyss of fire: and to the torment and the prison in which they shall be confined for ever."

Also, during this time period the fallen angel Azazel, and Semjaza, and others, may have taught knowledge and technology to humans based on what seems a historically accepted as reliable section (that Peter and Jude reference to) of First Enoch, in 1 Enoch 8:1-3:

"And Azazel taught men to make swords, and knives, and shields, and breastplates, and made known to them the metals of the earth and the art of working them, and bracelets, and ornaments, and the use of antimony, and the beautifying of the eyelids, and all kinds of costly stones, and all coloring tinctures. And there arose much godlessness, and they committed fornication, and they were led astray, and became corrupt in all their ways. Semjaza taught enchantments, and root-cuttings, 'Armaros the resolving of enchantments, Baraqijal (taught) astrology, Kokabel the constellations,

Ezeqeel the knowledge of the clouds, Araqiel the signs of the earth, Shamsiel the signs of the sun, and Sariel the course of the moon. And as men perished, they cried, and their cry went up to heaven . . ."

This may be confirmed in Gen 4:19-22 "Lamech married two women, one named Adah and the other Zillah. Adah gave birth to Jabal; he was the father of those who live in tents and raise livestock. His brother's name was Jubal; he was the father of all who play the harp and flute. Zillah also had a son, Tubal-Cain, who forged all kinds of tools out of bronze and iron. Tubal-Cain's sister was Naamah."

Technology, metallurgy, and weapon making, in any case, all did begin very early in the history of humanity, and technology may have originally been taught to humans by fallen angels. Technology did not originally "evolve" or develop slowly over tens or hundreds of thousands of years. But if so, this technology that was taught encouraged sin... adultery and fornication were encouraged in jewelry, ornamentation, and makeup, and murder and thievery were encouraged in the making of weapons. Idolatry was encouraged in the teaching of astronomy, and the attributes of the heavens, encouraging people to become fascinated and worship the created, instead of the Creator. The teaching of enchantments may refer to magic, and the worship of fallen angels and demons, praying to them, asking things of them, etc. This was all very bad. It seems that Peter and Jude would not have references to this section if it was not historically reliable. If it was, it is also clear that God punished the leader of the fallen angels who was teaching this destructive technology to humans as we read in 1 Enoch 10:

"And again the Lord said to Raphael: 'Bind Azazel hand and foot, and cast him into the darkness: and make an opening in the desert, which is in Dudael, and cast him therein. And place upon him rough and jagged rocks, and cover him with darkness, and let him abide there for ever, and cover his face that he may not see light. And on the day of the great judgment he shall be cast into the fire. And heal the earth which the angels have corrupted, and proclaim the healing of the earth, that they may heal the plague, and that all the children of men may not perish through all the secret things that the Watchers have disclosed and have taught their sons. And the whole earth has been corrupted through the works that were taught by Azazel: to him ascribe all sin..."

After all of this, God sent the worldwide flood. The proof of the worldwide flood is seen in the fossil layer found all over the Earth. All the animals, including dinosaurs, and people, which were all created on the sixth day, were all killed in the flood, save for those humans on the ark of Noah. All the Nephilim-descendents of the Nephilim were also killed in the worldwide flood. The account of the worldwide Flood is in Genesis 7, 8, and 9. For more information look into the information available through Creation Ministries International, and Kent Hovind of Creation Science Evangelism.

The Worldwide Flood of Noah's time ~ 3284 BC

Chapter Three

A Timeline of Demons and Fallen Angels

Post-Flood to the Time of Jesus - Part 1

~ 3180 BC The time of Peleg and afterwards

Gen 10:25 "Two sons were born to Eber: One was named Peleg, because in his time the earth was divided; his brother was named Joktan."

Gen 11:7-9 "Come, let Us go down and there confuse their language, so that they will not understand one another's speech." So the Lord scattered them abroad from there over the face of the whole earth; and they stopped building the city. Therefore its name was called Babel, because there the Lord confused the language of the whole earth; and from there the Lord scattered them abroad over the face of the whole earth."

Deut 32:8 "When the most High divided to the nations their inheritance, when he separated the sons of Adam, he set the bounds of the people according to the number of the sons of God." (Greek)

From these verses we can understand that God somehow separated all the people of the world after the Tower of Babel event. He set the "bounds" of the people. "Bounds" here is (1367) means "regions or boundaries". He set them according the number of the sons of God, which were angels. So all the people were divided, and given their boundaries or regions, according to the number of the angels.

Deut 32:9 "For the Lord's portion [is] his people; Jacob [is] the lot of his inheritance."

God took Israel as his personal inheritance. God was the God and ruler over Israel directly. God's relationship and covenant with Israel was special and unlike His relationship with the other nations and peoples. From the wording above, it can be inferred that the angels involved in the division of the nations might also have a ruling or responsibility role over the people whose inheritance was set by their number.

Some verses from the New Testament add credence to this idea:

Eph 6:12 "For we are not contending against flesh and blood, but against the principalities, against the powers, against the world rulers of this present darkness, against the spiritual hosts of wickedness in the heavenly places."

The "world rulers of this present darkness" who are not "flesh and blood" are those we battle against. This seems to clearly indicate that there are some spiritual beings that have ruling power in the world, and we are battling against them. Based on the role demons play in the New Testament, which does not seem to indicate that demons had any sort of ruling power to be called "world rulers", it would seem that some other sort of creature has to be referred to here. I would guess that it is angels, to be more specific fallen angels, which are referred to by Paul in Eph 6.

Heb 2:5 "It was not under angels that He put the world to come, about which we are speaking."

Paul's above statement is indicative of an implied contrast, that contrast being that unlike the world to come not being "under angels", the current world is "under angels". That the current world was "under angels" was apparently something Paul assumed would be understood by the reader, and apparently was common knowledge at the time for believers. The word here for "under" is "hupotaxis" (5293) which derives from "taxis" (5010) which means "an arranging or fixed order". This word is used in 1 Cor 14:40 to mean "orderly" as in orderly and unchaotic worship, referring to one person speaking at a time, etc. during church meetings. It also means "post, rank, or position". It is used in this sense in Heb 5:6 (and following verses) as "order" in the phrase "order of Melchizedek". The word hupotaxis itself is used in Phil 3:21, Rom 8:20, Heb 2:5, 8 (2x), 1 Cor 15:26, 27, 28. The exact spelling of the word "hupotaxis" is used as "subjected" in 1 Cor 15:26, which reads "for all things He subjected under the feet of Him".

A better translation would be "It was not subjected to angels that He put the world to come, about which we are speaking."

So the word hupotaxis implies a position of authority that is about things being arranged in an orderly manner. This is very reflective of Deut 32:8, that the nations were divided, ordered, and set under the angels, subjected to the angels, according to the number of the angels.

And so if the question is: When did the people of the world start being subjected and ordered "under angels?", then the answer would be "In the time of Peleg". What Paul spoke of in the New Testament began in the time of Peleg, and carries on to date. At the time of Peleg it can be assumed, because there is no indication otherwise, that when God arranged the nations under the angels, that the angels were all good. The time of Peleg was shortly after the worldwide flood, and also shortly after the time when the fallen angels who were the fathers of the Nephilim were imprisoned in Tartaros for their sin. The angels who were not punished might be best assumed to be on good terms with God, and there is no indication that I can find that at the time of Peleg that they had turned against God. So these sons of God, those remaining after the imprisonment of the fathers of the Nephilim, would still be considered Holy Angels at the time of Peleg when God divided the nations.

But, some of these sons of God, these angels, would later, as time passed, become part of the one third that fell that are mention in Rev 12:4 "His tail swept a third of the stars out of the sky and flung them to the earth. The dragon stood in front of the woman who was about to give birth, so that he might devour her child the moment it was born." We will get into that more, later. Now we are going to talk more about giants, the giants that lived after the Flood and after the Nephilim and Nephilim-giants were all long dead, when only humans remained.

Gen 10:8-11 "Now Cush became the father of Nimrod; he became a mighty one on the earth. He was a mighty hunter before the Lord; therefore it is said, "Like Nimrod a mighty hunter before the Lord."

In the Greek, the word here used for "mighty" is "gigan" derived from the Greek word "gigas" which means giant. There isn't a Strongs number for this word as far as I know (because the word isn't used in the New Testament). The Septuagint says Nimrod was a giant hunter. Not only that, but he was a giant hunter "before the Lord", as we read in Hebrew. This is (6440) "before" and (3068) "the Lord". "Before" means "facing or in the presence of" (the Lord), and is used hundreds of times, usually in a positive or neutral light. People made sacrifices "before the Lord", and burned incense "before the Lord", etc. This is actually the first usage of the phrase in the Old Testament.

Unlike the giants who were the Nephilim, Nimrod the giant seems to be mentioned in a positive light in the Hebrew, including a positive light in his relationship with God. These verses seem to lack any implication that Nimrod had a negative relationship with God, rather the verses suggest Nimrod had a positive relationship with God. Also, the verses lack any indication that Nimrod was to be considered a Nephilim, or a son of fallen angels. He is stated to be a giant, but he is not stated to be a Nephilim. He is not counted as a Nephilim, and it seems from the wording that he may have intentionally hunted "before the Lord", and as with such phrasing, Nimrod may have worshipped God. The phrase "before the Lord" is used many times in a positive light in the Hebrew.

However, in the Greek it says that Nimrod was a giant "against" the Lord. The word is "enantion" (1726) which means "contrary, opposed, opponent, adversary". It would be hard to say, with the Greek and Hebrew conflicting somewhat, whether Nimrod was seen in a positive or negative light in his relationship with God. But by the time of the translation of the Septuagint, which predates the birth of Jesus by hundreds of years, Nimrod was apparently viewed in a negative light. Or based on the difference between the Hebrew and Greek, perhaps giants in general were viewed in a negative light by the time of the translation of the Septuagint, verses the time when Moses wrote Genesis. There are reasons for that.

We read in Num 13:33, "We saw the giants there (the descendants of Anak come from the Nephilim). We seemed like grasshoppers in our own eyes, and we looked the same to them." From this we see that the sons of Anak or the Anakites, were giants that made the Israelites feel like they were grasshoppers in comparison to the size of the Anakite giants.

The first reason giants were held in a negative light would be the impact that giants, the Anakites or sons of Anak, had on Israel the first time they approached the promised land under Moses:

Deut 1:19-43 "Then, as the LORD our God commanded us, we set out from Horeb and went toward the hill country of the Amorites through all that vast and dreadful desert that you have seen, and so we reached Kadesh Barnea. Then I said to you, "You have reached the hill country of the Amorites, which the LORD our God is giving us. See, the LORD your God has given you the land. Go up and take possession of it as the LORD, the God of your fathers, told you. Do not be afraid; do not be discouraged." Then all of you came to me and said, "Let us send men ahead to spy out the land for us and bring back a report about the route we are to take and the towns we will come to." The idea seemed good to me; so I selected twelve of you, one man from each tribe. They left and went up into the hill country, and came to the Valley of Eshcol and explored it. Taking with them some of the fruit of the land, they brought it down to us and reported, "It is a good land that the LORD our God is giving us." But you were unwilling to go up; you rebelled against the command of the LORD your God. You grumbled in your tents and said, "The LORD hates us; so he brought us out of Egypt to deliver us into the hands of the Amorites to destroy us. Where can we go? Our brothers have made us lose heart. They say, 'The people are stronger and taller than we are; the cities are large, with walls up to the sky. We even saw the Anakites there.' " Then I said to you, "Do not be terrified; do not be afraid of them. The LORD your God, who is going before you, will fight for you, as he did for you in Egypt, before your very eyes, and in the desert. There you saw how the LORD your God carried you, as a father carries his son, all the way you went until you reached this place." In spite of this, you did not trust in the LORD your God, 33 who went ahead of you on your journey, in fire by night and in a cloud by day, to search out places for you to camp and to show you the way you should go. When the LORD heard what you said, he was angry and solemnly swore: "Not a man of this evil generation shall see the good land I swore to give your forefathers, except Caleb son of Jephunneh. He will see it, and I will give him and his descendants the land he set his feet on, because he followed the LORD wholeheartedly." Because of you the LORD became angry with me also and said, "You shall not enter it, either. But your assistant, Joshua son of Nun, will enter it. Encourage him, because he will lead Israel to inherit it. And the little ones that you said would be taken captive, your children who do not yet know good from bad – they will enter the land. I will give it to them and they will take possession of it. But as for you, turn around and set out toward the desert along the route to the Red Sea. " Then you replied, "We have sinned against the LORD. We will go up and fight, as the LORD our God commanded us." So every one of you put on his weapons, thinking it easy to go up into the hill country. But the LORD said to me, "Tell them, 'Do not go up and fight, because I will not be with you. You will be defeated by your enemies.' " So I told you, but you would not listen. You rebelled against the LORD's command and in your arrogance you marched up into the hill country. The Amorites who lived in those hills came out against you; they chased you like a swarm of bees and beat you down from Seir all the way to Hormah. You came back and wept before the LORD, but he paid no attention to your weeping and turned a deaf ear to you. And so you stayed in Kadesh many days – all the time you spent there."

So the Israelites were intimidated by the giants, the Anakites, and it greatly contributed to them refusing to enter the promised land the first time, and as a repercussion of their disobedience, wandering in the desert for 40 years. This wandering was not the fault of the Anakites of course, but the Israelites. Nevertheless there was some negative history between Israel and giants by the time the Israelites entered the promised land 40 years later under Joshua.

In Deut 2 we read more about giants after the flood, in the time of Joshua, also called the Rephaim, Rephaites, or Anakites. Apparently Anak was a famous giant, and there was a whole race of giants of his descendents called Anakites, to whom most other giants were compared. We read:

Deut 2:10-11 "A race of giants called the Emites had once lived in the area of Ar. They were as strong and numerous and tall as the Anakites, another race of giants. Both the Emites and the Anakites are also known as the Rephaites, though the Moabites call them Emites."

Deut 2:20-21 "That area was once considered the land of the Rephaites, who had lived there, though the Ammonites call them Zamzummites. 21 They were also as strong and numerous and tall as the Anakites. But the Lord destroyed them so the Ammonites could occupy their land."

There were races of giants, villages full of giants, throughout the area of Israel. In Deut 3:10-11 we read about a King named Og who was a giant:

"We had now conquered all the cities on the plateau and all Gilead and Bashan, as far as the towns of Salecah and Edrei, which were part of Og's kingdom in Bashan. (King Og of Bashan was the last survivor of the giant Rephaites. His bed was made of iron and was more than thirteen feet long and six feet wide. It can still be seen in the Ammonite city of Rabbah.)"

From the size of his bed, we can logically conclude that Og was probably about 13 feet tall. From the Guinness Book of World Records, the tallest man in recent history was Robert Wadlow, who was 8 feet and 11 inches tall. The tallest man living today is Xi Shun, who is 7 feet 9 inches tall. The late Andre Roussimoff, also known as Andre the Giant, or The Gentle Giant, who played the lovable Fezzik in the movie The Princess Bride, was about 7 feet tall. King Og was over 4 feet taller than the tallest of modern giants.

In 1 Sam 17:4-7 we read, "Then Goliath, a Philistine champion from Gath, came out of the Philistine ranks to face the forces of Israel. He was over 9 feet tall! He wore a bronze helmet, and his bronze coat of mail weighed 125 pounds. He also wore bronze leg armor, and he carried a bronze javelin on his shoulder. The shaft of his spear was as heavy and thick as a weaver's beam, tipped with an iron spearhead that weighed 15 pounds. His armor bearer walked ahead of him carrying a shield."

Goliath was over 9 feet tall. Though he was shorter than King Og, Goliath was still taller than the tallest of modern giants, though comparable in height. But Goliath lived about 300 years after King Og, and by that time giantism was more rare. God was with the Israelites under Joshua, and He had them completely destroy the tribes of giants in the area of Israel, who were the enemies of Israel. Of the giants, only a few stragglers here and there survived.

Josh 11:21-22 "At that time Joshua went and destroyed the Anakites from the hill country: from Hebron, Debir and Anab, from all the hill country of Judah, and from all the hill country of Israel. Joshua totally destroyed them and their towns. No Anakites were left in Israelite territory; only in Gaza, Gath and Ashdod did any survive."

The giant men, women, and children were all killed by the Israelites under Joshua. This was God's will, as we read later in Isaiah:

Isa 26:13-14 "O Lord our God, other masters besides You have ruled us; But through You alone we confess Your name. Let not the dead live, let not the giants [repha'im] rise again: therefore Thou hast visited and destroyed them, and hast destroyed all their memory."

Why did God want the races of giants (men, women, children) to all be killed, rather than taken prisoner and made servants?

We find the answer in Deut 9 and Num 13:

Deut 9:2 "a people great and tall, the sons of the Anakim, whom you know and of whom you have heard it said, 'Who can stand before the sons of Anak?'"

Num 13:33 "We saw the Nephilim there (the descendants of Anak come from the Nephilim). We seemed like grasshoppers in our own eyes, and we looked the same to them."

First off, the giants were so strong that of them it was said "Who can stand against them?" If The women and children had been spared, there would have been grown giant men in a few years, who would have been intimidating warriors against the Israelites. Giants wouldn't make good slaves or servants, they are so strong, they would surely have fought against the Israelites, and been a continuing problem, whether they had been slaves, servants, or allowed to go free and regain strength and numbers elsewhere.

This is confirmed in Psalm 105: 8-15, 42-44, "He has remembered His covenant forever, The word which He commanded to a thousand generations, The covenant which He made with Abraham, And His oath to Isaac. Then He confirmed it to Jacob for a statute, To Israel as an everlasting covenant, Saying, "To you I will give the land of Canaan As the portion of your inheritance," When they were only a few men in number, Very few, and strangers in it. And they wandered about from nation to nation, From one kingdom to another people. He permitted no man to oppress them, And He reproved kings for their sakes: "Do not touch My anointed ones, And do My prophets no harm."... For He remembered His holy word With Abraham His servant; And He brought forth His people with joy, His chosen ones with a joyful shout. He gave them also the lands of the nations, That they might take possession of the fruit of the peoples' labor"

The Anakites would have come to oppress the Israelites, and God would not permit that. Secondly, the "descendents of Anak come from the Nephilim" we read in Numbers 13:33. And as we know, the Nephilim were probably even larger giants, about 30 feet tall, who were the sons of fallen angels who mated with human women. But all the Nephilim were wiped out before the flood, killing each other off in battle as we read in First Enoch. All the fallen angels who had sired the Nephilim were imprisoned in Tartaros until the Judgement. So were there additional Nephilim sired by additional fallen angels after the Flood? Did the interbreeding start up again after the flood? No. Absolutely not.

Did any Nephilim survive the flood? No. But in a way, a part of them survived. Some of their genetics did survive on the Ark of Noah. And that is how the descendents of Anak come from the Nephilim, though the Nephilim were only born and lived in the time before the Flood. There were no Nephilim that lived after the flood.

Gary Bates makes an excellent point about this in his book "Alien Intrusion: UFOs and the Evolution Connection" in which he says,

"...The descendents of Anak (the Anakim/Anakites) were obviously a group of large people. However, in verse 28 the spies also reported that many of the other people in the land were "strong." There are several other passages that refer to the Anakim as a powerful group of people (Deut. 9:2 for example), but verse 33 in Numbers 13 is the only passage that suggests any Anakite relationship to the Nephilim. Once again, it should be remembered that these Anakim were descendents of post-Flood people. They could not be descended from the pre-Flood Nephilim. Chapter 10 of Genesis records the "Table of Nations"; that is, the descendents of Noah's sons, and there is no mention of Anak or the Nephilim, post-Flood.

"It should be noted that the spies brought back a bad, or "evil" (Hebrew dibbah, "to slander, whisper, or defame") report. That report included a parenthetic insertion that the large people known as the sons of Anak were descended from the Nephilim. The NIV simply puts it as: We saw the Nephilim there (the descendents of Anak come from the Nephilim)... (Num. 13.33).

"At first reading, this may seem like a factual account, but it is part of the quoted false report of the spies. Of the 12 spies, only Joshua and Caleb, trusting God, were keen to enter and take possession of the land; the other 10 did not want to. Because of the false report, the whole nation was too terrified to enter the Promised Land, and they turned against Moses for bringing them there. God responded:

The Lord said to Moses, 'How long will these people treat me with contempt?... I will strike them down with a plague and destroy them' (Num. 14:11)."

"How can we be sure that it was a false report? To start with, God intended to strike down all of the people with a plague for their unbelief, but Moses interceded on their behalf. However, there were some that were not going to escape God's justice. Why? Because they brought back an untruthful report. Numbers 14:36-37 says:"

"'Now the men whom Moses sent to spy out the land, who returned and made all the congregation complain against him by bringing a bad report of the land, those very men who brought the evil report about the land, died by the plague before the Lord' (New King James Version).'"

"Some Christians have actually added to the false account of the Nephilim in the Promised Land. They say that during the time that the children of Israel wandered in the desert (38 years), fallen angels were once again cohabiting with women to produce more Nephilim as part of a satanic strategy to prevent the Hebrews entering the land. This is unlikely because, although they encountered the Anakim, they defeated them, as well as many others inhabiting tribes. When they eventually entered the land of Canaan, there was no mention of the Nephilim or encounters with them. Surely, among the descriptions of all the battles that ensued, encounters with Nephilim would have been mentioned if they occurred. And it should be remembered, according to the fallen angel view, the original angels who stepped out of line in this manner were now in chains in Tartarus. There is no account of these supposedly post-Flood Nephilim having been destroyed, so where are they today?..."

Gary Bates, Alien Intrusion: UFOs and the Evolution Connection, pg. 363-364 (See: Recommended Resources)

I agree with Mr. Bates in his ideas that the report that Nephilim were seen after the Flood was false. I agree with his ideas that "We saw the Nephilim there" was a lie invented by the spies. I agree that there were no more Nephilim after the flood, and that interbreeding of fallen angels and women did not resume post-flood.

But, differing from Mr. Bates' view, I do not think it was also a false statement that "(the descendents of Anak come from the Nephilim)". Rather, I see this as a commonly accepted fact at the time, that the giantism they sometimes encountered was related to the Nephilim somehow, and that this fact was something commonly known at the time, which the spies were using to back up their lie of having seen actual Nephilim, to make that lie more believable in the telling of it. I do believe it was possible for them to have been seeing giants, descendents of the Nephilim which had lived before the Flood, but these were Human descendents.

Let's look at Gen 6:9 in the Greek again:

"And these [are] the generations of Noah. Noah was a just man; being perfect in his generation, Noah was well-pleasing to God."

The word here for "generation" is "genea" (1074) which means "fathered, birth, nativity, that which has been begotten, men of the same stock, a family, the several ranks of natural descent, the successive members of a genealogy". Noah's genealogical history, his paternal and maternal line, was perfect. Noah was 100% human, with no Nephilim or fallen angels in his ancestry.

But we are told nothing of his wife, or his daughters-in-law for that matter.

A fallen angel (male) and a human woman have a child, and that child is a giant Nephilim, all of whom were male. (This may relate to the fact that all angels are male.) He grows to be at least about 30 feet tall, destroys all the acquisitions of men, eats people, and lives no more than 500 years, dying from fighting with other Nephilim, before the flood. But before he dies he has children with a human female. Those children are ¼ fallen angel in their genetics, and were smaller giants. Those children were either male or female, and their paternal line went back to fallen angels, so they were all Nephilim giants, not human giants. The reason for them being counted as Nephilim when they were only ¼ fallen angel, and ¾ human in their genetics is because:

Lev 17:11,14 "For the life of a creature is in the blood, and I have given it to you to make atonement for yourselves on the altar; it is the blood that makes atonement for one's life... because the life of every creature is its blood. That is why I have said to the Israelites, "You must not eat the blood of any creature, because the life of every creature is its blood; anyone who eats it must be cut off."

The life of a person is in the blood. And as we covered in Chapter 1, God counts the life-blood as coming from the father of a baby; the paternal line.

And it is by this fact that a Nephilim child, male or female, could still be considered a Nephilim, although the giant child was ¾ human in genetics and only ¼ fallen angel. The life-blood is counted as coming through the paternal line, and the life is in the blood, so if the life-blood came from fallen angels, then the giant child was counted as Nephilim, the descendent of a fallen angel.

However, once there were female descendents of the Nephilim... then a human man could sire giant human children with a female descendent of the Nephilim (who herself would be counted as a Nephilim). If a human man, whose lineage traced back to Adam, had a child with a female Nephilim descendent, whose lineage traced back to fallen angels, the result would be giant human children, who were Human. These giant humans would be 1/8 fallen angel in genetics, and 7/8 human in genetics, they would be giants, and they would be human beings, and could be either male or female. And the rules I've just outlined of interbreeding would continue on down from there. Three generations later, there might be human women who were a little taller than average, but not noticeably so, who's paternal life-blood lineage traced back to Adam, but nevertheless were 1/64 fallen angel in their genetics.

And it is one of these Human female giants, or descendent of human female giants, that surely was on the ark. It might have been Noah's wife, or one or all of the daughters-in-law. But there was without a doubt a human woman on the Ark who had some fallen angel ancestry, although she was a human being, a human woman. And it is from her that Anak descended, Nimrod, Goliath, and Og, and all the other giants after the Flood. Giantism was a recessive characteristic then after the flood, just like it is today. However the giants were taller back then, because their genetics were not as diluted far away from fallen angels as the genetics of giant people today.

However, giant men and giant women were finding each other, having giant children, and the recessive of Giantism was becoming prominent, and whole races of giants were resulting. These giants were the Anakites, the Rephaim or Rephaites, and all the other races of giants mentioned in the Bible. If this human giantism continued, and the numbers of the giants continued to increase and spread, they would perhaps have come to rule over the entire Earth, or perhaps they would not have. But in the region of Israel the races of giants were a threat to oppress the Israelites. God had the Israelites destroy them for this reason. Of course, they were just human beings like anyone else. God does not hate giant humans, just like God does not hate normal sized humans; God loves all people whether they were born giants or not. Giant humans are humans too. So how could God treat the giant enemies of Israel different than the non-giant enemies of Israel, in having the women and children killed as well?

One thing was the situation: it was better for everyone who wasn't a giant to not be oppressed by a people of giants spreading all over the region and ruling shorter people by their greater physical strength. God is just, and omniscient, and loves all people. God did what was best for everyone. Still it may seem very harsh on the women and children with Giantism. Yet this is a much smaller event than the flood of Noah, which killed off many Nephilim giants and human giants. God never intended for humans and fallen angels to interbreed. Who was ultimately responsible for the deaths of the Nephilim, Nephilim giants, and human giants in the Old Testament?

I propose for you to consider what we read in Exodus 20:4-6:

"You shall not make for yourself an idol in the form of anything in heaven above or on the earth beneath or in the waters below. You shall not bow down to them or worship them; for I, the LORD your God, am a jealous God, punishing the children for the sin of the fathers to the third and fourth generation of those who hate me, but showing love to a thousand {generations} of those who love me and keep my commandments."

Although these human giants were human (because their life-blood paternal line was human) they still did have fallen angel "fathers" in their ancestry. It was the fallen angels who sired the Nephilim who brought this upon their descendents. Their mating was a horrible perversion… God never intended there to be giant people, God did not make giant people, though he loves giant people today, even as he also loved the giants who were the Anakites. The fallen angels who sired the Nephilim brought about punishment upon their descendents, the Anakites, by their sin. The fallen angels who sired the Nephilim are the ones who made this huge mess of perverted interbreeding, giving cause for the flood, and causing the human recessive dysfunction of the body which is "Pituitary Gigantism" today, and the need for the Anakites to be wiped out. The fallen angels are the wicked ones for mating with human women, not God for cleaning up the mess of things that resulted from their wickedness.

When it comes to the Anakites, it was the fallen angels that sired the Nephilim who were ultimately responsible for the unfortunate situation of their descendents.

And we know when Moses wrote that:

Gen 6:4 "The Nephilim were on the earth in those days—and also afterward—when the sons of God went to the daughters of men and had children by them. They were the heroes of old, men of renown."

Looking at the Hebrew, what Moses meant was that there were Nephilim on the earth from the time of the first interbreeding, up until the time of the Flood.

But looking at the Greek, the word is not "Nephilim" but "giganten" or Giants. In the Greek, Num. 13:33 reads "we saw the giants, the sons of Anak, which come of the Giants", and so what is meant in Gen 6:4 by "there were giants on the earth in those days, and also afterward" was that there were giants on the earth after that point of the first interbreeding. It does not mean that all giants came from ongoing fallen angel and human interbreeding, or that all the giants were Nephilim. Giantism continued down into human beings through genetics, although all fallen angel and human interbreeding stopped at or before the time of the Flood and imprisonment in Tartaros of the fallen angels responsible. There were no Nephilim after the flood, but there were Humans who were giants, and that trait of giantism did originate with the pre-flood Nephilim. In the Greek, both "Nephilim" (5303) and just "giants" (7497) in Hebrew are translated both to just "giants" in Greek, showing a connection, but leaving a vagueness based on simply size description, it does not mean that all "giants" and all "Nephilim" are the same thing.

It is unknown if besides giantism, if there are other genetic abnormalities that are currently part of the gene pool that are a result of the interbreeding of the fallen angels with human women. It could be that dwarfism, which is caused by problems with GH, the same hormone that causes giantism, is a later result of this interbreeding. Perhaps it is a genetic mutation related to giantism. It could be that some cancers, genetic diseases, and birth defects that would seem totally unrelated could also be a longterm result of this interbreeding, through the mutation of genes that originally came from fallen angels. For example, it seems likely that polydactylism, or having more than 5 digits, is related to giantism and the sin of the fallen angels now imprisoned in Tartaros. In David's time a man was encountered that was both a giant, and had 6 digits on his hands and feet. These were descendents of the few giants that remained past Joshua's time, and the relatives of Goliath, including his brother.

2 Sam 21:15-22 "Once again the Philistines were at war with Israel. And when David and his men were in the thick of battle, David became weak and exhausted. Ishbi-benob was a descendant of the giants; his bronze spearhead weighed more than seven pounds, and he was armed with a new sword. He had cornered David and was about to kill him. But Abishai son of Zeruiah came to David's rescue and killed the Philistine. Then David's men declared, "You are not going out to battle with us again! Why risk snuffing out the light of Israel?" After this, there was another battle against the Philistines at Gob. As they fought, Sibbecai from Hushah killed Saph, another descendant of the giants. During another battle at Gob, Elhanan son of Jair from Bethlehem killed the brother of Goliath of Gath. The handle of his spear was as thick as a weaver's beam! In another battle with the Philistines at Gath, they encountered a huge man with six fingers on each hand and six toes on each foot, twenty-four in all, who was also a descendant of the giants. 21 But when he defied and taunted Israel, he was killed by Jonathan, the son of David's brother Shimea. These four Philistines were descendants of the giants of Gath, but David and his warriors killed them."

1 Chr 20:6 "Again there was war at Gath, where there was a man of great stature who had twenty-four fingers and toes, six fingers on each hand and six toes on each foot; and he also was descended from the giants."

So it is clearly possible from these verses that polydactylism is related to giantism also. And there may be other genetic disorders that are related as well, which still cause people problems today. It is hard to say what all might be related. Many people of ordinary height, without giantism, or any visible abnormality, may be carrying recessive genes that in fact show that they had a fallen angel in their ancestry, a long, long, long, long, long, time ago. You or I might unbeknownst to us by any visible indication, have a miniscule amount of fallen angel genetics in our own DNA.

One thing is for certain: Giants today are human beings (and people with polydactylism, and people with silent fallen angel DNA, and whatever else).

We all have human spirits and souls. This is a very important point, because when the Nephilim died, their spirits became "evil spirits" upon the earth, which we also call demons. And the descendents of the Nephilim, the giants with a paternal life-blood line going back to a fallen angel, also became evil spirits when they died. When the Nephilim, or the Nephilim giants of further generations, died, their spirits became disembodied, and now roam the earth as demons. All of this happened prior to the flood of Noah.

However, all of the Human giants, whose paternal life-blood line traced back to Adam, were human beings. And as such when the Human giants died, their spirits did not become disembodied, they did not become evil spirits on the earth, they did not become demons. They had a human soul and spirit, and their spirit went to Sheol, just like any other human. Goliath was human. Og was human. Nimrod was human. Robert Wadlow was human, and Xi Shun, and other giants who live today are also human. Andre Roussimoff was also human, may he rest in peace.

Isa 14:9 "Hell from beneath is moved for thee to meet [thee] at thy coming: it stirreth up the dead for thee, [even] all the chief ones of the earth; it hath raised up from their thrones all the kings of the nations."

Here Isaiah is prophesying about the human king of Babylon, saying he is going to die. What is interesting about this verse is that in the Greek, "chief ones" is translated as "giganten" or in English, "giants". "Hell" here in the Hebrew is "Sheol". And so here we see that there are dead giants in Sheol. Those would be dead human-giants, not Nephilim-giants.

God did not allow fallen angel and human interbreeding after the time of the flood. There are no Nephilim that lived after the time of the Flood, nor Nephilim-giants who were paternal life-blood line descendents of the Nephilim. Fallen angel and human interbreeding was no longer allowed. Also, sexual interaction between human beings and fallen angels was heavily disapproved of by God, being a great wickedness, which we see in the story of Sodom and Gomorrah.

Gen 19:1-5 "The two angels arrived at Sodom in the evening, and Lot was sitting in the gateway of the city. When he saw them, he got up to meet them and bowed down with his face to the ground. "My lords," he said, "please turn aside to your servant's house. You can wash your feet and spend the night and then go on your way early in the morning."

"No," they answered, "we will spend the night in the square." But he insisted so strongly that they did go with him and entered his house. He prepared a meal for them, baking bread without yeast, and they ate. Before they had gone to bed, all the men from every part of the city of Sodom — both young and old — surrounded the house. They called to Lot, "Where are the men who came to you tonight? Bring them out to us so that we can have sex with them."

So the men of Sodom wanted to have sex with two Holy angels of the Lord. This was a great wickedness. We read in Jude:

Jude 6:6-7 "And angels who did not keep their own domain, but abandoned their proper abode, He has kept in eternal bonds under darkness for the judgment of the great day, just as Sodom and Gomorrah and the cities around them, since they in the same way as these indulged in gross immorality and went after strange flesh, are exhibited as an example in undergoing the punishment of eternal fire."

Apparently Sodom and Gomorrah were destroyed in part for the same reason the fallen angels who sired the Nephilim were imprisoned: they went after strange flesh. The men of Sodom tried to have sex with Holy angels of God, and this was not allowed, and the cities were destroyed. After the events leading up to the flood, and in keeping those events in mind, the reason behind God's destruction of Sodom and Gomorrah is more clearly seen. These people were so wicked they wanted to have sex with angels, despite the horrible history resulting from such sin.

Based on the fact that the giants after the flood were increasingly smaller, and none reached the great heights of the Nephilim, probably some 30 feet in height, it is clear that no Nephilim were sired after the flood. If Nephilim were sired after the flood, then there would have once again been 30 foot giants, living for 500 years, likely becoming cannibals again. God has forbidden this. And any fallen angels who did such a thing would undoubtedly also be thrown into Tartaros, just like the other fallen angels who practiced interbreeding. By the lack of 30 foot cannibalistic giants today, it is clear that fallen angel and human interbreeding is not taking place today.

Surely the only result to be produced from fallen angel and human interbreeding would be an enormous giant like the Nephilim. I say this because it logically follows that if fallen angels before the flood could have produced more normal looking offspring, instead of giants, they would have. And it would not be in the power of any fallen angel today to produce a child, a Nephilim, any different than the Nephilim before the flood of Noah.

Nephilim today would still be enormous cannibalistic giants of over 30 feet in height. And so we know there are not Nephilim being born today.

Also, what fallen angel would make this decision to sire a Nephilim, and then face the repercussion of being thrown into the darkest prison of Tartaros, held in chains until the Judgement, after seeing what happened to the other fallen angels who tried this? I offer that none would, because it would make no sense for one to do this.

Another point I would like to make involves this verse in Matthew:

Matt 24:36-44 "No one knows about that day or hour, not even the angels in heaven, nor the Son, but only the Father. As it was in the days of Noah, so it will be at the coming of the Son of Man. For in the days before the flood, people were eating and drinking, marrying and giving in marriage, up to the day Noah entered the ark; and they knew nothing about what would happen until the flood came and took them all away. That is how it will be at the coming of the Son of Man. Two men will be in the field; one will be taken and the other left. Two women will be grinding with a hand mill; one will be taken and the other left. "Therefore keep watch, because you do not know on what day your Lord will come. But understand this: If the owner of the house had known at what time of night the thief was coming, he would have kept watch and would not have let his house be broken into. So you also must be ready, because the Son of Man will come at an hour when you do not expect him."

I have seen it said that "as it was in the days of Noah" means that the Nephilim, and fallen angel and human interbreeding, will take place again just before the Lord Jesus returns. This reasoning is based off of this passage in Matthew. I do not see that demonstrated in this passage. The main point of this passage is that like people were not aware that the flood was upon them, neither will people be aware that Jesus is about to return. Just like people were not expecting the flood, they will not be expecting the rapture of the saints. However, there is nothing in this passage that indicates Jesus was in any way referring to the return of the Nephilim.

Now, when Jesus said that the people were "marrying and giving in marriage" up until the time the flood began, I do think he was referring to human men "marrying" Nephilim giants, and human women being "given in marriage" to fallen angels and Nephilim giants, right up until the end. This was a main cause for the flood, and a cause understood by the Jewish people Jesus was speaking to at the time. So it really was not a big deal that

Jesus mentioned the perverse sin of this interbreeding to the people he was speaking to in this section of Matthew: the people already knew what Jesus was talking about. And as such, the point of his mentioning it was that people would be engaged in horrible sin, sin bringing judgment, right up until the time judgment arrives, while not expecting the judgment when it comes. However, this does not mean that the sin people will be engaged in before Jesus' return is the same sin people were engaged in just before the flood began. That does not logically follow. The main point of the passage is that life will be business as usual, sinful as it might be, right up until the end most people wont be expecting. But we must be prepared and ready, and keep watch for his return. (In a later chapter on prophecy I will cover this topic of the impossibility of modern day fallen angel/human interbreeding from another angle.)

Now we are done with giants and how they relate to demons, and will resume a more focused look at the subject of fallen angels.

Chapter Four

A Timeline of Demons and Fallen Angels

Post-Flood to the Time of Jesus - Part 2

~2000-1800 BC The testing of Job

Stepping back a bit in time, to the time of Job (said to be a contemporary of Abraham), Satan is still allowed in the presence of God. As such Satan has not at this point technically done whatever sin would be necessary for him to not be allowed in Heaven in the presence of God. Satan could at the time of Job go back and forth between Heaven and Earth.

Job 1:6-7 "One day the angels came to present themselves before the LORD , and Satan also came with them. The LORD said to Satan, "Where have you come from?" Satan answered the LORD , "From roaming through the earth and going back and forth in it."

Job 2:1-2 "On another day the angels came to present themselves before the LORD , and Satan also came with them to present himself before him. And the LORD said to Satan, "Where have you come from?" Satan answered the LORD , "From roaming through the earth and going back and forth in it."

So in Job we see that the angels would gather in the presence of God, and even Satan, whom had been prophesied against back in Genesis, was still allowed in the presence of God in Heaven. As such we can clearly see that Satan had not yet fallen from Heaven, and cast down to earth, as is described in Revelation, because Satan was still allowed in Heaven at this point, in the presence of God.

Earlier we saw that the nations of humans were divided according to the number of the angels, and ordered, organized, and subjected under them. At the time when this began, the time of Peleg, the angels can be assumed to have all been in good standing with God, and not to have yet become fallen angels. But after the time of Peleg the relationship some of these angels had with God changed.

One thing that happened was that people started to worship the angels, idols, and the creation, instead of worshipping God the Creator. God warned the Israelites against this as early as the time of Moses

Deut 4:19 "And lest thou lift up thine eyes unto heaven, and when thou seest the sun, and the moon, and the stars, even all the host of heaven, shouldest be driven to worship them, and serve them, which the LORD thy God hath divided unto all nations under the whole heaven."

The people worshipping the angels instead of God was the fault of the people, not the angels, of course. However, this may have contributed to the angels doing things against God's will, or it could be angels were encouraging this worship, though we can't assume that from this passage. We read in a Psalm written about 300 years later, by Asaph a contemporary of David:

Psalm 82:1-8, "God has taken his place in the divine council; in the midst of the gods he holds judgment: "How long will you judge unjustly and show partiality to the wicked? Selah Give justice to the weak and the fatherless; maintain the right of the afflicted and the destitute. Rescue the weak and the needy; deliver them from the hand of the wicked." They have neither knowledge nor understanding, they walk about in darkness; all the foundations of the earth are shaken. I said, "You are gods, sons of the Most High, all of you; nevertheless, like men you shall die, and fall like any prince." Arise, O God, judge the earth; for you shall inherit all the nations!"

These gatherings of the angels before God, as mentioned in Job, are here referred to as "the divine council". The angels are here referred to as "gods" with a lower case "g". The angels apparently had the job of or ability to be judges in human affairs, and some of the angels were doing a poor job of it. They were showing partiality to the wicked, and here God was rebuking them for it, and telling them like men they would also die, and fall just like a human ruler eventually falls from power. This partiality to the wicked may have had something to do with the wicked (being wicked) worshipping the angels in place of God. This I couldn't say for certain. This was the state of affairs by the time of David. The once good angels, that God had set over the nations, were starting to fall.

We do know that people were worshipping idols and demons as "gods" and making human sacrifices to them.

Psalm 106:36-38 "They worshiped their idols, which became a snare to them. They sacrificed their sons and their daughters to demons. They shed innocent blood, the blood of their sons and daughters, whom they sacrificed to the idols of Canaan, and the land was desecrated by their blood."

We also know that arguments could and did break out between the angels:

Jude 1:9 "Yet Michael the archangel, when contending with the devil he disputed about the body of Moses, durst not bring against him a railing accusation, but said, The Lord rebuke thee."

From this verse we can see that disagreements were taking place between different angels, as early as the time of Moses, in this case Satan and Michael, in which Michael called upon God to rebuke Satan.

Pre-Birth of Jesus, in the time of Daniel about 600 BC
(about 400 years after David)

Were all of the angels starting to fall, or just some of the angels? Why were these angels turning against God and displeasing Him? To answer these questions, we must look ahead to the book of Revelation:

Rev 12:1-5 "And there appeared a great wonder in heaven; a woman clothed with the sun, and the moon under her feet, and upon her head a crown of twelve stars: And she being with child cried, travailing in birth, and pained to be delivered. And there appeared another wonder in heaven; and behold a great red dragon, having seven heads and ten horns, and seven crowns upon his heads. His tail swept a third of the stars out of the sky and flung them to the earth. The dragon stood in front of the woman who was about to give birth, so that he might devour her child the moment it was born. She gave birth to a son, a male child, who will rule all the nations with an iron scepter. And her child was snatched up to God and to his throne."

In this passage the "stars out of the sky" referred to are angels, who are symbolically represented as stars. The dragon is symbolic of and represents Satan. We see here that only one third of the angels were swept by Satan's tail out of the sky and down to earth. That means that two thirds of the total number of angels were Not affected by Satan's tail. So although the details are not revealed to us, from this passage in Revelation we can see that it is Satan who was somehow bringing these angels down. So whatever dynamics may have been occurring between humans and angels when it comes to idolatrous worship, or impartial judgments, Satan had a large responsible part in it. It can be assumed here that two thirds of the angels of the divine council stayed in good standing with God in their role over human affairs, still to be considered Holy angels, while only one third of them fell and thus would be called fallen angels.

It is also important to note that we see in this passage that these angels are described as having been flung to earth before Jesus was born, but after the woman was preparing to give birth to Jesus. It is Jesus who will rule all nations with an iron scepter. (Praise the Lord!) The woman with the twelve stars on her head must be Israel (though she might also be considered Eve, Sarah, and Mary as well in other perspectives). One thing is definite, which is that the angels fell after the woman existed, which would certainly be no earlier than Eve, because there were no women before Eve. But I would say the best interpretation would be that the woman was Israel, and that these angels fell after the time of Sarah and Abraham, when God first made his promise to Abraham to make a great nation of his descendents. This was not very long at all after the time of Peleg. So that is when the angels started to fall, propelled by Satan.

Satan had managed to appeal to one third of the total number of angels, and involve them in his evil activities and agendas on Earth. It can reasonably be assumed these fallen angels were able to go back and forth between Heaven and Earth, as was Satan, at this time. An angel was sometimes known as a "prince". By the time of Daniel the situation had gotten even worse than at the time of David. We read:

Daniel 10:5-14, 20-21 "I looked up and there before me was a man dressed in linen, with a belt of the finest gold around his waist. His body was like chrysolite, his face like lightning, his eyes like flaming torches, his arms and legs like the gleam of burnished bronze, and his voice like the sound of a multitude. I, Daniel, was the only one who saw the vision; the men with me did not see it, but such terror overwhelmed them that they fled and hid themselves. So I was left alone, gazing at this great vision; I had no strength left, my face turned deathly pale and I was helpless. Then I heard him speaking, and as I listened to him, I fell into a deep sleep, my face to the ground. A hand touched me and set me trembling on my hands and knees. He said, "Daniel, you who are highly esteemed, consider carefully the words I am about to speak to you, and stand up, for I have now been sent to you." And when he said this to me, I stood up trembling. Then he continued, "Do not be afraid, Daniel. Since the first day that you set your mind to gain understanding and to humble yourself before your God, your words were heard, and I have come in response to them. But the prince of the Persian kingdom resisted me twenty-one days. Then Michael, one of the chief princes, came to help me, because I was detained there with the king of Persia. Now I have come to explain to you what will happen to your people in the future, for the vision concerns a time yet to come." So he said, "Do you know why I have come to you? Soon I will return to fight against the prince of Persia, and when I go, the prince of Greece will come; but first I will tell you what is written in the Book of Truth. No one supports me against them except Michael, your prince."

All of the princes referred to here are angels, of the divine council we read about earlier. And what we see here is all out warfare. This is a picture of total chaos of angelic feudalism, with no regard for the will of God. Try to grasp how horrible this situation is! God sent a Holy angel, Gabriel, to Daniel. This is the same Gabriel who went to Mary and told her she would give birth to Jesus! He is a Holy angel of the Lord, and we see he is given assignments of great honor. And the situation with the divine council had deteriorated to such extremes that Gabriel, an angel delivering a message from God, the Most High Creator of the Entire Universe, was caused such delay by fallen angels that it took him 3 weeks to be able to deliver the message! Can you see how outrageous this is?! I'm only a human being, and I can Fedex a letter half way around the world to Moscow in 3 days! The fallen angels on the divine council were causing such problems that it took a Holy angel of God 3 weeks to be able to deliver a message! That's horrible!

And so I am also making the point here that God, being omnipotent, could have sent the message to Daniel directly and instantaneously. But God chose to send the message through the channels of the system He had put in place, the angels of the divine council. And so these verses in Daniel demonstrate to us just how corrupted that system had become because of Satan and the other fallen angels responsible for all this fighting. At this time, Satan and other fallen angels were still allowed in Heaven in the presence of God, though it is questionable as to how much time they spent in heaven, and how much time they chose to stay on Earth.

And this anarchistic dysfunctional system is what remained in place until the time of Jesus.

~0 AD Birth, Ministry, Death, and Resurrection of Jesus the Christ

The first major attack on Jesus was of course, Satan working through Herod, trying to kill Jesus right after his birth. This is part of what was referred to in Revelation 12. The next major event was when Satan tempted Jesus in the desert and failed.

Matt 4:1-11 "Then Jesus was led by the Spirit into the desert to be tempted by the devil. After fasting forty days and forty nights, he was hungry. The tempter came to him and said, "If you are the Son of God, tell these stones to become bread." Jesus answered, "It is written: "Man does not live on bread alone, but on every word that comes from the mouth of God."" Then the devil took him to the holy city and had him stand on the highest point of the temple. "If you are the Son of God," he said, "throw yourself down. For it is written: ""He will command his angels concerning you,

and they will lift you up in their hands, so that you will not strike your foot against a stone."" Jesus answered him, "It is also written: "Do not put the Lord your God to the test."" Again, the devil took him to a very high mountain and showed him all the kingdoms of the world and their splendor. "All this I will give you," he said, "if you will bow down and worship me." Jesus said to him, "Away from me, Satan! For it is written: "Worship the Lord your God, and serve him only."" Then the devil left him, and angels came and attended him."

Mark 1:12-13 "At once the Spirit sent him out into the desert, and he was in the desert forty days, being tempted by Satan. He was with the wild animals, and angels attended him."

Luke 4:1-13 "Jesus, full of the Holy Spirit, returned from the Jordan and was led by the Spirit in the desert, where for forty days he was tempted by the devil. He ate nothing during those days, and at the end of them he was hungry. The devil said to him, "If you are the Son of God, tell this stone to become bread." Jesus answered, "It is written: "Man does not live on bread alone."" The devil led him up to a high place and showed him in an instant all the kingdoms of the world. And he said to him, I will give you all their authority and splendor, for it has been given to me, and I can give it to anyone I want to. So if you worship me, it will all be yours." Jesus answered, "It is written: "Worship the Lord your God and serve him only."" The devil led him to Jerusalem and had him stand on the highest point of the temple. "If you are the Son of God," he said, "throw yourself down from here. For it is written: "He will command his angels concerning you to guard you carefully; they will lift you up in their hands, so that you will not strike your foot against a stone." Jesus answered, "It says: "Do not put the Lord your God to the test."" When the devil had finished all this tempting, he left him until an opportune time."

So from these verses we can gather that at this time, Satan tells Jesus that all the authority and splendor of all the kingdoms of the world has been given to him. Now, if all the peoples of the world had been divided according to the number of the angels, and only one third of the angels became fallen, how can this be? How could Satan have all the authority over the kingdoms of the world?

Well, one way to look at this is that Satan's power and authority has always been linked to the power of death, and Satan did not gain dominion until after Adam sinned. Satan held the position of the "mighty angelic guardian", as is written in Ezekiel 28. His dominion over the world of men was in place since Eden, long before the divine council was began in the time of Peleg. Although I do not fully understand Satan's position or it's relation to the divine council, Satan must have had a parallel power and authority, and influence, over the divine council. If Satan had his power because of death (or absence of life), and all people die, then this is the way in which he held jurisdiction over all peoples, even though they were subjected under other angels of the divine council.

Another thought is that it is obvious from the passage in Daniel that some angels were more powerful than other angels. Also, there are many angels, and God said he divided the nations according to the number of the sons of God. This method of proportionality is vague. It very well might be that the one third of the angels which fell were the more powerful angels on the divine council, and many of the angels which remained true to God were the less powerful angels in comparison. It could be that some angels were over other angels, in a hierarchal system. It could be the angels that fell were the angels at the top of the hierarchy, and the angels which remained true to God and Holy were those at the bottom of the hierarchy. The passages in Daniel 10 do not specify, nor do any other passages that I know of. But these possibilities I have listed show that there are ways in which this situation could make sense. And somehow, it does make sense that while only one third of the angels fell, nevertheless Satan had gained authority over all the kingdoms of the earth.

I tentatively (because we know Satan is the father of lies so one can't just believe anything he says) accept the presupposition that Satan was accurate about his claims of his authority, because of some things Jesus said:

A couple of days before his death on the cross Jesus said:

John 12:31 "Now is the time for judgment on this world; now the prince of this world will be driven out."

We will shortly get to what Jesus meant by "driven out".

John 14:30 "Hereafter I will not talk much with you: for the prince of this world cometh, and hath nothing in me."

John 16:11 "Of judgment, because the prince of this world is judged."

Three times Jesus refers to Satan as the "prince of this world". That seems to me to indicate that Satan had a position of being a prince over this world, more than just a prince over Greece or Persia, like the angelic princes mentioned in Daniel. Rather, Jesus says Satan is the prince of this World, implying the whole world, not just one country or people. And as such, he must somehow effectively be in a position over the divine council, because he is over the kingdoms of the world.

It is important to point out and make clear that when Satan said, "I will give you all their authority and splendor, for it has been given to me, and I can give it to anyone I want to.", that there is no indication that God is the one who gave Satan this authority over the world in any direct way. Rather it was the fallen angels of the divine council who gave this authority to Satan, handing over their once God-given authority to Satan. Satan was given this authority directly from other fallen angels, not directly from God.

Satan also was in a position of authority over demons (also called evil spirits, the disembodied spirits of dead Nephilim and their Nephilim descendents). Satan was called the "prince of demons", and also referred to as "Beelzebub". There is no doubt from the below verses that Satan had the demons working for him.

Matt 12:22-28 "Then they brought him a demon-possessed man who was blind and mute, and Jesus healed him, so that he could both talk and see. All the people were astonished and said, "Could this be the Son of David?" But when the Pharisees heard this, they said, "It is only by Beelzebub, the prince of demons, that this fellow drives out demons." Jesus knew their thoughts and said to them, "Every kingdom divided against itself will be ruined, and every city or household divided against itself will not stand. If Satan drives out Satan, he is divided against himself. How then can his kingdom stand? And if I drive out demons by Beelzebub, by whom do your people drive them out? So then, they will be your judges. But if I drive out demons by the Spirit of God, then the kingdom of God has come upon you."

It is in the Gospels we learn that demons, being disembodied spirits, are capable of entering into the bodies of other creatures, such as people and animals, and causing them problems. And here we see one of the most impactful aspects of Jesus' ministry. Jesus cast demons out of people by the

Spirit of God, healing the people. Also, we learn more about what the demons were capable of doing, and all sorts of conditions are attributed to people having demons, including muteness. We will cover the abilities of demons more in a later chapter. The important point for now was that Jesus had authority over the demons, which we see below:

Mark 1:27 "The people were all so amazed that they asked each other, "What is this? A new teaching — and with authority! He even gives orders to evil spirits and they obey him."

Luke 4:36 "All the people were amazed and said to each other, "What is this teaching? With authority and power he gives orders to evil spirits and they come out!"

Not only did Jesus have authority over demons, but he gave authority to his disciples as well:

Matt 10:1 "He called his twelve disciples to him and gave them authority to drive out evil spirits and to heal every disease and sickness."

Matt 10:7-9 "As you go, preach this message: 'The kingdom of heaven is near.' Heal the sick, raise the dead, cleanse those who have leprosy, drive out demons. Freely you have received, freely give."

And we know that the demons knew who Jesus was, that they knew he was the Son of God.

Mark 3:11 "Whenever the evil spirits saw him, they fell down before him and cried out, "You are the Son of God."

And we also know that the demons were aware that there was a time appointed for them to be judged and punished, as is recorded in First Enoch. And we also see verses confirming the demon's awareness of the Abyss or Tartaros, serving as a confirmation of what we read in the beginning chapters of First Enoch.

Luke 8:30-31 "Legion," he replied, because many demons had gone into him. And they begged him repeatedly not to order them to go into the Abyss."

Matt 8:29 "And they cried out, saying, "What business do we have with each other, Son of God? Have You come here to torment us before the time?"

Jesus anointed his disciples with the power to cast out demons, and cast out numerous demons personally, throughout His glorious ministry.

Chapter Five

Powers and Physics - Basic Concepts - God and Mankind

In this and following chapters we will cover the topic of the powers that demons and fallen angels have, using examples from the Bible, and will also cover the science and physics of these powers and the entities themselves. To start off, we will cover some basic concepts about space and time, and their dimensions.

In the terminology of science, we live in a world that verifiably has 4 dimensions. The first dimension is length, the second dimension is width, and the third dimension is height. These are the spatial dimensions. The fourth dimension is time. Everything in the universe is typically thought of as being 4 dimensional. Objects, living or nonliving, whatever they might be, pass through time, and are four-dimensional. Everything exists in these 4 dimensions, in what is called spacetime.

As human beings, we can remember the past, and cannot see the future, but are bound in our perception to the present. At least that is how things normally are for us.

However, God is eternal, infinite, omnipresent, omniscient, and all-powerful. God was here before the beginning of creation, and before the beginning of time. God is above time, and outside of time, as well as being active inside of it. God created time. We perceive time as a defining boundary of our existence, but God does not. From God's perspective all of human history from Adam and Eve, to Moses, to the time of Jesus, to the present, and the future, the endtimes, and the New Kingdom of Heaven; all these times are seen by Him at the same time. God can look over all time like we would a simple written timeline on a piece of paper, but with total detailed knowledge of all things going on at each time and place. God is above time. So though we are 4 dimensional, God is not.

I have heard it said before that "God does not exist: God IS", and that is true. We "exist". All of creation "exists" because God made us, and everything, into being. We have being, and we have nonbeing, we exist and then we don't exist, we are here for a time, and then we pass away. But God does not, He always was, He is, and He always will be. As such, God just IS. As God said, "I AM".

So how many dimensions is God? There is nothing above Him, and no limiting Him. It would suffice to say that God is infinitely dimensional. It really is beyond our understanding to define God, so I think it is best to say He is infinitely dimensional and just leave it at that.

As Christians, we know that Jesus was here from before the beginning, and will be here at the end. He is the Alpha and Omega, the First and the Last, whom all things were created through.

John 1:1-4, 10 "In the beginning was the Word, and the Word was with God, and the Word was God. He was in the beginning with God. All things came into being through Him, and apart from Him nothing came into being that has come into being. In Him was life, and the life was the Light of men. He was in the world, and the world was made through Him, and the world did not know Him."

Rev 21:5-7 "And He who sits on the throne said, "Behold, I am making all things new " And He said, "Write, for these words are faithful and true." Then He said to me, "It is done I am the Alpha and the Omega, the beginning and the end I will give to the one who thirsts from the spring of the water of life without cost. He who overcomes will inherit these things, and I will be his God and he will be My son."

Jesus Himself stands as the marker for the beginning and end of time itself. He is part of the three persons that are God, yet Jesus is not God the Father, exactly. We know that there are some things that God the Father knows that Jesus does not know (or did not know at one time). Jesus Himself said he did not know the exact time of His return, that only the Father in Heaven knew this.

Matt 24:36 "No one knows about that day or hour, not even the angels in heaven, nor the Son, but only the Father."

Mark 13:32 "No one knows about that day or hour, not even the angels in heaven, nor the Son, but only the Father."

So it would suffice to say that Jesus is infinitely dimensional minus 1. (Haha.... that equals that Jesus is still infinitely dimensional, just like God, for those of you that aren't familiar with the math). What I mean is that while Jesus is God, He also is just a little lower than God the Father, but still far above everyone and everything else. For in John 8:58, "Jesus said unto them, Verily, verily, I say unto you, Before Abraham was, I am." This shows us that Jesus, one person of the Godhead, the trinity that is God, is God and is above and outside of time in some ways, almost exactly like God the Father. We also know that time passes differently for Jesus from this verse:

2 Pet 3:8 "But, beloved, be not ignorant of this one thing, that one day [is] with the Lord as a thousand years, and a thousand years as one day."

Rom 8:34 and Heb 8:1 may add understanding for us as to why this is:

"Who [is] he that condemneth? [It is] Christ that died, yea rather, that is risen again, who is even at the right hand of God, who also maketh intercession for us."

"Now of the things which we have spoken [this is] the sum: We have such an high priest, who is set on the right hand of the throne of the Majesty in the heavens;"

Jesus is constantly making intercession for us, hearing our prayers, and is our high priest at God's right hand. Hearing the prayers of all Christians on earth, and responding to those prayers, surely is a lot of work. What if 3000 Christians were praying at the same time, making requests? I don't think I could keep track of 3000 requests, or 3000 people talking to me at the same time. I suppose that a day might be like a thousand years to the Lord Jesus, so that He can handle very well and with great efficiency the task of being the Head of His church. That's just one idea though. In any case, the Bible teaches that time passes differently for Jesus, and that God and Jesus are above time. The Bible shows that time is not always the concrete dimension that we perceive it to be, when it comes to God, in any of His persons. And we know that God is spirit from John 4:24, "God [is] a Spirit: and they that worship him must worship [him] in spirit and in truth." This shows us that when it comes to God, who is spirit, time is not always concrete. The dimension of time is therefore possibly experienced differently by a being that is spirit, whether that being actually is a spirit, or that being only has a spirit. Without a doubt time is experienced differently for God, who is spirit and the Creator of all other things.

We will go into more about time issues for other spirits later, but for now let's just talk more about other spirits. We will cover other kinds of spirits who are not God, but were created by God, starting with humans. We humans ourselves have spirits, though until we are born again spiritually, the spirits that we have are dead. That is because when Adam sinned, his spirit died, and all humanity has lived with dead spirits ever since.

1 Cor 15:22 "For as in Adam all die, so in Christ all will be made alive."

So every human has a human spirit, but it is dead. But upon being born again by the Holy Spirit when one accepts Jesus as their Lord and Savior, our spirits are made alive. Rom 5:12-19,

"Therefore, just as sin entered the world through one man, and death through sin, and in this way death came to all men, because all sinned-- for before the law was given, sin was in the world. But sin is not taken into account when there is no law. Nevertheless, death reigned from the time of Adam to the time of Moses, even over those who did not sin by breaking a command, as did Adam, who was a pattern of the one to come. But the gift is not like the trespass. For if the many died by the trespass of the one man, how much more did God's grace and the gift that came by the grace of the one man, Jesus Christ, overflow to the many! Again, the gift of God is not like the result of the one man's sin: The judgment followed one sin and brought condemnation, but the gift followed many trespasses and brought justification. For if, by the trespass of the one man, death reigned through that one man, how much more will those who receive God's abundant provision of grace and of the gift of righteousness reign in life through the one man, Jesus Christ. Consequently, just as the result of one trespass was condemnation for all men, so also the result of one act of righteousness was justification that brings life for all men. For just as through the disobedience of the one man the many were made sinners, so also through the obedience of the one man the many will be made righteous."

But whether a human has a live spirit or a dead spirit, all humans have a human spirit. This is clearly shown in the Bible,

Job 32:8 "But [there is] a spirit in man: and the inspiration of the Almighty giveth them understanding."

Psalm 31:5 "Into thine hand I commit my spirit: thou hast redeemed me, O LORD God of truth."

We each have a human spirit. The word for spirit in Hebrew is "ruwach" (7307). There is a different Hebrew word which means "soul" which is "nephesh" (5315). The terms are both used here in Job:

Job 7:11 "Therefore I will not refrain my mouth; I will speak in the anguish of my spirit (ruwach); I will complain in the bitterness of my soul (nephesh)".

So we humans not only each have a spirit, we each have a soul.

In 1 Thes 5:23 we further read, "Now may the God of peace Himself sanctify you entirely; and may your spirit and soul and body be preserved complete, without blame at the coming of our Lord Jesus Christ."

From this we see that for us humans, we each have a spirit, we each have a soul, and we each have a body.

Also in Luke 10:27 we read, "He answered: " 'Love the Lord your God with all your heart and with all your soul and with all your strength and with all your mind'; and, 'Love your neighbor as yourself.'"

So Jesus acknowledged that we each have a heart, a soul, strength, and a mind, which we have power of choice over.

It seems that a human spirit, which is dead, would not be capable of doing much, nor would a person's will be able to command much control over their own spirit, if their spirit was in a dead state. As such it seems that a person's heart, soul, and mind is not part of their spirit, nor is a person's strength defined by a person's own spirit. The spirit is different from the heart, the mind, the body, and the soul of a person. More detail on how we humans are composed is found in Hebrews:

Heb 4:12, "For the word of God is living and active. Sharper than any double-edged sword, it penetrates even to dividing soul and spirit, joints and marrow; it judges the thoughts and attitudes of the heart."

From this we can gather that the soul and spirit can be divided, and thus are different, though the verse implies the soul and spirit are normally found together. Because the verse says, "it penetrates even to dividing soul and spirit", what is implied is that normally the soul and spirit are so meshed together that it is difficult to separate one from another. Perhaps like a wick in a candle, though they are 2 different things, it is hard to divide one from the other. The soul and spirit of a human are normally closely together. We are told in Prov 27:19 of the heart that, "As in water face {reflects} face, so the heart of man {reflects} man." This may mean that an image of the heart of a person reflects the entirety of who that person is, in their soul and spirit, mind and heart, and in all non-bodily ways.

Whether a person has a dead spirit or not, every person has a heart, a mind, and a soul which is intertwined with their spirit.

I think the heart, soul, and mind of a person were designed by God to interact with a person's living spirit. The heart, mind and soul of each of us are open to receive and communicate with our spirit, though that communication would do nothing if our own spirit was dead. Our soul mind and heart are attuned to communicate with our own spirit, but as such they are also attuned to communicate with other spirits, such as God who is

Spirit. We know the Holy Spirit interacts with the dead spirit of a human, causing a rebirth, and bringing the spirit of a human to life, this is shown in John 3: 3-8

"In reply Jesus declared, "I tell you the truth, no one can see the kingdom of God unless he is born again." "How can a man be born when he is old?" Nicodemus asked. "Surely he cannot enter a second time into his mother's womb to be born!" Jesus answered, "I tell you the truth, no one can enter the kingdom of God unless he is born of water and the Spirit. Flesh gives birth to flesh, but the Spirit gives birth to spirit. You should not be surprised at my saying, 'You must be born again.' The wind blows wherever it pleases. You hear its sound, but you cannot tell where it comes from or where it is going. So it is with everyone born of the Spirit."

Also in Eph 1:13-14 we read that the Holy Spirit remains in the born again Christian, sealing them. "And you also were included in Christ when you heard the word of truth, the gospel of your salvation. Having believed, you were marked in him with a seal, the promised Holy Spirit, who is a deposit guaranteeing our inheritance until the redemption of those who are God's possession—to the praise of his glory."

In 2 Cor 1:21-22 we read that the Holy Spirit stays in the hearts of Christians, "Now it is God who makes both us and you stand firm in Christ. He anointed us, set his seal of ownership on us, and put his Spirit in our hearts as a deposit, guaranteeing what is to come."

So the Holy Spirit is in the heart of a Christian, the heart that is what reflects all of whom a person is (Prov 27:19), in all non-bodily ways. The human body itself is mortal, and dies. During life, the body is somehow intertwined with the spirit, soul, heart, and mind of a person. Can these separate from each other, and be untwined?

On the soul, we read in Gen 2:7 "And the LORD God formed man of the dust of the ground, and breathed into his nostrils the breath of life; and man became a living soul." From this we see that the substance of life to the soul came through the body, the breath of God that gave life came into Adam through his nostrils, and then Adam became a living soul. (Prior to the fall and the first sin, Adam had a living spirit as well as a living soul. After Adam sinned his spirit died, and all humanity has had dead spirits since, unless God as the Holy Spirit has in His grace has given rebirth to a human's spirit. After Adam sinned, Adam did not have a living spirit, but Adam still had a living soul.) The life of Adam was tied to his body, and through his body life came about in his soul. So the life of the soul comes through the body.

In Lev 17:11-14 we read, "For the life of a creature is in the blood, and I have given it to you to make atonement for yourselves on the altar; it is the blood that makes atonement for one's life. Therefore I say to the Israelites, "None of you may eat blood, nor may an alien living among you eat blood." " 'Any Israelite or any alien living among you who hunts any animal or bird that may be eaten must drain out the blood and cover it with earth, because the life of every creature is its blood. That is why I have said to the Israelites, "You must not eat the blood of any creature, because the life of every creature is its blood; anyone who eats it must be cut off." So the life of the body comes through the blood.

First God breathed the breath of life into Adam's nostrils, then second the life was in his blood, and then third Adam had and was a living soul. A soul being alive in the physical world, in this life, is dependent on the person's body having life in it. A soul being alive in the spiritual world, after this life, is dependent on the person's spirit having life in it. Still, the soul of a human being was designed to have a body. Without a human being having a body, I believe a person cannot do much. Without the body, there is no life and no consciousness, no awareness. Because there is no life in the soul apart from life in the body and blood, it is therefore it is impossible for a person's soul (and the related heart and mind) to detach, during life, from the body and remain alive and/or have consciousness. What about during death?

When the Christian person's body dies, that person's soul and spirit go to Heaven to wait with God for the resurrection. This is shown in Rev 6:9-11. "When he opened the fifth seal, I saw under the altar the souls of those who had been slain because of the word of God and the testimony they had maintained. They called out in a loud voice, "How long, Sovereign Lord, holy and true, until you judge the inhabitants of the earth and avenge our blood?" Then each of them was given a white robe, and they were told to wait a little longer, until the number of their fellow servants and brothers who were to be killed as they had been was completed." Whether every Christian is conscious, or only the martyrs remain conscious, or the martyrs only have consciousness for a time, I do not know. Paul often refers to Christians in death as being asleep, so it is possible it is like being asleep.

At the (second) resurrection of the dead, that Christian will receive back their reconstituted body from life, but it will be transformed into an immortal physical body, also described as a spiritual body, just like Jesus' mortal body was transformed at His resurrection from the dead. A spiritual body, but having flesh and bone like Jesus had after His resurrection (Luke 24:39). But only those saved in Jesus Christ will continue living in this newly transformed immortal spiritual body like Jesus had after His resurrection, which ties to the fact that they have a living spirit, and during this life that their dead spirit was reborn into life by the Holy Spirit of God. They are saved. That they receive this resurrected Jesus-like body is a choice made by God, and is a gift from Him. But people who do not have a living spirit, but still have a dead spirit, will be made conscious in their soul to experience judgment, likely by a simple reconstitution of their mortal bodies. Rom 14:11 says, "It is written: " 'As surely as I live,' says the Lord, 'every knee will bow before me; every tongue will confess to God.' ". Every one will have a knee to bow with and a tongue to confess with, whether saved or unsaved. Then the unsaved will experience the second death in their reconstituted mortal body, and they will be thrown into the Lake of Fire after they are judged by Jesus Christ.

Rev 20:11-15, "Then I saw a great white throne and him who was seated on it. Earth and sky fled from his presence, and there was no place for them. And I saw the dead, great and small, standing before the throne, and books were opened. Another book was opened, which is the book of life. The dead were judged according to what they had done as recorded in the books. The sea gave up the dead that were in it, and death and Hades gave up the dead that were in them, and each person was judged according to what he had done. Then death and Hades were thrown into the lake of fire. The lake of fire is the second death. If anyone's name was not found written in the book of life, he was thrown into the lake of fire."

This is called the "second death", and as such I believe that some people may become unconscious after a while, like in the first death. But their dead bodies will remain for ever and ever. Isa 66:24 "And they will go out and look upon the dead bodies of those who rebelled against me; their worm will not die, nor will their fire be quenched, and they will be loathsome to all mankind."

But those who (in the Great Tribulation) take the Mark of the Beast on their forehead or hand we are told in Revelation 14 will experience conscious torment day and night without rest for ever and ever. "A third angel followed them and said in a loud voice: "If anyone worships the beast and his image and receives his mark on the forehead or on the hand, he, too, will drink of the wine of God's fury, which has been poured full strength into the cup of his wrath. He will be tormented with burning sulfur in the presence of the holy angels and of the Lamb. And the smoke of their torment rises for ever and ever. There is no rest day or night for those who worship the beast and his image, or for anyone who receives the mark of his name." This calls for patient endurance on the part of the saints who obey God's commandments and remain faithful to Jesus." (It is better to die without the Mark of the Beast, than to accept it and live, for any reason whatsoever. This is where Matt 18:8 may someday take a literal meaning rather than its typically interpreted non-literal meaning today.) Whereas believers who do not take the Mark of the Beast, but would rather die instead, will be raised at the (first) resurrection, receive their spiritual bodies earlier than everyone else, and will reign with Christ personally for 1000 years with a great and wondrous glory.

One thing to learn from how all this operates is that life is tied to the body. When the human body is dead, the human soul and spirit are inactive and unconscious. When the human body is alive, the soul and spirit only remain active and conscious when tied to the person's body. A person's soul and spirit cannot be separated from their body and still be alive. For the life is in the blood, and the blood is in the body. This is except that the rules are a bit different for Christians, who have a living spirit, so their living spirit tied to their soul, allows their soul to go to God upon the death of the Christian's body. But in death the soul cannot just wander around. The soul of the dead Christian is tied to spirit of the dead Christian, and the Christian spirit goes to rest with God. The unsaved soul is tied to a dead spirit, and would just be lost, save that God remembers that person, and they will be resurrected with some sort of body (with life in it) at the Judgment.

We have talked about the heart, soul, mind, and spirit in relation to how they interact with each other in general, and in how they are tied to the body in human beings. Though it is difficult to know all the details, and I do not know them all, nor do I think anybody knows for sure. Somehow the life of a soul and consciousness is tied to the body, the soul is tied to the heart and mind, which are tied to the body as well, and the soul heart and mind are all tied to the spirit as well. The connection of the body to the spirit seems to come once removed through their respective ties to the soul, heart, and mind. Like this: (Spirit)-(Heart/Soul/Mind/Will)-(Body) The 5 dimensional spirit is something each of us has, and it ties into our minds, hearts, and our souls directly: but it however does Not tie into our bodies directly. The human spirit ties into the human body through the heart, soul, and mind. Otherwise, how could the heart, soul, and mind of a person stay in existence, tied to their spirit, after the body has died and disintegrated away? For this reason the spirit and mortal body cannot be directly connected, but the connection has to come through the soul, mind, and heart of a person.

We have also talked about how God is spirit, though God is a vastly different spirit than us humans are in each having spirits. A human spirit is very different from God, who is also a spirit. Part of this difference is obviously shown in how time is experienced very differently for God and Jesus, and for us humans. God is infinite and an infinite spirit, but we humans are finite and only part of us is our own finite spirit. Next I want to focus more on talking about the finite spirit itself, how to describe finite spirits in substance, its attributes, and then move on to talking about other kinds of finite spirits (or all non-God spirits) besides humans.

First off, to explain finite spirits like a human spirit, there is a necessity for the existence of a 5th dimension, beyond height, width, length, matter, mass, energy, and time. This is the dimension of the spirit, or spiritual dimension; a 5th, spiritual, dimension. Spirits are things that don't have any substance in the basic 3 spatial dimensions, and have no matter, energy, or mass. A spirit exists in the 4th dimension of time, and does pass through time. Human spirits are not in any way directly impacted by the physical 3 dimensional world as it passes through time. For instance, one can't hit a human spirit with a rock and hurt it. The only impact that can be had on a human spirit through the 3 dimensional world must come through the soul, heart, mind and body that the human spirit is intertwined with.

Human beings all have spirits. Most people have dead spirits, and born-again Christians have living spirits, Thank the Lord Jesus Christ! But whether a human being has a living or dead spirit, we each still have a spirit. And that spirit is not a 3 dimensional object affected by the 4th dimension, but rather a 5th dimensional "thing" (or spiritual realm "thing") affected by the 4th dimension. So there is a spiritual dimension. Our spirit is finite, and explainable with a 5th (or more) dimension(s), but God who is spirit is not limited to the 5d. God's spirit is infinite. So there is a difference between finite spirits, and God.

By 5th dimension here, I am not saying exactly what dimension this might be in a science sort of way. Right now, I am using this term loosely: by 5th dimension I mean a spiritual realm aspect to us that is distinctly different from the 3d physical world we know, or the 4th dimension of time; something that is not matter, or energy, but spirit, of the spiritual realm. Under modern science theories, tiny curled up 5th dimensional balls smaller than the size of a cell are possible - perhaps we humans each have one of those (made to come alive, or still dead), which are unshakably tied to our souls and bodies. Or perhaps our spirits are something else. I don't know: please just understand I am using the term loosely here. (I will talk about dimensions in a much more concretely defined way in later chapters.)

Why did God give us a spirit? Because God made us in His image, and God is Spirit. And God meant for us to worship Him in spirit and in truth.

We were created to be both alive and receptive spiritually for this reason: for our relationship with God. Nowadays, people are born spiritually dead but still receptive. When a person is born-again they become spiritually alive and receptive, as we were originally intended to be, like Adam and Eve had living spirits before the fall. 1 Cor 15:22, "For as in Adam all die, so also in Christ all will be made alive."

So we originally were created for our spirit to be alive and receive from God, and Christians can do this today, for their spirits have been born again and are alive. We can pray and worship in spirit to God, which is what He originally designed us to do, He created us to have a two-way relationship with Him. But as for the unsaved, or Christians, our hearts, souls, and minds were made to be able to receive from our own 5d spirits, and from God, who is Spirit. God created us to have a spirit for the purpose of using our spirits to have a direct relationship with Him.

Another thing we can know about the spirit of a human is that, as a class, human spirits have no supernatural or paranormal powers. God is Spirit, and God has infinite power and ability. Our spirits do not.

This can be seen in that Christians in the Bible, in order to partake in the doing of miraculous things, had to have received the Gifts of the Holy Spirit. God was the one that did these miracles. Miraculous healings took place with the apostles after Jesus ascended, but this was not by their own power spiritually. Rather this was God's power working through them. If the Gifts of the Holy Spirit include miraculous things, supernatural things, like healing, speaking in unknown tongues, amazing signs following them, prophecy of events to come, etc. then we can see that the apostles could not have done these things themselves by any means.

So this shows that the nature of a human spirit is such that it has absolutely

NO supernatural powers inherent in it's abilities. God did not make the human spirit to have supernatural powers inherent in itself in how God created it. So although we have a spirit, being made in God's image, for God is Spirit, unlike God, we do not have any spiritual supernatural powers inherent in us. But as Christians God gives us Gifts by His Holy Spirit who lives within us.

The key point here is that human beings have no paranormal or supernatural powers of their own. We were not created to have powers such as these, and we still don't today.

However, the world is not just full of human spirits, and God. There are also Holy angels who work for God in accordance to His Will. Holy angels are also spirits, different than God, and different than humans. They have supernatural powers inherent in their spirits, in themselves that God created them with, which we humans do not have.

And unfortunately, there are also fallen angels, spirits who have supernatural powers as well, and use them for evil. And as discussed earlier in this book, there are also demons. Demons are different than human spirits, and fallen angels, having a mix of the abilities of both. In this chapter we covered the supernatural abilities of humans (namely none). In the next few chapters we will cover the supernatural powers of fallen angels and demons, and modern science ideas which may explain how these powers work, or

Chapter Six
Powers and Physics of Fallen Angels

We are going to take a look at the abilities demonstrated by angels in the Bible.

It would make sense that the abilities of fallen angels would be the same as the abilities of Holy angels. As such I'm going to be using examples found in the Bible of both Holy angels and fallen angels, to establish what the Bible says are the abilities of angels in general.

Angelic Apparitions

The first category of angelic encounters is "Mental Envelopments" or "Mental Attacks". This angelic ability is demonstrated in the following passage:

Dan 10: 1-12 "In the third year of Cyrus king of Persia a thing was revealed unto Daniel, whose name was called Belteshazzar; and the thing was true, but the time appointed was long: and he understood the thing, and had understanding of the vision. In those days I Daniel was mourning three full weeks. I ate no pleasant bread, neither came flesh nor wine in my mouth, neither did I anoint myself at all, till three whole weeks were fulfilled. And in the four and twentieth day of the first month, as I was by the side of the great river, which is Hiddekel; Then I lifted up mine eyes, and looked, and behold a certain man clothed in linen, whose loins were girded with fine gold of Uphaz: His body also was like the beryl, and his face as the appearance of lightning, and his eyes as lamps of fire, and his arms and his feet like in colour to polished brass, and the voice of his words like the voice of a multitude. And I Daniel alone saw the vision: for the men that were with me saw not the vision; but a great quaking fell upon them, so that they fled to hide themselves. Therefore I was left alone, and saw this great vision, and there remained no strength in me: for my comeliness was turned in me into corruption, and I retained no strength.

Yet heard I the voice of his words: and when I heard the voice of his words, then was I in a deep sleep on my face, and my face toward the ground. And, behold, an hand touched me, which set me upon my knees and upon the palms of my hands. And he said unto me, O Daniel, a man greatly beloved, understand the words that I speak unto thee, and stand upright: for unto thee am I now sent. And when he had spoken this word unto me, I stood trembling. Then said he unto me, Fear not, Daniel: for from the first day that thou didst set thine heart to understand, and to chasten thyself before thy God, thy words were heard, and I am come for thy words."

What can we observe from this passage?

Daniel calls what he experienced a "great vision" (Daniel 10:8) caused by an angel. While having this "vision":

It was real to the bodily senses: Daniel was in his body, he saw with his eyes, he heard with his ears, he felt a hand touch his body, felt being on his hands and knees and later standing up, he felt bodily trembling,

The vision Daniel saw was overlaid on top of the reality everyone else could see, but others could not see it. (Daniel 10:7)

What Daniel saw was unusual, and even impossible-seeming, such as a face with the "appearance of lightning". Also the voice of the singular being he was seeing sounded like a multitude of voices.

Daniel was awake, and not dreaming, nor in a trance.

So Daniel's body is still surrounded by objective reality, the river, the landscape, the men fleeing from something they can't see, but feel emotionally. However Daniel's mind is also seeing a vision from an angel overlaid onto this objective reality, and this vision that he is interactive with feels completely real to his bodily senses.

Another example is in Acts 10:9-17, "On the morrow, as they went on their journey, and drew nigh unto the city, Peter went up upon the housetop to pray about the sixth hour: And he became very hungry, and would have eaten: but while they made ready, he fell into a trance, And saw heaven opened, and a certain vessel descending upon him, as it had been a great sheet knit at the four corners, and let down to the earth: Wherein were all manner of fourfooted beasts of the earth, and wild beasts, and creeping things, and fowls of the air. And there came a voice to him, Rise, Peter; kill, and eat. But Peter said, Not so, Lord; for I have never eaten any thing that is common or unclean. And the voice spake unto him again the second time, What God hath cleansed, that call not thou common. This was done thrice: and the vessel was received up again into heaven. Now while Peter doubted in himself what this vision which he had seen should mean, behold, the men which were sent from Cornelius had made enquiry for Simon's house, and stood before the gate."

Observations:

Peter had this "vision" in a "trance", while awake, and not asleep. The "trance" is not described as "dreaming". It seems likely that those preparing for lunch with Peter saw Peter in this trance state. However, this trance state is not described as "dreaming". Peter was awake, and not asleep.

Peter observed being in his body - this is implied by his optionally being able to "rise, kill, and eat". Peter also is seeing with his eyes, and hearing with his ears.

Peter, like Daniel, sees unusual or impossible-seeming things.

What Peter experienced during this trance the Bible calls a 'vision' ("horama" Strong's 3705). Earlier in Acts 10:3, Cornelius also receives a "horama" vision, specified to be caused by an angel. Later, in Acts 12, Peter is unsure whether or not he is having another vision, when an angel is present:

"Peter followed him (an angel) out of the prison, but he had no idea that what the angel was doing was really happening; he thought he was seeing a vision" Acts 10:9 NIV

So there is really no doubt that 'visions', which communicate a message, are Biblically associated as being caused by angels - Holy angels who are God's messengers. (The Greek word angelos means "messenger".)

The word above in Acts 10 for 'trance' is "ekstasis" (1611 in the Strong's). The second definition is "a throwing of the mind out of its normal state, alienation of mind, whether such as makes a lunatic or that of a man who by some sudden emotion is transported as it were out of himself, so that in this rapt condition, although he is awake, his mind is drawn off from all surrounding objects and wholly fixed on things divine that he sees nothing but the forms and images lying within, and thinks that he perceives with his bodily eyes and ears realities shown him by God."

So, even the Strong's Concordance defines this trance as an experience in the mind, which is perceived with "bodily eyes and ears", or in other words is real to the bodily senses. In Peter's case, he describes perceiving hearing with his ears, seeing with his eyes, and speaking with his mouth. This indicates he perceives himself as being in his body, experiencing something which seems real to all the bodily senses. However, it is implied that those around Peter perceive him as being in a trance state.

Another kind of partial vision, as Daniel had, arguably and likely facilitated by a Holy angel messenger (Se Rev 1, 1:1) happened to Paul and the men with him in Acts 9 (related again in Acts 22).

Acts 9:3-8, "And as he journeyed, he came near Damascus: and suddenly there shined round about him a light from heaven: And he fell to the earth, and heard a voice saying unto him, Saul, Saul, why persecutest thou me? And he said, Who art thou, Lord? And the Lord said, I am Jesus whom thou persecutest: it is hard for thee to kick against the pricks. And he trembling and astonished said, Lord, what wilt thou have me to do? And the Lord said unto him, Arise, and go into the city, and it shall be told thee what thou must do. And the men which journeyed with him stood speechless, hearing a voice, but seeing no man. And Saul arose from the earth; and when his eyes were opened, he saw no man: but they led him by the hand, and brought him into Damascus."

Acts 22:6-11, "And it came to pass, that, as I made my journey, and was come nigh unto Damascus about noon, suddenly there shone from heaven a great light round about me. And I fell unto the ground, and heard a voice saying unto me, Saul, Saul, why persecutest thou me? And I answered, Who art thou, Lord? And he said unto me, I am Jesus of Nazareth, whom thou persecutest. And they that were with me saw indeed the light, and were afraid; but they understood not the voice of him that spake to me. And I said, What shall I do, LORD? And the Lord said unto me, Arise, and go into Damascus; and there it shall be told thee of all things which are appointed for thee to do. And when I could not see for the glory of that light, being led by the hand of them that were with me, I came into Damascus."

Observations:

Paul and the men saw the light, though no one saw to whom the voice which was speaking belonged.

Paul saw the glory of the light, and it was so intense he was blinded by it, but the men with him did not even see it..

Paul heard and understood the voice that was speaking.

The men heard the voice that was speaking, but did not understand it

In this case the vision was waking, and very partial (in that sight and vision were affected but not other senses).

What is most interesting is that the vision was experienced in one way by Paul, and in another, more limited way, by the men with him. This implies that group waking mental attack visions are possible, in which one person sees A but another person sees B.

Another kind of mental vision caused by angels is simply seeing the angel in a dream, such as in the case of Joseph the husband of Mary, surrogate father of Jesus Christ:

Matt 1:20 But while he thought on these things, behold, the angel of the Lord appeared unto him in a dream, saying, Joseph, thou son of David, fear not to take unto thee Mary thy wife: for that which is conceived in her is of the Holy Ghost.

Matt 2:13 And when they were departed, behold, the angel of the Lord appeareth to Joseph in a dream, saying, Arise, and take the young child and his mother, and flee into Egypt, and be thou there until I bring thee word: for Herod will seek the young child to destroy him.

This summarizes as:

First Category of Angelic Encounters: Mental Envelopments

1. Visions – are completely real to the bodily senses

    a. Fully, or partially, overlaying objective reality

    b. fully awake, or a waking trance state

    c. experienced by one person or multiple people

2. Dreams – are not real to the bodily senses, and happen while asleep

I categorize these kinds of angelic encounters as "mental attacks" (for fallen angels) or "mental envelopments" (for Holy angels), and also simply call them "visions". They are real to the bodily senses, but other people cannot see them.

Mental Envelopments can be full visions (as in Peter's case) in which a trance is involved. Objective (or "normal") reality is no longer seen, but rather only the landscape of the vision, which is real to the bodily senses.

Mental Envelopments can be partial visions (as in Daniel's case), in which the vision is overlaid onto objective reality, and both are perceived with the bodily senses at the same time.

Mental Envelopments can happen to one person alone, or to several people at the same time (as with Paul on the Damascus Road).

Mental Envelopments can also occur while in a dream, which is not real to the bodily senses, and happens while asleep in a dream. This is not the same as a waking vision, whether full or partial, whether in a trance state or not, and dreams are not real to the bodily senses in the same way as a waking or trance vision.

When it comes to the perception of time, in these cases the subjective perception of the passing of time of Daniel and Peter seemed to match the objective amount of time that had passed for other people around them. However, this is arguably not always the case with angelic encounters. (More on that later.)

The second category of angelic encounters is Physical Attacks or Experiences.

Acts 12:5-12, 18-19, "Peter therefore was kept in prison: but prayer was made without ceasing of the church unto God for him. And when Herod would have brought him forth, the same night Peter was sleeping between two soldiers, bound with two chains: and the keepers before the door kept the prison. And, behold, the angel of the Lord came upon him, and a light shined in the prison: and he smote Peter on the side, and raised him up, saying, Arise up quickly. And his chains fell off from his hands. And the angel said unto him, Gird thyself, and bind on thy sandals. And so he did. And he saith unto him, Cast thy garment about thee, and follow me. And he went out, and followed him; and wist not that it was true which was done by the angel; but thought he saw a vision. When they were past the first and the second ward, they came unto the iron gate that leadeth unto the city; which opened to them of his own accord: and they went out, and passed on through one street; and forthwith the angel departed from him. And when Peter was come to himself, he said, Now I know of a surety, that the LORD hath sent his angel, and hath delivered me out of the hand of Herod, and from all the expectation of the people of the Jews. And when he had considered the thing, he came to the house of Mary the mother of John, whose surname was Mark; where many were gathered together praying. .... Now as soon as it was day, there was no small stir among the soldiers, what was become of Peter. And when Herod had sought for him, and found him not, he examined the keepers, and commanded that they should be put to death. And he went down from Judaea to Caesarea, and there abode."

In this case an angel is sent to free Peter from Herod's prison. At first Peter thinks he is experiencing a vision, but soon realizes the events have truly taken place. Peter had visions before, and his confusion proves the point that visions are real to the bodily senses - as real as objective reality - which is why Peter was not sure if what was happening was a vision or not. But the events did take place in objective reality.

The angel materialized in a physical way and caused lasting physical changes in objective reality. Other people, such as the guards, Herod, and Peter's friends were all affected by these lasting physical changes to objective reality.

Not only that, but the angel was able to defy physics in objective reality, or seem to have supernatural powers, by doing things such as causing a light to shine, chains to fall off, likely opening what was a locked gate, and moving a very heavy door with apparently supernatural strength, as well as appearing and disappearing seemingly out of nowhere.

Another case is seen in Gen 19:

Gen 19:1-7, 10-13, 24-28, "And there came two angels to Sodom at even; and Lot sat in the gate of Sodom: and Lot seeing them rose up to meet them; and he bowed himself with his face toward the ground; And he said, Behold now, my lords, turn in, I pray you, into your servant's house, and tarry all night, and wash your feet, and ye shall rise up early, and go on your ways.

And they said, Nay; but we will abide in the street all night. And he pressed upon them greatly; and they turned in unto him, and entered into his house; and he made them a feast, and did bake unleavened bread, and they did eat. But before they lay down, the men of the city, even the men of Sodom, compassed the house round, both old and young, all the people from every quarter: And they called unto Lot, and said unto him, Where are the men which came in to thee this night? bring them out unto us, that we may know them. And Lot went out at the door unto them, and shut the door after him, And said, I pray you, brethren, do not so wickedly....But the men put forth their hand, and pulled Lot into the house to them, and shut to the door. And they smote the men that were at the door of the house with blindness, both small and great: so that they wearied themselves to find the door. And the men said unto Lot, Hast thou here any besides? son in law, and thy sons, and thy daughters, and whatsoever thou hast in the city, bring them out of this place: For we will destroy this place, because the cry of them is waxen great before the face of the LORD; and the LORD hath sent us to destroy it...Then the LORD rained upon Sodom and upon Gomorrah brimstone and fire from the LORD out of heaven; And he overthrew those cities, and all the plain, and all the inhabitants of the cities, and that which grew upon the ground. But his wife looked back from behind him, and she became a pillar of salt. And Abraham gat up early in the morning to the place where he stood before the LORD: And he looked toward Sodom and Gomorrah, and toward all the land of the plain, and beheld, and, lo, the smoke of the country went up as the smoke of a furnace."

Some observations: All of the men of the city could see the angels, not just Lot. The angels caused all the men who were harassing Lot to become blind. The angels likely turned Lot's wife into a pillar of salt. The angels also destroyed the city of Sodom and Gomorrah, and Abraham was able to observe the smoke from the city's destruction from far away. Today some people (see arkdiscovery.com) say they have found the destroyed city, and no doubt some evidence of this angelic event remains to this day, somewhere.

In the case of Sodom and Gomorrah the angels were seen by men and interacted with them. However, angels can also interact with objective reality without being seen, as in the case of Job.

Job 1:12-19, "And the LORD said unto Satan, Behold, all that he hath is in thy power; only upon himself put not forth thine hand. So Satan went forth from the presence of the LORD.
And there was a day when his sons and his daughters were eating and drinking wine in their eldest brother's house: And there came a messenger unto Job, and said, The oxen were plowing, and the asses feeding beside them: And the Sabeans fell upon them, and took them away; yea, they have slain the servants with the edge of the sword; and I only am escaped alone to tell thee. While he was yet speaking, there came also another, and said, The fire of God is fallen from heaven, and hath burned up the sheep, and the servants, and consumed them; and I only am escaped alone to tell thee. While he was yet speaking, there came also another, and said, The Chaldeans made out three bands, and fell upon the camels, and have carried them away, yea, and slain the servants with the edge of the sword; and I only am escaped alone to tell thee. While he was yet speaking, there came also another, and said, Thy sons and thy daughters were eating and drinking wine in their eldest brother's house: And, behold, there came a great wind from the wilderness, and smote the four corners of the house, and it fell upon the young men, and they are dead; and I only am escaped alone to tell thee".

In this case God effectively removed a "hedge of protection" around Job and allowed everything but Job's life to be put "into Satan's hands"

(Job 1:12). Satan then inspired people to kill Job's servants, caused a fire from heaven to come down and kill his sheep and servants, and caused a great wind to demolish a house on top of Job's children, killing them all. Though Satan was effectively invisible in all of these events, nevertheless the events Satan caused occurred in objective reality with multiple witnesses as to what had occurred.

Another subset of Physical Attacks, of physical illness or injury, is seen in Acts and in Job:

Acts 12:21-23, "And upon a set day Herod, arrayed in royal apparel, sat upon his throne, and made an oration unto them. And the people gave a shout, saying, It is the voice of a god, and not of a man. And immediately the angel of the Lord smote him, because he gave not God the glory: and he was eaten of worms, and died. "

In this case in Acts the angel was invisible, at least his public appearance to the crowd is not recorded, and the angel caused a physical ailment resulting in death to the body of a person.

Job 2:6-7, "And the LORD said unto Satan, Behold, he is in thine hand; but save his life. So went Satan forth from the presence of the LORD, and smote Job with sore boils from the sole of his foot unto his crown. "

In this case in Job, the angel, Satan, was invisible, but in objective reality caused real and visible injury/disease to the body of a person.

Observations on Physical Attacks

1.   Multiple witnesses of angels

2.   Multiple witnesses to lasting physical effects, including illnesses, and sometimes even death

3.   Supernatural occurrences, that seem to defy physics, in objective reality

4.   Objective reality generally follows normal physical laws, except for actions of angels

This summarizes as:

Physical Attacks:

> 1. Lasting physical effects in objective reality with multiple witnesses caused by both
>
> > a. Visible angels, and
> >
> > b. Invisible angels

The third category of angelic encounters is "Combination Experiences".

Let's look at some scriptural examples for the third category of angelic encounters. The first two scriptural examples say "he carried me away in the spirit".

Rev 17:3, "So he carried me away in the spirit into the wilderness: and I saw a woman sit upon a scarlet coloured beast, full of names of blasphemy, having seven heads and ten horns."

Rev 21:10, "And he carried me away in the spirit to a great and high mountain, and shewed me that great city, the holy Jerusalem, descending out of heaven from God,"

The "he" that is referenced here is an angel of the Lord, a messenger of Jesus Christ. This is established in

Rev 22:8-9, "And I John saw these things, and heard [them]. And when I had heard and seen, I fell down to worship before the feet of the angel which shewed me these things. Then saith he unto me, See [thou do it] not: for I am thy fellow servant, and of thy brethren the prophets, and of them which keep the sayings of this book: worship God."

So we know "he" is an angel of the Lord.

From these passages, we see that angels can "carry someone away in the spirit". These two passages say so specifically, however other passages in scripture are a little more unclear in terminology as to whether the "Spirit of the Lord" or an "angel of the Lord" is involved. But as we know an angel was doing the "carrying away in the spirit" in the above verses in Revelation, we can reasonably conclude that this angel was also doing the things mentioned in other passages in Revelation. Such as:

Rev 1:10-19, "I was in the Spirit on the Lord's day, and heard behind me a great voice, as of a trumpet, Saying, I am Alpha and Omega, the first and the last: and, What thou seest, write in a book, and send [it] unto the seven churches which are in Asia; unto Ephesus, and unto Smyrna, and unto Pergamos, and unto Thyatira, and unto Sardis, and unto Philadelphia, and unto Laodicea. And I turned to see the voice that spake with me. And being turned, I saw seven golden candlesticks; And in the midst of the seven candlesticks [one] like unto the Son of man, clothed with a garment down to the foot, and girt about the paps with a golden girdle. His head and [his] hairs [were] white like wool, as white as snow; and his eyes [were] as a flame of fire; And his feet like unto fine brass, as if they burned in a furnace; and his voice as the sound of many waters. And he had in his right hand seven stars: and out of his mouth went a sharp twoedged sword: and his countenance [was] as the sun shineth in his strength. And when I saw him, I fell at his feet as dead. And he laid his right hand upon me, saying unto me, Fear not; I am the first and the last: I [am] he that liveth, and was dead; and, behold, I am alive for evermore, Amen; and have the keys of hell and of death. Write the things which thou hast seen, and the things which are, and the things which shall be hereafter…"

Altogether, the entire imagery John recorded in the book of Revelation was caused by an angel of the Lord showing him these things (though I'm not going to quote the entire book of Revelation here). What John experienced was real to all the bodily senses, even including taste, and he was in his body.

Rev 4:2-3, "After this I looked, and, behold, a door [was] opened in heaven: and the first voice which I heard [was] as it were of a trumpet talking with me; which said, Come up hither, and I will shew thee things which must be hereafter. And immediately I was in the spirit: and, behold, a throne was set in heaven, and [one] sat on the throne. And he that sat was to look upon like a jasper and a sardine stone: and [there was] a rainbow round about the throne, in sight like unto an emerald."

Rev 10:10, "And I took the little book out of the angel's hand, and ate it up; and it was in my mouth sweet as honey: and as soon as I had eaten it, my belly was bitter."

Rev 10:4, "And when the seven thunders had uttered their voices, I was about to write: and I heard a voice from heaven saying unto me, Seal up those things which the seven thunders uttered, and write them not."

Notable is that in Revelation John ate a scroll which was part of the vision, tasted it, and it was "bitter to his stomach". Also, John was writing down what he saw and heard throughout his experience on a paper, and this paper remained with him after the experience had ended.

John did not write down the experience after it had ended, but while it was ongoing. Whether John was given the paper to write on and the writing instrument during the vision, or if John carried these things into the experience and out of the experience later, is unknown. But in either case a different level of physicality is shown here than in mental envelopments, or physical attacks.

Unlike the other two categories, John did not record that he had a "vision", nor was "in a trance", the terms used to refer to "mental envelopments", nor was it an "Physical Attack". Instead, the key phrases used are "carried away" and "in the spirit".

Another angelic encounter in a passage with similar terminology is:

Luke 4:5, "And the devil, taking him up into an high mountain, shewed unto him all the kingdoms of the world in a moment of time."

The Greek word here for 'moment' is "stigme" (4743) which literally means a "point" of time. This word is used only once in the New Testament, but is used in the Greek Old Testament, the Septuagint, in Isaiah 29:5. The word that is translated as "stigme" is "petha`" (6621) in Hebrew. According to Thayer's Lexicon, "petha" means "the opening of the eyes", hence the meaning "a moment of time".

The amount of time referenced to here, is the amount of time it takes to open your eyes. This is no more than the time it would take to blink.

It takes humans 300 to 400 milliseconds, that is 3/10ths to 4/10ths of a second, to blink.

How could Jesus see "all the kingdoms of the world" in the time it takes to blink? It would seem that to be shown all the kingdoms of the world should take at least a couple hours, if not days, if a thorough tour was done. But even snapshot pictures in quick succession would take several minutes, and this without any time to comprehend or think about what one was seeing, the necessary amount of time is still incredibly more than 400 milliseconds.

Obviously another attribute of this kind of angelic encounter is time perception manipulation of the person having the experience. This passage implies that one second passed in time, but Jesus experienced subjectively a much longer period of time during that one second.

Some observations about these passages:

Like other kinds of angelic encounters, the experience is physically real to all the bodily senses, and the person is in their body.

The person is carried or taken "in the spirit", implying they have been "carried" or "taken" in some fashion of a spiritual nature.

The person is in a place of fantastically unrealistic scenery and/or a place in which out of the ordinary or impossible-seeming things occur.

In John's case, he is writing on a real scroll during the entire experience, and the real scroll remains with him afterwards. So objects taken into the experience can be altered and retained afterwards. This also implies that objects obtained by a person during the experience could remain afterwards, and/or that objects brought into the experience could be lost.

In John's case he eats a scroll that is part of the encounter, and his stomach is upset by it, as such the experience can physically go inside the human body and have internal effects.

Time perception manipulation of the person having the experience.

I categorize these types of angelic encounters as "Combination". There are two reasons for doing so.

The first is the different terminology the Bible uses: "carried away" or "taken up in the spirit".

The second is there seems to be more physicality in these cases than in "Mental envelopment visions" and less physicality than in "Physical Attacks".

So, interpreting from the Bible, the three categories of fallen angel attacks are: Mental Attacks in visions or dreams, Physical Attacks, and Combination Attacks

Types of Fallen Angelic Apparitions

Mental Attacks

> 1. Visions – real to the bodily senses
>
>> a. Fully, or partially, overlaying objective reality
>>
>> b. fully awake, or a waking trance state
>>
>> c. one person or multiple people
>
> 2. Dreams – not real to bodily senses, and happen while asleep

Physical Attacks

Lasting physical effects in objective reality with multiple witnesses

> 1. Visible angels
>
> 2. Invisible angels

Combination Attacks

> 1. Normal or Manipulated perception of time
>
> 2. Objects carried in/taken with, or not

I have tried to organize Fallen Angelic Apparitions into categories that are as well defined as possible, so as to be easier to understand. However, there are limitations on the accuracy of these categories.

The main problem is that angels have such expansive powers that it is possible to combine these categories, or have overlap between them.

For instance, it may be possible to have multiple people experience a Combination attack at the same time. Also, if a person is alone, it is very difficult to discern a Combination attack from a Mental Attack. Additionally, it would make sense that a manipulated perception of time could occur in a Mental Attack, as well as a Combination experience.

It can be confusing to categorize exactly what happened, especially between the Mental Attack and Combination Attack categories.

I believe the Bible speaks on this difficulty, with firm guidance on how we should view this difficulty in 2 Corinthians 12:2-4:

"I knew a man in Christ above fourteen years ago, (whether in the body, I cannot tell; or whether out of the body, I cannot tell: God knoweth;) such an one caught up to the third heaven. And I knew such a man, (whether in the body, or out of the body, I cannot tell: God knoweth;) How that he was caught up into paradise, and heard unspeakable words, which it is not lawful for a man to utter."

Here Paul expresses he doesn't know whether the man was "caught up" inside his body (a Mental Envelopment) or outside of his body (a Combination experience (or possibly real travel). However, God knows, and we really don't need to know which it was, it's not that important. The Bible essentially tells us that it may be impossible for us to figure out, so there's no need to dwell on it.

So, ultimately the abilities and attacks of fallen angels that people experience are like the parable of the blind men and the elephant.

The first held its trunk, and said, "It's like a snake." The second leaned against its belly and said "it's like a wall" and the third held its tail and said, "it's like a rope". In truth, the elephant was like all of those things, and a lot more.

In truth, fallen angels have expansive powers, and that is the bottom line. One person would say its like a vision, another would say its a holodeck-like experience, and in another case we would say it was completely real… but they are all real experiences, and like the elephant, fallen angels have expansive powers which we cannot understand, which are not limited by our individual perceptions of them.

This level of power in the hands of fallen and evil angels is staggering to conceptualize. I thank God that they are limited in what they can do, and who they can do it to, by God's laws of spiritual authority grounds. A fallen angel can only attack someone if they have spiritual authority grounds and rights to do so. God places his protection on people, limiting whom the fallen angels can harass and harm, and limiting the extent of the harm that they can do to a person. (See Job 1 and 2, also the New Testament is full of this concept. I will cover more on this in the next chapter and in a later chapter on spiritual warfare.) It is also a relief to know that for every fallen angel, there are 2 Holy angels working for God and Jesus; the fallen angels are outnumbered two to one.

Chapter Seven
Powers, Physics and Science - Part 1

Next we are going to move onto the Physics. The goal of this portion is to explain how fallen angels could do these things, conceptualize their abilities, using modern physics terminology and theories. The main point of doing this is to show that science does not preclude the existence of fallen angels, nor rule out their Biblically described abilities. I believe modern science actually completely allows for fallen angels and their Biblically described abilities.

All of the categories of angelic apparitions would be called supernatural events.

There are some words in the Bible to describe the "supernatural" activities of God, Holy angels, and fallen angels.

Greek - signs "semeion" (4592), wonders "teras" (5059), and miracles "dynamis" (1411).

These same 3 words are all used in the context of:

God - the power of God, in signs, wonders, and miracles that God, Jesus Christ, and the Holy Spirit through the gift of miracles, as seen throughout the Bible

Angels

Holy angels. (Acts 2:22, 5:12, 2 Peter 2:11, Heb 2:4)

Fallen angels, of the dragon and beast, and the "3 evil spirits like frogs". (Matt 24:24, 2 Thes 2:9, Rev 13:2, 14, 16:14)

From the Bible it is clear that God in His three persons, Holy angels, and also Fallen angels, are all capable of performing signs, wonders, and miracles.

How, in physics terminology, might God work signs, wonders, and miracles?

Gen 1:1 In the beginning God created the heaven and the earth.

Eph 3:18 May be able to comprehend with all saints what [is] the breadth, and length, and depth, and height

Rev 1:8 I am Alpha and Omega, the beginning and the ending, saith the Lord, which is, and which was, and which is to come, the Almighty.

We live in an observably 4 dimensional universe. The universe is made of space(3) + and time(1) dimensions, of the Spacetime we can see. God made all the 3 dimensions of space that we see (length, width, and height), when God "created the heaven and the earth". God made the dimension of time "in the beginning", which marked the creation of time itself, the dimension of time as we know it. God is eternal, and having made time itself, God is outside of time, and was here before time was created. God has complete authority and control over the dimension of time. God also made the three dimensions of space, and is also outside of them. So, God made it all, and is outside of the entire universe, having created it.

Are there more dimensions that God made, besides the 4 we can perceive? Maybe.

The term "heaven" is used in several different ways in the Bible, referring to the atmosphere, the sky, outerspace, the place where the angels dwell, and God's throne where the angels can go. Although the angels can be in the presence of God, God created the angels, as God created mankind. We are 4 dimensional in our physicality, being made for 4 dimensions. Angels are spirits, and Jesus said after His Resurrection in Luke 24:39:

"Behold my hands and my feet, that it is I myself: handle me, and see; for a spirit hath not flesh and bones, as ye see me have."

This could be taken, that truly angels are not physical life of the 3 physical dimensions we live in, as we are. Rather, angels are spirits of the heavenly realm, and their "bodies" exist in another dimension, a spirit or a heaven dimension. It would make sense that their bodies are composed of the substance of this spirit or heaven dimension they live in, as human bodies are composed of the stuff of the 3 physical dimensions we live in.

1 Cor 15:40, 44 [There are] also celestial bodies, and bodies terrestrial: but the glory of the celestial [is] one, and the [glory] of the terrestrial [is] another... It is sown a natural body; it is raised a spiritual body. There is a natural body, and there is a spiritual body.

The word in 1 Cor 15, "celestial" (epouranios 2032) means "existing in heaven". The Bible acknowledges that there are living beings in heaven, and there can be bodies made of spirit. As our human terrestrial bodies are composed of 4-dimensional physical matter, it would make sense that living spirit or heavenly bodies would be composed of the "matter" of the realm of heaven. Angels have such heavenly bodies, and were created with such. It would make sense that there is at least a 5th dimension, if not more, and that the angels bodies are composed of the analogy to our "4d matter" in that heavenly realm. The heavenly realm might be composed of several heavenly dimensions, in the scientific sense of the term, such as a heavenly realm width, length, and height. But even if the heavenly realm is just 1 heavenly dimension, in the scientific sense of the term, heaven would still be a 5th dimension, 1 more dimension that the 4 dimensional physical world we perceive.

The additional dimension(s) that the angels have bodies in, bodies which are composed of that extra dimension or dimensions, would be an extra dimension more than the 4 dimensions that we perceive. Thus it would be fair to call angels "extra-dimensional", meaning of more dimensions than us.

1 Kings 8:27 But will God indeed dwell on the earth? behold, the heaven and heaven of heavens cannot contain thee; how much less this house that I have builded?

Deut 10:14 Behold, the heaven and the heaven of heavens [is] the LORD'S thy God, the earth [also], with all that therein [is].

"The heaven and the heaven of heavens" is an interesting phrase, which implies no less that 4 heavens.

The heaven (1)

+ and the heaven (1)

+ of heavens (1+1 = (2) minimum)

_____

= at least 4 heavens.

The Bible may speak of extra dimensions, even multiple extra dimensions, in relation to the heavenly realm. The phrase heaven and the heaven of the heavens may describe at least 4 heavens.

If the atmosphere was the first heaven, and outerspace was a second heaven, and God's throne was the third heaven, then there is still room for one more heaven, which could be where the angels exist when they are not at God's throne, and the angel's bodies could be made of the "stuff" of this heavenly dimension.

It is also important to note from these scriptures, that God Himself cannot be contained within the heavens, and they are His, because God made them all. The heaven of God's throne, where the angels can be in the presence of God, is also a dimension of heaven that God made. An additional heaven where angels exist when they are not at God's throne is also a heaven that God made. God himself cannot be contained in any of heavens or the dimensions of heaven or earth that God made. God is therefore, not extra-dimensional. The Bible seems to say that angels are "extra-dimensional", but God cannot be "extra-dimensional".

God is eternal, and therefore is what I call "outer-dimensional". It's not just that God is in another additional dimension, or dimensions, which would make God extra-dimensional, No, God is outside of dimensionality, being eternal and the Creator of everything that is, including all dimensions of heaven and earth, and everything living in them. So to coin a term, God is "outer-dimensional". This is an important distinction between the God the Creator, and His creation.

So the Bible may be interpreted to indicate that angels are extra-dimensional and have extra-dimensional bodies. What would modern physics have to say about this?

Modern physics actually does include the topic of extra dimensions, and talk from scientists about extra dimensions has to do with something called "string theory" or "superstring theory".

Some branches in modern physics are well established through experiments, such as gravity, relativity, quantum mechanics, much of particle physics, electromagnetism, and the weak and strong nuclear forces. String theory is not established, but rather is an attempt to bring all these branches of the tree of physics together, to connect them, to draw and see the trunk that all the branches stem from. String theory is highly theoretical, unproven, likely improvable and unverifiable, highly mathematical, and requires 10-11 dimensions to theoretically be able to describe the trunk of the tree of modern physics.

Here is quote from Lisa Randall PhD, a leading theoretical physicist and expert on particle physics, string theory, and cosmology:

"How many dimensions of space are there? Do we really know? By now, I hope you would agree that it would be overreaching to claim that we know for certain that extra dimensions do not exist. We see three dimensions of space, but there could be more that we haven't yet detected.

You know now that extra dimensions can be hidden either because they are curled up and small, or because spacetime is warped and gravity so concentrated in a small region that even an infinite dimension is invisible. Either way, whether dimensions are compact or localized, spacetime would appear to be four-dimensional everywhere, no matter where you are."

-Lisa Randall PhD, Warped Passages: Unraveling the Mysteries of the Universe's Hidden Dimensions, pg. 437

Lisa Randall is saying, according to modern physics, that there may be very large, even infinitely large, invisible dimensions that do exist, although we can only perceive the 4 dimensions of space-time.

And here is a quote from Stephen Hawking Phd, one of the most famous scientists and theoretical astrophysicists of our time, commenting his thoughts on Randall's work:

"In fact, in order to explain the rate in which stars orbit the center of our galaxy, it seems there must be more mass than is accounted for by matter we observe. This missing mass might arise from some exotic species of particles in our world such as WIMPs (weakly interacting massive particles) or axions (very light elementary particles). But missing mass could also be evidence of the existence of a shadow world with matter in it... Instead of the extra dimensions ending on a shadow brane, another possibility is that they are infinite but highly curved, like a saddle. Lisa Randall and Raman Sundrum showed that this kind of curvature would act rather like a second brane: the gravitational influence of an object on the brane would be confined to a small neighborhood of the brane and not spread out to infinity in the extra dimensions. As in the shadow brane model, the gravitational field would have the right long-distance falloff to explain the planetary orbits and lab measurements of the gravitational force, but gravity would vary more rapidly at short distances. There is however an important difference between this Randall-Sundrum model and the shadow brane model. Bodies that move under the influence of gravity will produce gravitational waves, ripples of curvature that travel through spacetime at the speed of light. Like the electromagnetic waves of light , gravitational waves should carry energy, a prediction that has been confirmed by observations of the binary pulsar PSR1913+16. If we indeed live on a brane in a spacetime with extra dimensions, gravitational waves generated by the motion of bodies on the brane would travel off into the other dimensions. If there were a second shadow brane, gravitational waves would be reflected back and trapped between the two branes. On the other hand, if there was only a single brane and the extra dimensions went on forever, as in the Randall-Sundrum model, gravitational waves could escape altogether and carry away energy from our brane world. This would seem to breach one of the fundamental principles of physics: The Law of Conservation of Energy. The total amount of energy remains the same. However, it appears to be a violation only because our view of what is happening is restricted to the brane. An angel who could see the extra dimensions would know that the energy was the same, just more spread out."

-Stephen Hawking PhD, The Universe in a Nutshell, pgs. 184-192

While giving credence to Randall's statement, basically Hawking says that very large extra-dimensions are possible, and would not violate the known laws of physics. In fact, their existence might help explain some rather large befuddling questions in science that are still unanswered, such as missing mass. As such, science allows for the existence of a heavenly dimension, potentially one in which angels are, and the bodies of angels could be composed of the stuff of this heavenly extra dimension.

The branch of physics called quantum mechanics deals with particles which are subatomic (that is smaller than an atom). Quantum mechanics has been well-established through scientific experimentation. Unlike string theory, quantum mechanics is a field of practical experimentation. It is in quantum physics that we find the Heisenberg Uncertainty Principle:

"In quantum physics, the Heisenberg uncertainty principle states that certain pairs of physical properties, like position and momentum, cannot both be known to arbitrary precision. That is, the more precisely one property is known, the less precisely the other can be known. It is impossible to measure simultaneously both position and velocity of a microscopic particle with any degree of accuracy or certainty. This is not a statement about the limitations of a researcher's ability to measure particular quantities of a system, but rather about the nature of the system itself and hence it expresses a property of the universe." -Wikipedia, Uncertainty Principle

This basically means that on a subatomic level, that of electrons, quarks, photons, etc. there seems to be a fundamental principal of randomness. Particles go where they seem to want to go. Particles almost seem to choose what they are doing. However, these choices do form an overall pattern, of statistically calculable probabilities.

One of the most well-know and respectable scientists in recent history, instrumental in the development of quantum mechanics, was Richard Feynman PhD. He worked on the Manhattan project developing the atomic bomb, was a recipient of the Nobel Prize in Physics, and is also known for demonstrating the O-ring defects resulting in the space shuttle Challenger tragedy.

To quote Richard Feynman PhD:

"One might still like to ask: "How does it work? What is the machinery behind the law?" No one has found any machinery behind the law. No one can "explain" any more than we have just "explained." No one will give you any deeper representation of the situation. We have no ideas about a more basic mechanism from which these results can be deduced.

"We would like to emphasize a very important difference between classical and quantum mechanics. We have been talking about the probability that an electron will arrive in a given circumstance. We have implied that in our experimental arrangement (or even in the best possible one) it would be impossible to predict exactly what would happen. We can only predict the odds! This would mean, if it were true, that physics has given up on the problem of trying to predict exactly what will happen in a definite circumstance. Yes! physics has given up. We do not know how to predict what would happen in a given circumstance, and we believe now that it is impossible—that the only thing that can be predicted is the probability of different events. It must be recognized that this is a retrenchment in our earlier ideal of understanding nature. It may be a backward step but no one has found a way to avoid it.

No one has figured a way out of this puzzle. So at the present time we must limit ourselves to computing probabilities. We say "at the present time," but we suspect very strongly that it is something that will be with us forever—that it is impossible to beat that puzzle—that this is the way nature really is."

-Richard P. Feynman, PhD, The Feynman Lectures on Physics, Vol. 3, pgs.1-10,1-11

So why is it that at the scale of the tiniest parts of the universe, that there is all this randomness? Why has science given up on predictability, and accepted that uncertainty and chance rule the microscopic domain of the most basic and fundamental building blocks of the universe?

"With the advent of quantum mechanics, we have come to recognize that events cannot be predicted with complete accuracy but that there is always a degree of uncertainty. If one likes, one could ascribe this randomness to the intervention of God, but it would be a very strange kind of intervention: there is no evidence that it is directed toward any purpose. Indeed, if it were, it would by definition not be random. In modern times, we have effectively removed the third possibility above by redefining the goal of science: our aim is to formulate a set of laws that enables us to predict events only up to the limit set by the uncertainty principle."

-Stephen Hawking PhD, The Illustrated Brief History of Time, Pg 224

"There is always an element of uncertainty or chance, and this affects the behavior of matter on a small scale in a fundamental way. Einstein was almost singlehandedly responsible for general relativity, and he played an important part in the development of quantum mechanics. His feelings about the matter are summed up in the phrase "God does not play dice." But all the evidence indicates that God is an inveterate gambler and that He throws the dice on every possible occasion."

-Stephen Hawking PhD, Black Holes and Baby Universes, pg. 70

Regarding quantum physics, Einstein said that "God does not play dice", and Stephen Hawking says, "God throws the dice on every possible occasion".

But what does the Bible say on the topic of dice and God?

Prov 16:33

"We may throw the dice, but the LORD determines how they fall."

Assuming that whether it is us or matter that throws the dice, it makes no difference, then what the Bible indicates is that God set up the universe to "play dice" on a quantum level, but at the same time, God is the one that determines how those "quantum dice" fall. By "quantum dice" I am referring to all of the subatomic particles/energies and their activities on the microscopic scale of the quantum level.

However, if the uncertainty principle of quantum physics is correct, then the Bible assures us that God still sets the rules and outcomes for the seeming "randomness" of the "quantum dice".

Some Christians who are Scientists speak on this very issue:

John Byl has a PhD in Astronomy, is the author of the book "God and Cosmos: A Christian View of Time, Space, and the Universe", and is Professor of Mathematics and Head of the Department of Mathematical Sciences at Trinity Western University.

"W.G. Pollard and, more recently, Nancey Murphy advocate that the apparently random events at the quantum level are all specific, intentional acts of God. God's action at this level is limited in that

(1) He respects the integrity of the entities with which He co-operates (e.g., He doesn't change the electron's mass arbitrarily) and

(2) He restricts His action to produce a world that, for all we can tell, is orderly and law-like.

God is the hidden variable. Murphy asserts that this position is not only theologically preferable to indeterminism, but has the further advantage of consistency with the principle of sufficient reason. Of course, if God is directly responsible for quantum events this entails that these are therefore predictable by God. Hence we are left with a deterministic universe, at least at the quantum level."

"God's sovereignty rules out the possibility of agents acting independently of Him. In particular, quantum mechanics does not imply ontological indeterminism, given that determinist interpretations of quantum mechanics are possible, that non-physical secondary causes cannot be ruled out and that God is the primary cause for all events."

-John Byl PhD, "Indeterminacy, Divine action and Human Freedom"

William Pollard PhD, is a Nuclear Physicist and Episcopal Priest, with a PhD in Physics and Honorary doctorates in science, divinity, law, and humane letters. He is the author of "Chance and Providence: God's Action in a World Governed by Scientific Law". The entire book is on God operating, instead of "chance", in quantum mechanics.

"In the next chapter I will begin the presentation for your consideration of a quite different approach to this problem which seems to me to offer an entirely adequate solution for it. Under it, as we shall attempt to show, there can emerge again in all of its ancient power the fullness of the Biblical response to the living God who is ever active in the whole of His creation sustaining, providing, judging, and redeeming all things, both in heaven and in earth, in accordance with the mysterious and hidden purposes of His might will. At the same time, however, this is accomplished in such a way that the essential integrity and unity of science, both as it is now and as in principle it may become, is fully preserved."

"To Einstein's famous question expressing his abhorrence of quantum mechanics, "Does God throw dice?" the Judeo-Christian answer is not, as so many have wrongly supposed, a denial, but a very positive affirmative. For only in a world in which the laws of nature govern events in accordance with the casting of dice can a Biblical view of a world whose history is responsive to God's will prevail."

-William Pollard PhD, "Chance and Providence: God's Action in a World Governed by Scientific Law", pg. 35, pg. 97

Nancey Murphy PhD, Theologian, is Professor of Christian Philosophy at the Fuller Theological Seminary. She also serves as an editorial advisor for Theology and Science, Theology Today, and Christianity Today. She is the author of "Divine Action In The Natural Order".

"The second strategy for giving an account of the locus of divine action explores quantum physics and seeks to give an account of God's action throughout the natural and human world by means of action at the quantum level (either alone or in conjunction with top-down action). My proposal is motivated theologically. If God is immanent in and acting in all creatures, then necessarily God is acting at the quantum level. Emphasis on this fact has the advantage of sidestepping the problem of interventionism: the laws of quantum mechanics are only statistical and therefore not subject to violation. If, as most interpreters conclude, events at this level are genuinely indeterminate, then there need be no competition between divine action and physical causation. It is possible from a theistic perspective to interpret current physics as saying that the natural world is intrinsically incomplete and open to divine action at its most basic level."

-Nancey Murphy PhD, Dive Action In The Natural Order, pg. 131

The Bible may also present an argument of God controlling the "quantum dice" in Col 1:16-17, referring to Jesus Christ,

"For by him were all things created, that are in heaven, and that are in earth, visible and invisible, whether [they be] thrones, or dominions, or principalities, or powers: all things were created by him, and for him: And he is before all things, and by him all things consist."

The word here for "consist" is "synistemi" (4921) and it means, "to consist of or be composed of, to cohere, put together, hold together or band together".

According to physics, it is the subatomic force particles of bosons, and gluons that hold together atoms themselves, and particles like photons and electrons that hold together different atoms. As such, this verse in the Bible could be referring to, that it is by God's control over the "quantum dice" that makes the observations of quantum mechanics as they are, which is that particles we are composed of Do hold together. As such, by His actions all things hold together or "by Him all things consist".

Assuming it is true that God does allow randomness at a quantum level of physics, but also constantly controls the outcome of that randomness, besides "upholding all things", like the universe, "by the word of His power", (as we read in Heb 1:3) is there another possible reason for God creating the universe to be this way? Could it relate to miracles, signs and wonders? It could be.

Not only does quantum physics allow for existing particles that we can observe in experiment to act in random way, but it also allows for particles and antiparticles (antimatter) to pop in and out of existence, seemingly randomly. These particles usually only exist for a very short time, and are called "virtual particles".

"Down at the very tiniest length scale and trillions of times smaller than atoms, is what is known as the Planck scale where the concept of length loses its meaning and quantum uncertainty rules. At this level all known laws of physics break down and even space and time become nebulous concepts. Any and all conceivable distortions of spacetime will be popping in and out of existence in a random and chaotic dance which is going on all the time everywhere in the universe. Terms such as "quantum fluctuations" and the "quantum foam" which are used to describe this chaotic activity certainly do not do it justice."

-Jim Al-Khalili PhD, Black Holes, Wormholes, and Time Machines, pg. 207

PhD in Theoretical Nuclear Physics, theoretical physicist at the University of Surrey

The existence of these seemingly random particles does not violate the laws of physics, especially the Law of Conservation of Energy:

"Where did all these particles come from? The answer is that relativity and quantum mechanics allow matter to be creates out of energy in the form of particle/antiparticle pairs. And where did the energy come from to create this matter? The answer is that it was borrowed from the gravitational energy of the universe. The universe has an enormous debt of negative gravitational energy, which exactly balances the positive energy of the matter."

-Stephen Hawking, PhD, Black Holes and Baby Universes, Pg. 97

Virtual particles have been shown, through experiments, to exist, as seen in the Lamb shift and the Casimir Effect.

"These particles are called virtual because, unlike "real" particles, they cannot be observed directly with a particle detector. Their indirect effects can nonetheless be measured, and their existence has been confirmed by a small shift (the "Lamb shift") they produce in the spectrum of light from excited hydrogen atoms."

-Stephen Hawking PhD, Black Holes and Baby Universes, Pg 107

Regarding the Casimir Effect,

"As we saw in Chapter 7, even what we think of as "empty" space is filled with pairs of virtual particles and antiparticles that appear together, move apart, and come back together and annihilate each other. Now, suppose one has two metal plates a short distance apart. The plates will act like mirrors for the virtual photons or particles of light. In fact they will form a cavity between them, a bit like an organ pipe that will resonate only at certain notes. This means that virtual photons can occur in the space between the plates only if their wavelengths (the distance between the crest of one wave and the next) fit a whole number of times into the gap between the plates. If the width of a cavity is a whole number of wavelengths plus a fraction of a wavelength, then after some reflections backward and forward between the plates, the crests of one wave with coincide with the troughs of another and the waves will cancel out.

"Because the virtual photons between the plates can have only the resonant wavelengths, there will be slightly fewer of them than in the region outside the plates where virtual photons can have any wavelength. Thus there will be slightly fewer virtual photons hitting the inside surfaces of the plates than the outside surfaces. One would therefore expect a force on the plates, pushing them toward each other. This force has actually been detected and has the predicted value. Thus we have experimental evidence that virtual particles exist and have real effects."

-Stephen Hawking PhD, The Illustrated Brief History of Time, pgs. 204-206

Virtual particles can include all types of particles, including photons, electrons, gluons, bosons, and quarks. According to physicists, under certain conditions in the universe, virtual particles can exist for longer periods of time and therefore become "real" particles. This particular example relates to conditions of space near a black hole, but in principle this shows that science does generally allow for the possibility of virtual particles popping into existence and becoming real particles.

"We can understand this in the following way: what we think of as "empty" space cannot be completely empty because that would mean that all the fields, such as the gravitational and electromagnetic fields, would have to be exactly zero. However, the value of a field and its rate of change with time are like the position and velocity of a particle: the uncertainty principle implies that the more accurately one knows one of these quantities, the less accurately one can know the other. So in empty space the field cannot be fixed at exactly zero, because then it would have both a precise value (zero) and a precise rate of change (also zero). There must be a certain minimum amount of uncertainty, or quantum fluctuations, in the value of the field. One can think of these fluctuations as pairs of particle of light or gravity that appear together at some time, move apart, and then come together again and annihilate each other. These particles are virtual particles like carry the gravitational force of the sun: unlike real particles, they cannot be observed directly with a particle detector. However, their indirect effects, such as small changes in the electron orbits in atoms, can be measured and agree with the theoretical predictions to a remarkable degree of accuracy. The uncertainty principle also predicts that there will be similar virtual pairs of matter particles, such as electrons or quarks. In this case, however, one member of the pair will be a particle, and the other an antiparticle (the antiparticles of light and gravity are the same as the particles).

"Because energy cannot be created out of nothing, one of the partners in a particle/antiparticle pair will have positive energy, and the other partner negative energy. The one with negative energy is condemned to be a short-lived virtual particle because real particles always have positive energy in normal situations. It must therefore seek out its partner and annihilate with it. However, a real particle close to a massive body has less energy than if it were far away, because it would take energy to lift it far away against the gravitational attraction of the body. Normally, the energy of the particle is still positive, but the gravitational field inside a black hole is so strong that even a real particle can have negative energy there. It is therefore possible, if a black hole is present, for the virtual particle with negative energy to fall into the black hole and become a real particle or antiparticle. In this case it no longer has to annihilate with its partner. Its forsaken partner may fall into the black hole as well. Or, having positive energy, it might also escape from the vicinity of the black hole as a real particle or antiparticle. To an observer at a distance, it will appear to have been emitted from the black hole."

-Stephen Hawking PhD, The Illustrated Brief History of Time, Pgs. 134-137

According to science it is possible that physical particles can randomly pop into existence seemingly out of nowhere.

Modern Physics teaches that elementary particles, of all kinds, can and do randomly pop in and out of existence. This includes photons, which are particles of light. This also includes gravitons, which are theoretical and theoretically instrumental in gravity, as well as gluons, bosons and other force carrying particles.

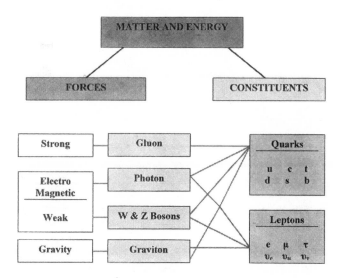

Some force carrying particles are what hold quarks together to form neutrons and protons, and other force particles hold together atoms. All of these particles can pop into existence out of nowhere, seemingly randomly, the universe allows for this, and the universe was created by God intentionally to be the way it is.

What are quarks and electrons? They are the particles that are the building blocks of atoms.

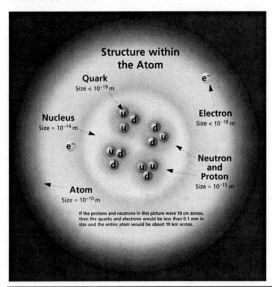

Different types of atoms make up all of the elements of matter, as seen in the periodic table of the elements.

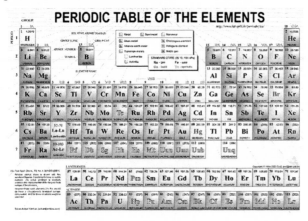

Atoms are the building blocks of all the matter we see, and our bodies are made of atoms.

So assuming God, who is omnipotent, one way or another, controlled the randomness of the quantum world... then this means that God could choose to have a large number of quarks, gluons, electrons, etc. pop into existence very quickly, and assemble into atoms. God could also do this in such a way that many atoms were formed, and would assemble into much larger objects, even objects large enough that we could see them.

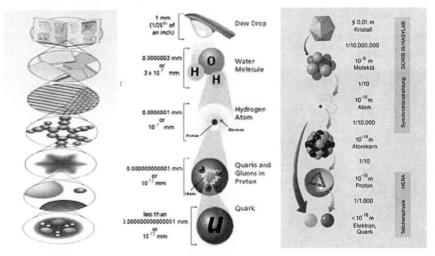

This might include things like oil and grain popping into existence out of nowhere:

1 Kings 17:8-16, "And the word of the LORD came unto him, saying, Arise, get thee to Zarephath, which belongeth to Zidon, and dwell there: behold, I

have commanded a widow woman there to sustain thee. So he arose and went to Zarephath. And when he came to the gate of the city, behold, the widow woman was there gathering of sticks: and he called to her, and said, Fetch me, I pray thee, a little water in a vessel, that I may drink. And as she was going to fetch it, he called to her, and said, Bring me, I pray thee, a morsel of bread in thine hand. And she said, As the LORD thy God liveth, I have not a cake, but an handful of meal in a barrel, and a little oil in a cruse: and, behold, I am gathering two sticks, that I may go in and dress it for me and my son, that we may eat it, and die. And Elijah said unto her, Fear not; go and do as thou hast said: but make me thereof a little cake first, and bring it unto me, and after make for thee and for thy son. For thus saith the LORD God of Israel, The barrel of meal shall not waste, neither shall the cruse of oil fail, until the day that the LORD sendeth rain upon the earth. And she went and did according to the saying of Elijah: and she, and he, and her house, did eat many days. And the barrel of meal wasted not, neither did the cruse of oil fail, according to the word of the LORD, which he spake by Elijah."

God provided oil and grain for 3 years, though the land was in a drought with famine. This oil and grain appeared seemingly out of thin air. But another way to put it might be that it appeared out of "seemingly random quantum foam". And there are many miracles, signs, and wonders in the Bible, done by God, which are similar to this, such as Jesus Christ feeding the multitudes.

Also, there are miraculous healings mentioned many times in the Bible. According to science, our bodies are made up of molecules of atoms, which are made from quarks and electrons and such. Consider the cases of sight being restored to the blind, the healing of the disfigured hand, the healing of lepers, and the healing of all manner of sicknesses; miracles done by Jesus Christ. Control over the "quantum dice" would be one way to explain how sick flesh was instantaneously changed into healthy flesh.

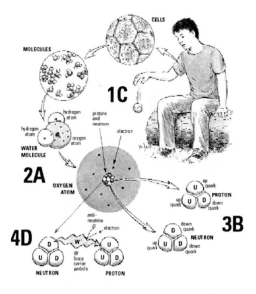

And so this is one way to describe, in modern physics concepts, how God does miracles, signs, and wonders. Though God does do them, whether control of quantum physics is truly and specifically how, or not.

But the Bible also says that Holy angels, and Fallen angels, also work miracles, signs and wonders. (Acts 2:22, 5:12, 2 Peter 2:11, Heb 2:4, Matt 24:24, 2 Thes 2:9, Rev 13:2, 14, 16:14) So it could be an accurate description to say that how fallen angels also do miracles, signs, and wonders is because they too somehow have control over the "quantum dice", though definitely on a more limited scale than God does.

The Bible teaches that God is everywhere in the universe, and there is nowhere that He is not. Whereas fallen angels have a set, limited, location for their body, and are only in one place at a time, much like mankind. Under this line of reasoning, God has power, and "quantum power" everywhere in the universe, but fallen angels only have power or "quantum power" in their immediate location. Also, God has power over the fallen angels bodies themselves, as their bodies are part of the creation, whereas fallen angels have no such power over God.

It does make some analogous sense that all angels would have powers like God, but limited, for the Bible several times in the Old Testament calls angels the "sons of God". (Gen 6, Job 1:6, Job 2:1, Psalm 29:1, 89:6)

It may be that the extra-dimensionality of angels is what would make possible them having limited control over the "quantum dice" in their immediate location.

"Today, however, physicists are following a different trail-the one leading to superstring theory. Unlike previous proposals, it has survived every blistering mathematical challenge ever hurled at it. Not surprisingly, the theory is a radical-some might say crazy-departure from the past, being based on tiny strings vibrating in 10-dimensional space-time... In superstring theory, the subatomic particles we see in nature are nothing more than different resonances of the vibrating superstrings, in the same way that different musical notes emanate from the different modes of vibration of a violin string."

-Michio Kaku PhD, "Into the Eleventh Dimension", author of Hyperspace: A Scientific Odyssey through the 10th Dimension, Oxford University Press.

According to String Theory, particles in the 4d spacetime we observe, are the result of vibrations of 1 dimensional strings that exist in an additional 6-7 dimensions, in the scientific sense of the word, or 10-11 dimensions total.

As such, speaking generally, according to science in principle, it is possible that the extradimensionality of angels would allow for their altering of particles in our 4 dimensional world, on the subatomic quantum level. As such, their extradimensionality, in the heavenly realm, may be tied directly to their ability to work "miracles, signs, and wonders", possibly through being able to determine how the "quantum dice" fall (on a limited scale in their immediate locality).

Chapter Eight

Powers, Physics and Science - Part 2

Let's review the Biblically described abilities of fallen angels:

Mental Attacks, Physical Attacks, and Combination Attacks.

Fallen Angelic Apparitions

Mental Attacks

> 1. Visions – real to the bodily senses √
>> a. Fully, or partially, overlaying objective reality, √
>> b. fully awake, or a waking trance state √
>> c. one person or multiple people √
> 2. Dreams – not real to bodily senses, and happen while asleep

√

Physical Attacks- Lasting physical effects in objective reality with multiple witnesses

> 1. Visible angels √
> 2. Invisible angels √

Combination Attacks

> 1. Normal or Manipulated perception of time ?
> 2. objects carried in/taken with, or not √

I think that fallen angels being able to control (in a limited sphere of influence) how the "quantum dice" fall, would work as a way to explain Physical Attacks very easily, both with visible angels materializing, or seeing the physical effects of invisible angels, including the Physical aspects of Combination Attacks. Excepting time perception manipulation, I also think this "quantum dice" idea explains all varieties and aspects of Mental Attacks quite well, as well as the Mental aspects of Combination attacks.

"The human brain, however, is also subject to the uncertainty principle. Thus, there is an element of the randomness associated with quantum mechanics in human behavior. But the energies involved in the brain are low, so quantum mechanical uncertainty is only a small effect."

-Stephen Hawking PhD, Black Holes and Baby Universes, Pg. 133

Although the quantum mechanical uncertainty effect is normally small in the human brain, if fallen angels can determine how the "quantum dice" fall, then a fallen angel could make the effect quite large and noticeable.

Regarding Mental Visions, and the Mental aspects of Combination attacks, all of our physical senses are dependant on how our brain interprets them. By fallen angels generating electrical impulses in the brain, and such things like that, fallen angels would be able to make us "see" things that are not actually in front of our eyes, and "hear" things that are not there to make any sound, "feel" things that are not touching our bodies, "smell" things not before our noses, and "taste" things that are not on our tongues. These things would seem completely real to all of the bodily senses. They could occur awake or in a waking trance state, and could fully or partially overlay objective reality. Fallen angels could cause this to happen to more than one person at a time. So that covers Mental Visions, and the Mental aspects of Combination Attacks. Mental Dreams could be explained much in the same way, but the attack occurring while the person is asleep and dreaming.

Let's look at the example of time perception manipulation mentioned earlier:

Luke 4:5, "And the devil, taking him up into an high mountain, shewed unto him all the kingdoms of the world in a moment of time."

The case of Jesus Christ mentioned in the Bible was likely at least hours in less than 1 second.

What we are going to cover next is the aspect of fallen angelic apparitions still remaining to be covered - the time perception manipulation abilities of fallen angels, as seen in Mental and Combination attacks. I will first be covering what time perception manipulation is Not,before I get into what it is.

As the brain of the victim of an attack is an integral part of how fallen angels carry out these attacks, and the memories of these attacks are stored in the brain, then the time perception manipulation aspect of these attacks must be explainable in a way that is consistent and not conflicting with the physical human brain and how it functions. And so any explanation of time perception manipulation must be limited and confined to explanations that do not conflict with the science of the human brain.

If we were to assume that time perception manipulation involves a compacting or compressing of extensive experiences into a short period of time, then this would require the human brain in one second to handle somewhere from a hundred to a thousand times more information than the brain usually processes in one second. The brain processes information by the firing of neurons.

The only information I could find on neurons firing more rapidly than normal were studies on psychoactive drugs, heroin especially. As people attacked by fallen angels do not report experiencing a heroin-like sensation, this is experimental evidence that overly-rapid neuronic firing in the normal passage of time will not work to explain this time perception manipulation.

And as such, time perception manipulation does not involve a compacting or compressing of extensive experiences into a short period of time. The only other option is that these experiences actually do take as much time as subjectively perceived by the person who is victim of fallen angelic attack, though objective time passage for the rest of the world is much shorter.

A major example for this may be seen in the theory of general relativity. According to relativity, no matter what speed a person moves, time is perceived to pass at the same rate. However, less time will comparatively pass for an accelerated person than for a (relatively) stationary person. Yet either person will feel time passing at the same rate. It could be argued from a theological standpoint that God designed the human brain to need a consistent flow of actual time in order to function correctly, and designed a universe in which time passage would remain consistent, no matter to what speed a human might accelerate.

Because the person's brain is involved in the process, yet their body does not go anywhere, many theoretical physics concepts dealing with time would not work to explain how the brain can experience more time while the body experiences less time.

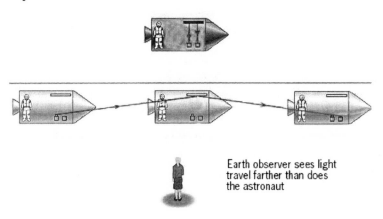

Earth observer sees light travel farther than does the astronaut

Could general relativity, and time dilation explain how this works? Relativistic Time Dilation would not work, because it would require the body to feel acceleration (or its gravitational equivalent) in comparison to the brain, at over 99% the speed of light. This speed would be necessary to produce a 100 or 1000 seconds to 1 second ratio. This is not what is reported by witnesses of the person under attack's body, that see it does not go anywhere, so this cannot be the case, aside from the fact that such a thing would likely kill the person.

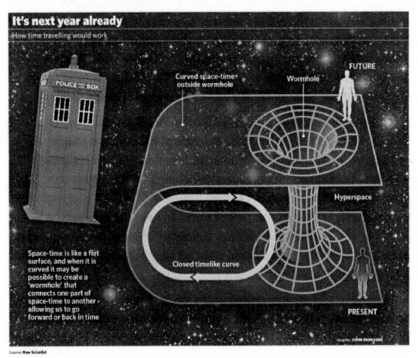

Could time travel gained by travel to the future, and then the past, explain this extra time?

Although there is a type of theoretical wormhole, called a CTC, which could be used in this way, if many detailed criteria were met, but according to the current consensus of scientists, a CTC would not work for time travel to the past. This manner specifically would involve moving a brain to another location in 4d spacetime, spending a real amount of time in that other location, and then the brain traveling back in time to the same moment it left. Even if this could work without killing the person, a CTC wormhole still would not work for returning the brain to the past, as a CTC will not work for time travel to the past.

Kip Thorne and Stephen Hawking had an ongoing debate for about 20 years over the subject of time travel into the past, using a CTC wormhole, for time travel, involving 2 locations in this 4d universe. The debate, based on their books, seems to have become settled, with Thorne (pro-possibility of time travel) coming to agree with Hawking (anti-possibility of time travel). Here are some highlights:

"Perhaps fortunately for our survival (and that of our mothers), it seems that the laws of physics do not allow such time travel. There seems to be a Chronology Protection Agency that makes the world safe for historians by preventing travel into the past. What seems to happen is that the effects of the uncertainty principle would cause there to be a large amount of radiation if one traveled into the past. This radiation would either warp space-time so much that it would not be possible to go back in time, or it would cause space-time to come to an end in a singularity like the big bang and the big crunch. Either way, our past would be safe from evil-minded persons. The Chronology Protection Hypothesis is supported by some recent calculations that I and other people have done. But the best evidence we have that time travel is not possible, and never will be, is that we have not been invaded by hordes of tourists from the future." -Stephen Hawking PhD, Black Holes and Baby Universes Pg. 154 (1994)

"Translating back the viewpoint of an observer at rest in the wormhole (the observer that Kim and I had relied on), Hawking's conjecture meant that the quantum gravity cutoff occurs 10^{-95} second before the wormhole becomes a time machine, not 10^{-43} second – and by then, according to our calculations, the vacuum fluctuational beam is strong enough, but just barely so, that it might indeed destroy the wormhole." -Kip S. Thorne PhD, Black Holes and Time Warps pg. 520 (1994)

"Hawking suspects that the growing beams of vacuum fluctuations is nature's way of enforcing chronology protection: Whenever one tries to make a time machine, and no matter what kind of device one uses in one's attempt (a wormhole, a spinning cylinder, a "cosmic string", or whatever), just before one's device becomes a time machine, a beam of vacuum fluctuations will circulate through the device and destroy it. Hawking seems ready to bet heavily on this outcome. I am not willing to take the other side in such a bet. I do enjoy taking bets with Hawking, but only bets that I have a reasonable chance of winning. My strong gut feeling is that I would lose this one. My own calculations with Kim, and unpublished calculations that Eanna Flanagan (a student of mine) has done more recently, suggest to me that Hawking is likely to be right. Every time machine is likely to self-destruct (by means of circulating vacuum fluctuations) at the moment one tries to activate it." -Kip S. Thorne PhD, Black Holes and Time Warps pg. 521 (1994)

That was all from 1994, but a more recent quote from 2001 shows the issue has generally been settled:

"... Since the sum-over-histories calculations in these backgrounds are mathematically equivalent, one can conclude that the probability of these backgrounds goes to zero as they approach the warping needed for time loops. In other words, the probability of having sufficient warping for a time machine is zero. This supports what I have called the Chronology Protection Conjecture: that the laws of physics conspire to prevent time travel by macroscopic objects.

"Although time loops are allowed by the sum over histories, the probabilities are extremely small. Based on the duality arguments I mentioned earlier, I estimate the probability that Kip Thorne could go back and kill his grandfather as less than one in ten with a trillion trillion trillion trillion trillion zeroes after it... As gambling men, Kip and I would bet on odds like that. The trouble is, we can't bet each other because we are now both on the same side." -Stephen Hawking PhD, The Universe in a Nutshell, pgs. 152-153 (2001)

One problem with time travel to the past between 2 locations in 4d spacetime is that, put simply, electromagnetic vacuum fluctuations would build up traveling in a loop from the present to the past, an infinite loop, and this would destroy any pathway from the present to the past. Stephen Hawking and Kip Thorne have said, CTC wormholes won't work for time travel to the past.

As such, this is also not a possibility for time perception manipulation during abductions, and it can summarily be concluded that peoples' brains do not go anywhere, or time travel. Time gained by traveling to the future, and then the past, is not allowed by physics in any way that would fit this time perception manipulation scenario.

Biblically, this can be understood in that God created the universe so as to not allow time travel into the past. God controls both sides of the wormhole, and it is God who would make it so electromagnetic vacuum fluctuations in a loop from the wormhole mouths would destroy the wormhole before it would make possible time travel into the past.

God created time, as did Jesus Christ, as all things were created through him. Jesus Christ says:

Rev 22:13, "I am the Alpha and the Omega, the First and the Last, the Beginning and the End."

As such God has complete authority over time, and simply does not allow time travel to the past, or the future and then the past again.

So what is going on?

The key verse is Luke 4:5

"And the devil, taking him up into an high mountain, shewed unto him all the kingdoms of the world in a moment of time."

This verse does not describe time travel to the past. In contrast, this verse describes a long period of time passing during a second, or less than a second.

Or another way to say this is that some extra time was perceptually gained by the person, more than the objective passage of time that God controls.

This verse describes a long period of time passing during a second, or less than a second. Or another way to say this is that some extra time was perceptually gained by the person, more than the objective passage of time that God controls. So how would a fallen angel do this? How might this work?

The answer is that there is simply more to the dimension of time than we normally think of there being. I believe the Bible sets precedence for this concept, and this is how I would interpret Joshua's Long Day.

Josh 10:12-14, "Then spake Joshua to the LORD in the day when the LORD delivered up the Amorites before the children of Israel, and he said in the sight of Israel, Sun, stand thou still upon Gibeon; and thou, Moon, in the valley of Ajalon. And the sun stood still, and the moon stayed, until the people had avenged themselves upon their enemies. Is not this written in the book of Jasher? So the sun stood still in the midst of heaven, and hasted not to go down about a whole day. And there was no day like that before it or after it, that the LORD hearkened unto the voice of a man: for the LORD fought for Israel."

I have read several theories to explain how this worked, but here is mine: When God made the dimension of time, He made it to have both its flow in length, as we normally perceive, and draw as a line, but also to have a width to it, at right angles to its length. This width is normally small and tight like a string. But the width of time is like a stretchy material, like a rubber band, and so if God wants to, God can stretch out the width of time. The width of time is not affected by the 3 dimensions of space, or things like gravity or speed. The length of time is what is referred to in "spacetime", but the width of time exists unaffected by the things that would normally affect the length of time.

In Joshua's Long Day, it was the width of time that God stretched out, around the surface of the earth, and for the people on the earth. As such the people on earth experienced long time passage in the width of time, during what was a brief moment in the length of time.

I believe that according to physics this is possible. Although the concept of time having a dimension of "width" I think is in its infancy, there is some information to be found on it. The concept which parallels the "width" of time in modern theoretical physics is the concept of "imaginary time":

"…One of these is that it is easier to do the sum if one deals with histories in what is called imaginary time rather than in ordinary, real time. Imaginary time is a difficult concept to grasp, and it is probably the one that has caused the greatest problems for the readers of my book. I have also been criticized fiercely by philosophers for using imaginary time. How can imaginary time have anything to do with the real universe?

"I think these philosophers have not learned the lessons of history. It was once considered obvious that the earth was flat and that the sun went around the earth, yet since the time of Copernicus and Galileo, we have had to adjust to the idea that the earth is round and that it goes around the sun. Similarly, it was long obvious that time went for the same rate for every observer, but since Einstein, we have had to accept that time goes for at different rates for different observers. It also seemed obvious that the universe had a unique history, yet since the discovery of quantum mechanics, we have had to consider the universe as having every possible history. I want to suggest that the idea of imaginary time is something that we will also have to come to accept. It is an intellectual leap of the same order as believing that the world is round. I think that imaginary time will come to seem as natural as a round earth does now. There are not many Flat Earthers left in the educated world." -Stephen Hawking, Black Holes and Baby Universe, Pg. 81-82

"Imaginary time is already a commonplace of science fiction. But it is more than science fiction or a mathematical trick. It is something that shapes the universe we live in." -Stephen Hawking, Black Holes and Baby Universes, Pg. 83

Though it is a newer concept, it seems that imaginary time shapes the universe we live in.

According to physics, what is it like?

"You can think of ordinary, real time as a horizontal line, going from left to right. Early times are on the left, and late times are on the right. But you can also consider another direction of time, up and down the page. This is the so-called imaginary direction of time, at right angles to real time.

"What is the point of introducing the concept of imaginary time? Why doesn't one just stick to the ordinary, real time that we understand? The reason is that, as noted earlier, matter and energy tend to make space-time curve in on itself. In the real time direction, this inevitably leads to singularities, places where space-time comes to an end. At the singularities, the equations of physics cannot be defined; thus one cannot predict what will happen. But the imaginary time direction is at right angles to real time. This means that it behaves in a similar way to the three directions that correspond to moving in space. The curvature of space-time caused by the matter in the universe can then lead to the three space directions and the imaginary time direction meeting up around the back. They would form a closed surface, like the surface of the earth. The space directions and imaginary time would form a space-time that was closed in on itself, without boundaries or edges. It wouldn't have any point that could be called a beginning or end, any more than the surface of the earth has a beginning or end."

-Stephen Hawking PhD, Black Holes and Baby Universes, Pg 82

"When one tried to unify gravity with quantum mechanics, one had to introduce the idea of "imaginary" time. Imaginary time is indistinguishable from directions in space. If one can go north, one can turn around and head south; equally, if one can go forward in imaginary time, one out to be able to turn round and go backward. This means that there can be no important difference between the forward and backward directions of imaginary time. On the other hand, when one looks at "real" time, there's a very big difference between the forward and backward directions, as we all know."

-Stephen Hawking PhD, The Illustrated Brief History of Time, Pg 182

Imaginary time does not follow the forward direction of time, but instead forms a closed loop, in which there is no distinguishable forward or backward direction. This concept seems to parallel a stretchy width to time very well. A person experiencing imaginary time could gain time, going around a closed loop on the width of time, and ending up where they started. This would allow time to be gained, and experienced, by the person, without that person moving forward on the length of time.

Time Perception Manipulation? Could Imaginary Time/Width of Time explain time perception manipulation? ...Yes.

As I have mentioned before, the Bible calls the angels the "sons of God" in several places, and this may relate to that angels can do many of the same things that God can do, but on a more limited and local basis.

For instance, God can perform miracles, signs and wonders, and Joshua's Long Day was one of these miraculous events. If this analogy holds true in this case, as it has in other cases, then it would make sense that fallen angels may also be able to stretch out the width of time on a limited basis. The length of time God keeps all authority over, and the additional time is from fallen angels stretching out the width of time, but they cannot alter the length of time.

In fallen angelic apparitional experiences, this could be visualized as a fallen angel stretching out the width of time around the brain of the person under attack. The person's brain does Not leave their body, nor move forwards and backwards along the length of time, but does experience a gain of time from a period in which the width of time is stretched out around their brain. This allows for a gain of perceived passage of time, and would allow for a 100 seconds to 1 second, or 1000 seconds to 1 second ratio of perceived time passage.

This scenario would allow the brain to function at its normal speed, with decision making processes working as they normally do in the brain-mind-soul-spirit connection.

And so this is how I would explain fallen angels accomplish time perception manipulation. This explanation of stretching the width of time around the brain of the person would work to explain time perception manipulation in Mental and Combination Attack scenarios.

I find a good analogy to conceptualize an extra dimension or dimensions is the green code in the Matrix movie. Like the agents in the Matrix movie, fallen angels can alter the "code" ("quantum dice") to change what is there and alter the green code inside a person's mind, to change what the person is perceiving.

As such I often try to represent the three categories of Fallen Angelic Apparitions using Matrix imagery. I use a red sphere of code to represent the invisible extradimensional or heavenly realm fallen angel.

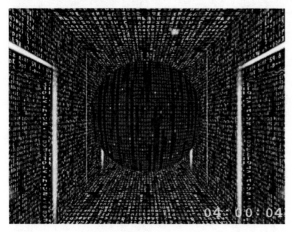

As an example, this is a close up of a fallen-angel-caused vision of an "alien abduction". Remember that the entire vision, all 3 aliens, and the setting, are all caused by 1 fallen angel.

And here are the 3 categories of Fallen angelic apparitions side by side

Fallen Angel Apparitions - Three ways Fallen Angels can atack and Apparate.
Green code area is God Reality; Red holodeck area is Fallen Angel; human is in white.

 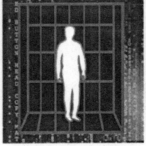 

| Mind Envelopment | Full Body Envelopment | Actual Materialization |

In conclusion, for Christians, the Bible does establish the kinds of things that fallen angels can do. Taking the Bible as the authoritative Word of God, on faith, there really is no need to question that fallen angels have these abilities. The Bible says fallen angels have these abilities, and I think Christians should be able to accept that, whether modern science has caught up to the Truth of the Word of God, or not. Theories in Science are always changing, in a progressive accumulation of knowledge: they are not truth. Where the Bible and science seem to contradict, I believe the Bible should always be deferred to as Correct and Truth, no matter what science teaches or scientists say.

I've touched on topics involved with big bang theory, quantum mechanics, black holes, worm holes, extra dimensional planes, and string theory.

But I agree with what Russell Grigg, from CMI-Australia has to say on this:

"It has truly been said that Christians married in their thinking to today's science (e.g. big bang, ten dimensions, etc.) will be widowed tomorrow."

-Russell M. Grigg M.Sc. (Hons.), Creationist Chemist and Missionary
www.creation.com, CMI–Australia

That being said, I'm not entirely convinced about any of these theoretical things, but the aim of this was to conceptualize in modern physics terminology and theories. The main point of doing this is to show that science does not preclude the existence of fallen angels, nor their Biblically described abilities, but rather I believe modern science actually completely allows for fallen angels and their Biblically described abilities.

It is clear that the Bible says fallen angels can do things as are described in many different types of supernatural accounts. Rather than disprove this seemingly supernatural activity is impossible, science actually completely allows for all of this to be possible... Modern physics shows that God created the universe to leave room for the miraculous to occur, without violating the laws of physics that He set up and maintains.

In any case, God is infinitely dimensional, without any question, having created all dimensions and everything in them, and as we know, God, in His three persons, can do anything and is All-powerful.

A fallen angel is more powerful than a human. But Jesus Christ is the Son of God, fully God and fully man, and also infinitely dimensional. So Jesus Christ is more powerful than any fallen angel, and even more powerful than all fallen angels combined. This is just another way of looking at what we already know, that Jesus Christ is seated at the right hand of God, with all power, above every other power, principality, authority, above every angel, Holy or fallen.

Angels can only be in one place at once, as we see in Daniel 10. Angels were created by God, as Genesis says "God created the heavens and all the host of them".

But Jesus Christ is the fullness of the Godhead in human form, and Jesus Christ said "before Abraham was, I AM", and John tells us "All things were made by him; and without him was not any thing made that was made", showing Jesus Christ's infinite dimensionality as the Son of God.

And the Bible tells us,

Acts 4:10-12, "Be it known unto you all, and to all the people of Israel, that by the name of Jesus Christ of Nazareth, whom ye crucified, whom God raised from the dead, [even] by him doth this man stand here before you whole. This is the stone which was set at nought of you builders, which is become the head of the corner. Neither is there salvation in any other: for there is none other name under heaven given among men, whereby we must be saved."

And we see this in supernatural harassment and attacks stopping in the name of Jesus Christ. Jesus Christ can help, and does help, those who call out to Him for His help, and who have faith in Him, and believe upon the power of His Name.

So Jesus Christ is more powerful than fallen angels, in whatever form they take, no matter how powerful they seem, Jesus Christ is more powerful.

Chapter Nine
Powers and Physics of Demons

This chapter will be covering the powers and abilities of "Demons", which are also called "Evil Spirits". We have already covered where demons come from: they are the disembodied spirits of dead Nephilim giants, paternal life-blood descendents of the Nephilim, or the first generation of Nephilim themselves, the paternal life-blood descendents of fallen angels. This unique heritage necessitates an accompanying uniqueness in the powers and abilities of demons.

Are demons spirits just like human spirits? No, demon spirits are different from human spirits. We can see some major differences in these passages:

A demon gave fortune-related orations to this demonized girl, and the demon knew who God's servants were, and knew that they were telling people how to be saved, in Acts 16:16-19, "It happened that as we were going to the place of prayer, a slave-girl having a spirit of divination met us, who was bringing her masters much profit by fortune-telling. This girl followed Paul and the rest of us, shouting, "These men are servants of the Most High God, who are telling you the way to be saved." She kept this up for many days. Finally Paul became so troubled that he turned around and said to the spirit, "In the name of Jesus Christ I command you to come out of her!" At that moment the spirit left her. When the owners of the slave girl realized that their hope of making money was gone, they seized Paul and Silas and dragged them into the marketplace to face the authorities." (Note: there is nothing here that verifies that this demon could predict the future, or that the fortune-telling of this girl was any different in vagueness and accuracy than fortune-tellers today.)

Demons in the NT knew who Jesus was, as seen in:

Mark 5:6-8 "When he saw Jesus from a distance, he ran and fell on his knees in front of him. He shouted at the top of his voice, "What do you want with me, Jesus, Son of the Most High God? Swear to God that you won't torture me!" For Jesus had said to him, "Come out of this man, you evil spirit!".

Luke 8:28-31 "When he saw Jesus, he cried out and fell at his feet, shouting at the top of his voice, "What do you want with me, Jesus, Son of the Most High

God? I beg you, don't torture me!" (For Jesus had commanded the evil spirit to come out of the man. For oftentimes it had caught him: and he was kept bound with chains and in fetters; and he brake the bands, and was driven of the devil into the wilderness.) Jesus asked him, "What is your name?" "Legion," he replied, because many demons had gone into him. And they begged him repeatedly not to order them to go into the Abyss."

Here we see that demons also have knowledge of the Abyss where their fallen angel fathers (or paternal life-blood ancestors) are imprisoned.

Demons travel through dry desert places, without a body, which Jesus says in Luke 11:24-26, "When an evil spirit comes out of a man, it goes through arid places seeking rest and does not find it. Then it says, 'I will return to the house I left.' When it arrives, it finds the house swept clean and put in order. Then it goes and takes seven other spirits more wicked than itself, and they go in and live there. And the final condition of that man is worse than the first." Also Jesus says in Matt 12:43-45, "When an evil spirit comes out of a man, it goes through arid places seeking rest and does not find it. Then it says, 'I will return to the house I left.' When it arrives, it finds the house unoccupied, swept clean and put in order. Then it goes and takes with it seven other spirits more wicked than itself, and they go in and live there. And the final condition of that man is worse than the first. That is how it will be with this wicked generation." These dry arid places seem to refer to a desert location, and points on Earth on a 3d spatial plane.

Although translated as "possession" in the KJV, the Greek word is actually "demonized" (1139), meaning, "to be under the power of a demon" according to Thayer's. Demons get inside of people, demonizing them, and causing the afflicted person a variety of potential problems. We know that the demons that are demonizing a person are inside the person somehow, because Jesus always told the demons to "come out" (1831, Greek exerchomai) of a demonized person.

Demons work for Satan. Demons could be driven out of a person by the power of God, healing the people, and this is what Jesus did and explained in Luke 11:14-20, "Jesus was driving out a demon that was mute. When the demon left, the man who had been mute spoke, and the crowd was amazed. But some of them said, "By Beelzebub, the prince of demons, he is driving out demons." Others tested him by asking for a sign from heaven. Jesus knew their thoughts and said to them: "Any kingdom divided against itself will be ruined, and a house divided against itself will fall. If Satan is divided against himself, how can his kingdom stand? I say this because you claim that I drive out demons by Beelzebub. Now if I drive out demons by Beelzebub, by whom do your followers drive them out? So then, they will be your judges. But if I drive out demons by the finger of God, then the kingdom of God has come to you." So it is by the power of God that demons are driven out.

So what do we see in these passages? It seems that demon spirits are not like human spirits. Living human spirits, those of deceased Christians, do not travel around the earth, nor do they have the ability to get inside of living people, (nor would we if we could as it is a violation of a person), and it simply does not happen. We go to sleep, unconscious, until one of the Resurrections. Or our spirit is with God, which He brings to Himself, in the Third Heaven at His throne (Rev 6:9-11). But we do not have the ability to travel where we will. We have no choice in this, Christian or not. Dead human spirits do not have this ability. Neither in the state of life, or death, of the human body can human spirits (living or dead (see Chapter 5)) separate from the body, or do anything apart from the body. For the spirit is tied to the soul, the soul has the awareness and consciousness of life, and the life is in the blood, and the blood is in the body. So there can be no consciousness and separation. Separation from the body would mean unconsciousness. For the unsaved, the human spirit is dead and can't do anything, let alone travel away from the body. For the Christian, the human spirit is alive, but the soul, mind and heart are tied in life with consciousness, to the body with the life in the blood. So a living Christian spirit also could not travel outside of that Christian's body. In death we sleep, or God keeps us by Him, possibly also asleep. In either case, dead Christian spirits don't have bodies (until one of the Resurrections) and are in God's hand. So in summary, none of us humans can get inside of anyone else, person or animal, with our human spirits.

Nor can human spirits know and instantly recognize Jesus as the Son of God (if only all lost people could, but it doesn't work that way, their spirits being dead). Demon spirits are different than human spirits, and have more power than human spirits.

It is Very important to note that demons have no physical bodies. Demons' giant bodies died a long time ago, before the flood. Demons do not have physical 3d bodies anymore. However, like human spirits are not physical, neither are demon spirits. Demon spirits are simply more powerful than human spirits, but they have no direct physical presence in the basic 3 spatial dimensions in and of themselves. Yet, they can get inside of living beings, and then they have a potential physical power, but only through inhabiting some person or animal's body. (More on this "inside" a person a little later.) Demons have no physical body made out of matter, mass, or energy, but rather in and of themselves they exist entirely on the spiritual dimensional plane.

Can demons do all the things that fallen angels can do? No. Whereas fallen angels have something along the lines of extradimensional spirit "bodies", demons used to have mortal giant human-looking physical bodies, and those bodies died before the Flood. And as such, while fallen angels have expansive supernatural powers in their "bodies", demons don't have bodies like fallen angels do, and as such there are things they can't do.

For instance, demons cannot physically manifest external to a living body. A demon could not move a chair, bend a spoon, cause a mass sighting of a UFO or multiple people to see a ghost, sit on someone putting pressure on their chest, leave Bigfoot tracks on the ground, etc. A demon can only have a physical presence in the 3d world by gaining control over the body of an animal or person. Then a demon could move a chair, bend a spoon, etc., by causing a demonized person or animal's body to manually physically do such things.

Demons are thousands of years old. Although they came into existence after fallen angels, demons have this in common with fallen angels: longevity. Fallen angels are immortal or near-immortal spirits. Fallen angels which have a sort of spirit, life and body that they are not mortal like humans. Demons did not inherit the immortal bodies of their fathers, but however they do have an immortal sort of soul/spirit as their fathers do. The soul (mind/will/emotions) of a demon is attached to their spirit of life, independent of a body. For angels, their bodies themselves are made of the stuff of the spirit or heavenly realm. For demons, their bodies were made of the stuff of the earthly physical realm (but now they don't have their own bodies).

And so demons inherited some qualities of fallen angels, and some of humans.

It could be argued that humans are a physical body, with a soul (mind/will/emotions) that is part physical and part spiritual in consciousness, and a spirit. (And human spirits are either dead or made alive by the Holy Spirit of Jesus.)

Fallen angels have a spirit body, a soul (mind/will/emotions or equivalents) of spirit (of such immortal independent life that only God could snuff it out).

But demons have qualities of both. Demons had physical bodies, they have a soul (mind/will/emotions) of spirit, seemingly immortal and independent in having life, apart from their now-and-long-dead physical bodies.

As such it seems that how demons work their demonization is for the demon soul (mind/will/emotions) to try to replace the authority/position of the soul (mind/will/emotions) of a human in that own human's body. This can result in internal struggle, confusion, and also potentially the human's will or self-control being pushed to the side.

Fallen angels seem to have supernatural abilities based on their spirit bodies. From the previous chapters, fallen angels may be extradimensional in every aspect of them. Demons had 3 dimensional physical bodies, so there seems to be nothing supernatural in ability there. But demons also seemed to have extradimensional souls/spirits which are not part physical, or physically tied for life, such as the souls of human beings. Or to put another way, for human beings, "the life of the flesh is in the blood" and without our bodies, we cease from activity. But it is not so with demons, as their life seems at least partially independent of their blood/bodies, as they did and have remained active after their physical bodies died.

So, whatever supernatural abilities demons could have, rests not in their bodies, but in their soul/spirits. And so if the supernatural powers of fallen angels could be said to come from extradimensionality conceptually (or heavenly realm-ness), then it would be true of demons that their supernatural abilities would have to come from a similar extradimensional aspect to their soul/spirits. But it is very obvious that demons cannot cause supernatural occurrences, except for when they gain control over the body of a human or animal. And when this happens, the supernatural abilities of a demon are limited to causing supernatural changes within the natural system of the body they are in. It could be that the substance of the souls/spirits of demons is of an extradimensional nature, which allows them limited supernatural abilities within a bodily system, according to how it is. This might be how they can cause muteness, deafness, blindness, insanity, seizures, ailments, and cause supernatural strength in a body. In any case, the Bible makes clear in the New Testament that demons can do these things (Matt. 9, 12; Luke 8, 11, 13; Mark 9). And I want to make clear, these are the most physically supernatural abilities that are attributed to demons in the Bible. I don't see any firm Biblical examples of any more pronouncedly physical effects that demons can cause.

How could a demon, inside a person, cause things such as blindness, deafness, seizures, or supernatural strength? And by supernatural strength, the Bible speaks of simply being strong enough to take on several people in a fight (as in Acts 19), or escape from chains and fetters (Luke 8). There is no firm indication that these chains were metal, but might have been leather straps or ropes. This is not "leaps tall buildings in a single bound" sort of strength. And in this case, it was the case of Legion, in which the man had many, many demons inside of him. And the demonized man was also prone to causing intentional injury to himself. So in the case of supernatural strength to escape from fetters and chains, it is possible that the demons had the man cause injury to himself in doing so. But another way to explain great strength might be found in adrenaline. It could be that a demon, or many demons, could supernaturally cause a sharp and high increase in natural bodily adrenaline, which would have enabled the man to show amazing strength. Here is an excerpt from "How Can Adrenaline Help You Lift a 3,500 Pound Car?" by Josh Clark of HowStuffWorks.com:

"In 2006 in Tucson, Ariz., Tim Boyle watched as a Chevrolet Camaro hit 18-year-old Kyle Holtrust. The car pinned Holtrust, still alive, underneath. Boyle ran to the scene of the accident and lifted the Camaro off the teenager, while the driver of the car pulled him to safety. In 1982, in Lawrenceville, Ga., Angela Cavallo lifted a 1964 Chevrolet Impala from her son, Tony, after it fell off the jacks that had held it up while he worked underneath the car. Mrs. Cavallo lifted the car high enough and long enough for two neighbors to replace the jacks and pull Tony from beneath the car. Marie "Bootsy" Payton was cutting her lawn in High Island, Texas, when her riding mower got away from her. Payton's young granddaughter, Evie, tried to stop the mower, but was knocked underneath the still-running machine. Payton reached the mower and easily tossed it off her granddaughter, limiting Evie's injuries to four severed toes. Curious, Payton later tried to lift the mower again and found she couldn't move it.

What accounts for feats of superhuman strength like these? Are they glimpses into the lives of superheroes' alter egos? Or are all of us imbued with amazing strength?

Although well-documented when they do occur, feats of hysterical strength -- unnatural and amazing strength tapped during high-stress situations -- are not recognized by medical science. This is largely due to the problem of gathering evidence: Instances like these come about without warning, and to reproduce these situations in a clinical setting would be unethical and dangerous. But we are aware of the effects of adrenaline, a hormone shown to increase strength to amazing degrees for short periods of time."
- "How Can Adrenaline Help You Lift a 3,500 Pound Car?" by Josh Clark

If a demon were able to stimulate the brain directly, to cause a strong adrenaline response throughout the body, then great temporary strength might result. This implies that a demon spirit/soul inside a person can at least cause some sort of physical stimulation of the brain. Blindness, deafness, and seizures would also perhaps necessitate that the demon possessing the person was able to cause neurons/nerves in the brain to fire, and also to supernaturally block other neurons or nerves from working properly. This would entail that demons can cause physical operational malfunctions inside a living person's brain (or animal).

The key thing to keep in mind here is that it is the living state of the person or animal that allows for a demon to come inside. If a person or animal is dead, there is nothing in the Bible that indicates a demon can gain control of their body. The independent immortal life "energy" that a demon has/is cannot directly plug into a human body to animate it, in the case of a living human soul being absent. This indicates that the demon is not capable of directly interacting, or plugging into, the body, or the physical, but rather that the demon is plugging into the part of the person that is "a living soul". In short, demons are parasitic on the living souls of human beings. Demons do not enter through people's bodies, or animal's bodies, but rather their souls; souls being composed of the mind, the will, and the emotions. And once a demon gets inside the soul, then they are inside the body that the soul is tied to. At least this is as best as I understand it. And when the demon has gotten inside having control over the body, not directly but through the soul, then the demon can cause physical effects to the body. By this I mean things such as supernaturally induced blindness, deafness, ailments, etc.

But probably the most prominent aspect of demonization is not anything as sharp as blindness, but rather psychological warfare. If a demon can think thoughts using a person's brain, firing the appropriate neurons for those thoughts, mental images, words, etc., then a demon can cause mental oppression of a great degree. Also, if a demon can block the auditory nerves in the brain, so that the person cannot receive external sounds, then who is to say that demons cannot do the opposite? What I mean by that is that is it possible that demon would be able to cause false sounds, fake auditory stimulus in the brain, which to the person would seem to be external auditory noises? Could this even include seemingly auditory voices that speak intelligently?

Although the Bible does not specify that demonized people heard voices, it does indicate that demons can cause deafness, and therefore can manipulate the auditory centers of the brain. And so if demons can block real sounds, supernaturally causing deafness, then it stands to reason that they could also cause pseudo-sounds that seem to be authentic auditory stimulations. The same reasoning would seem to hold as equally for blindness. If a demon can supernaturally block the optic nerves/center of the brain in the demonized person, to cause blindness, then why couldn't a demon also generate false visual stimulus, that seems to originate externally, but does not? Hearing auditory or seeing visual "hallucinations" is a well-known symptom today of various mental disorders. Among mental disorders today, "hallucinations" are seen as an extreme symptom on the range of mental illness symptoms, and sometimes occur as part of psychosis, which is an acute period of insanity. And somewhat milder symptoms of mental disorders seem to commonly include emotional disturbance (depression, mania, fear, etc.), anxiety and paranoia, and especially, delusional thinking.

One commonly known symptom of schizophrenia is delusional paranoia, in one example, the belief that someone or something is out to get you. (As Christians, we know there are beings out to get us, they are called demons and fallen angels).

One passage I find very interesting in the Bible is John 7:20-21,

Jesus said, "Did not Moses give you the law, and [yet] none of you keepeth the law? Why go ye about to kill me?"
"The people answered and said, Thou hast a devil: who goeth about to kill thee?"

So Jesus said openly that people were trying to kill him, and the people responded by saying he "had a demon". Funny, if I walked around saying people were out to get me, and trying to kill me, I think people might respond by thinking or saying I was "paranoid" or "crazy". Which would be a normal response these days. What few people would think or say to me is "you have a demon". Yet in the days of Jesus, it seems the terms were synonymous. People today are not so different from people 2000 years ago. Another interesting verse of what people said of Jesus: "Many of them were saying, "He has a demon and is insane. Why do you listen to Him?" (John 10:20) There is no doubt that demons can cause insanity, and crazy behavior. The man demonized by "Legion", whose behavior while demonized was insane, greatly changed after Jesus cast the demons out of him, as seen in Luke 8: "Then they went out to see what was done; and came to Jesus, and found the man, out of whom the devils were departed, sitting at the feet of Jesus, clothed, and in his right mind: and they were afraid. Then those who had seen what happened told the others how the demonized man had been healed." After the demons had left the man, he was healed to again having a "sound mind" or in his "right mind" (the term can be translated both ways).

While demons cannot cause a chair to move across a room, or a spoon to bend, demons can cause physical effects to a living body, once inside that body. For instance, in cases of muteness or seizures of demoniacs in the Bible, the demon on the inside was able to cause a supernatural ailment to the body physically. Nevertheless, this is a physicality that can effect a person's body only from the inside out. A demon would have to have spiritual authority grounds to be inside the person, having strong influence, in order to cause these supernatural physical ailments in the body.

Most prevalently: demons internally telepathically communicate with people, and cause them to have dreams or visions in the mind, whether in a sleeping or awake state, or in a state between asleep and awake, demons have the ability to telepathically project words, thoughts, images, and emotions. Also, instances of astral projection and remote viewing are evil illusions that could be caused by demons (or fallen angels). Demons use their abilities to oppress, attack, deceive, torment, disable, and destroy people. Such methods may include telepathy, mental visions, dreams, hearing voices in the mind, physical ailments of the body, for instance: muteness, seizures, illnesses, deafness, perhaps even hearing auditory voices or seeing things, etc., projecting thoughts/emotions/images into a person's mind, inducement of insanity, depression, heavy mental/emotional/psychological oppression and harassment, and control over the person's physical body. What they can do can include many, many things, in that the attack can be tailored to suit the individual person under attack.

At least this is how it can work, and these descriptions could fit all people, excepting where God's presence changes things.

I want to next talk about the scenarios possible for a Christian.

A born-again Christian has a living spirit, born of the Holy Spirit. A born-again Christian has the Holy Spirit living within their heart. As we read earlier, the heart reflects the entire person. The Holy Spirit is the spirit of God Himself, the Spirit of Jesus, and I would consider the Holy Spirit to have a dimensionality comparable to God and Jesus, being summarily infinite in dimensionality. As such, potentially, no demon spirit can take over the heart of a Christian, because the Holy Spirit is in that person's heart, covering the reflection of their entire self.

This principle is shown by Jesus in, Matt12:28-19 "But if I drive out demons by the Spirit of God, then the kingdom of God has come upon you. Or again, how can anyone enter a strong man's house and carry off his possessions unless he first ties up the strong man? Then he can rob his house." And also Luke 11:20-26, "But if I drive out demons by the finger of God, then the kingdom of God has come to you. "When a strong man, fully armed, guards his own house, his possessions are safe. But when someone stronger attacks and overpowers him, he takes away the armor in which the man trusted and divides up the spoils. "He who is not with me is against me, and he who does not gather with me, scatters. "When an evil spirit comes out of a man, it goes through arid places seeking rest and does not find it. Then it says, 'I will return to the house I left.' When it arrives, it finds the house swept clean and put in order. Then it goes and takes seven other spirits more wicked than itself, and they go in and live there. And the final condition of that man is worse than the first."

Once the Holy Spirit is in your house, your heart, no demon can conquer the strong man of the Holy Spirit and get in your house (heart). But if its just you in your house (heart), a demon could enter in. In general, we know "The heart is deceitful above all things, and desperately corrupt, who can understand it?" (Jer 17:9). But with the Holy Spirit inside the heart of a born-again Christian, there is a circumcision of the person's heart by the Holy Spirit (Rom 2:29). God writes his laws upon the Christian's heart, and their mind. (Heb 10:16-17). In this way the heart, and the mind to some extent, of a born-again Christian are different and changed from those of an unsaved person. The Holy Spirit is in the house of their heart. The heart and mind have God's laws written on them. Therefore, A demon cannot take control over a born-again Christian's heart, as the Holy Spirit is inside and will allow no demon to have control over it, or get in it. Also, a Christian's born-again spirit is independent, and cannot be violated by a demon. This means that both the heart and spirit of a Christian is protected from demons.

But a demon can still get in soul or the mind, will, and even emotions of a Christian. Christians can still unfortunately have demons harassing them, which can lead to influence, torment, and even potentially control over the body, I think primarily through the mind. But fortunately, the best case also includes that demons cannot enter and have power over the heart of a Christian. Also, the spirit of a Christian person is of course their own and a demon cannot control or influence a Christian's spirit. The heart and spirit of a Christian are safe.

If in the course of the life of a person, they acquire a demon that gains power and influence over their system, what then happens when that person becomes a born-again Christian and the Holy Spirit comes inside and dwells in that new Christian's heart?

The demon is already inside of the person's heart, mind, and soul. Is the demon automatically forced to withdraw its influence and control at the moment the person becomes Christian? Yes, from the heart. No, not necessarily from the mind, will, or even emotions.

Somehow in the person's life, the person sinned in such a way that allowed the demons to have legal spiritual authority grounds to be there in the person. By the person's own free will, they allowed the demon 'inside' and to gain control and influence over them. In the same way, the same person, now a new Christian, must use their same free will to no longer allow the demon to remain 'inside', having influence or control. The Christian has all the authority they need, through Jesus, and the power of God through the Holy Spirit of Jesus, to command the demon to get out and stay out, and refuse to let the demon influence or control them any longer. But the Christian person must choose this by his or her own free will. God does not violate our free will, and the Christian must choose of their free will to kick the demon out of their system and self.

But, I would say it is arguable that it makes sense that most of the demons in a person do automatically leave a person as or after they become Christian, as part of the process of repentance and healing. "Submit yourselves then to God. Resist the devil and he will flee from you." (James 4:7) Yet I think stragglers are possible, specifically demons that specialize in harassing or tempting a person in areas of sin they have strong problems with; I have heard people call them "Satanic Strongholds". Other potential demons might be ones that gained the authority to be there in the first place because of generational curses, the result of sins of ancestors going back to the immediate 3rd or 4th generations (Ex 20:5), or non-immediately from even earlier generations that never had the curses on them broken. These curses can be broken by God and Jesus in Jesus' name, and the associated demons can also be told to get out and stay out by a Christian with the authority and power of Jesus' name and His Holy Spirit. So this cleaning house can be, and I think often is, a gradual process for the new Christian. As the Christian repents of more sin, and asks for forgiveness, and to be filled with the Holy Spirit, whatever demons are left quietly flee, as the Holy Spirit fills more of the Christian's mind, and soul. Ultimately, the Holy Spirit can so fill the heart, soul, and mind of a person that there is no place for a demon, and resisted, they must flee. I believe this gradual process is a common scenario, and not the worst case scenario.

Ultimately, we Christians and our bodies belong to God. A demon cannot "own" or "possess" us, as truly we are owned or possessed by God, purchased by the blood of Jesus Christ. The Bible says in 1 Cor 6:19-20, "What? know ye not that your body is the temple of the Holy Ghost [which is] in you, which ye have of God, and ye are not your own? For ye are bought with a price: therefore glorify God in your body, and in your spirit, which are God's." So Christians are owned by God, and demons are just squatters or burglars that can cause trouble; they can always be evicted by the true landowner, Jesus Christ the Lord.

But in this life, we are not yet made perfect, and this means that as Christians, in this world, we are never entirely free from the possibility of harassment from demons. I would think they are always looking for some grounds or weakness by which to gain the authority to enter back inside and gain influence over the soul or mind directly. In this way they can be like annoying flies to the Christian who is strong in the Lord, occasionally buzzing around, but no real threat to the strong in the Lord who will resist them. (It is interesting in this that one root meaning of Beelzebub (954) is "lord of flies".) Though I don't believe that they ever give up entirely, I would argue they eventually choose to rarely target such a person, because they know it is probably pointless and they can do more harm and damage focusing their efforts on some other person.

Having covered some relatively brighter scenarios, there is a worst case scenario for Christians. That is the one in which a Christian uses their free will to allow new demons to gain influence and control over their system and enter 'into' them, after they have become a born-again Christian. Although the Holy Spirit, using the model above, can so completely fill the person that there is no room for any demon, the Holy Spirit, who is God, does not violate a Christian person's free will. If a Christian willingly chooses to get involved with demons, and sin, and invite demons into their self, and desires that the Holy Spirit not interfere, then the Holy Spirit will not violate the Christian's free will. In this worst case scenario, a Christian would still have their living human spirit inviolate, and the Holy Spirit would still be inside their heart.... but their mind and soul could be infiltrated by a demon, causing the demon to have strong influence or control over that Christian.

But please understand, this scenario requires that the Christian be working against the Holy Spirit, and strongly choosing evil over good, likely doing things to violate their conscience, sinning, or it is possible this could only come through decided choice to get involved with demons and the occult. I'm not sure what it takes for a Christian to get to this level, but it takes choosing evil, and not seeking God's protection and help. I do not think it matters as to whether the person gets involved with the occult, demons, and evil things in ignorance of the danger, or with good intentions, the result is the same. At this level, which is possible for a Christian to reach by their free will and God's respect of their free will, a Christian could become so demonized that they might be hardly distinguishable from an unbeliever who is so demonized as to be called "possessed" by Biblical standards.

Pastor Chris Ward, an experienced deliverance minister (or exorcist), in his book "Case Files of an Internet Exorcist" says,

"I cannot find any scripture that undeniably states that a true believer can or cannot be demonically possessed, but I do know that a Christian can be so spiritually oppressed that the average person cannot tell the difference. I know this fact from experience. In many cases I have worked where it would take a very discerning and experienced deliverance minister to know the difference between possession and oppression. What I do know is that when we give our life to Jesus, we keep our free will. Free will allows Satan to get a foothold in any person, believer or non-believer, in order to oppress and confuse the spiritual life of the believer. Obviously some of the church is confused. I have heard all the scriptures that argue that a born again Christian cannot be demon possessed. These theological arguments ignore the reality of the many believers who come to me for deliverance." Pg. 171

"It is my opinion that the best way to understand the difference between demon possession and spiritual oppression is this: when I am dealing with an unbeliever who demonstrates supernatural phenomena, I assume, for the moment, that he is demon possessed. When I am dealing with a professing believer, who is demonstrating supernatural phenomena, I assume, for the moment, that they are spiritually oppressed. This is an oversimplification of course, but as I begin to investigate and interview the person, I make a more discerning diagnosis. Sometimes it will take prayer and fasting to discern the difference between possession and oppression. Sometimes the person is both. Other times I may discern that the professing Christian is not a Christian at all, but masking his evil in religion as Dr. M. Scott Peck reported in his book The People of the Lie." Pg. 172

Using the strong man analogy, if a Christian wants the Holy Spirit to stand aside and let the demon in the mind, will, or even emotions, He will. This would grieve God, Jesus, and the Holy Spirit greatly. (The Holy Spirit stays in the heart, sealing it, and will not leave, no matter what, so the heart has no room for a demon. God will not break His side of the New Covenant, even if a person tries to break it.)

But even in this state, the Christian could always choose to seek God's help, cry out to Jesus, repent, and be cleansed and healed of all of their demons. Also, in this state, a Christian still has a measure of internal protection greater than that of an unbeliever, because the Holy Spirit is dwelling in their heart, always working to comfort them and teach them the Truth. With this level of demonization, a born-again Christian might even need the help of a Deliverance ministry (or Exorcism ministry), to get the demon out of themselves and to stop it from having influence and control any longer, the same as an unsaved person.

About the Deliverance ministry or Exorcism field, in his book, Pastor Chris Ward also says,
"The ministry of deliverance is a ministry of intercession. It is a ministry of mercy. I often refer to it as the gift of evangelism (Ephesians 4:11) because such a high percentage of the people who come for help have never before given their active free will over to the Lord. I also refer to the ministry of deliverance as the gift of miracles, see Mark 9: 39. Some professing believers know Jesus as Lord, but they have never made Jesus the Lord of their life. Another reason I refer to deliverance ministry, as the gift of evangelism, is that I start every deliverance session with a clear declaration of commitment to the Lord Jesus Christ whenever this is possible.
"Also, Phillip was the only person in the New Testament identified as an evangelist and his ministry was marked by the demons crying out (Acts 8:7). To me, deliverance ministry is the highest form of evangelism. The New Testament refers to deliverance ministry as: the "discerning of spirits" (1 Corinthians 12:10), as the "gift of mercy" (Romans 12:8), as "evangelists" (Ephesians 4:11), as "exorcists" (Acts 19:13), and as "spiritual intercession" (Ephesians 6:18). The Lord loves the intercessory man or woman. In Psalm 99:6 the Lord declares, "Moses and Aaron were among the priests, and Samuel was among those who called upon His name; they called upon the Lord, and He answered them." I find it interesting that the Lord keeps track of those ministers who conduct intercessory prayer for the people. The Lord recalls the names of Moses, Aaron, and Samuel as intercessors for the people. Intercession is so important to the Lord that He cherishes the intercessory minister. Deliverance ministry is intercession."

"Some deliverance ministers feel it is necessary to classify their client's behavior as spiritual oppression, demonic activity, demonic oppression, demon possession, or full demon possession. I personally do not do this. I do not care at what level of spiritual wickedness the person is. I do not care if they are oppressed or possessed. I do not care if they are believers or non-believers. I do not argue if a Christian can or cannot be demon possessed. These questions are moot when a person needs intercession for spiritual attack in his life. The only thing that goes through my mind is: are they having spiritual problems, and do they want help from Jesus?

"I was involved with deliverance ministry for over twenty years before I even knew that most of these theological arguments existed. It has only been within the last couple of years since I started my web page, The Origin of Demons, when I discovered so many churches reject or ignore deliverance ministry. You may visit the Origin of Demons at my web site at http://www.logoschristian.org/demon.html. It is apparent from what we have studied together so far in this book, that rejecting the ministry of healing and deliverance is the same as rejecting the ministry of Jesus.

"Do not let theology, denominational bias, or fear keep you from one of the most wonderful ministries that Jesus has appointed to the Body of Christ. Do not let theological opinions prevent you from intercessing for people who need help. The Lord cherishes deliverance and intercession ministry. Go and act with authority, the authority that Jesus gave us and the authority that God planned from the beginning."

- Case Files of an Internet Exorcist, Pastor Chris Ward, Pgs. 173,174

There is no doubt in my mind that Jesus and His disciples cast out demons in the Gospels and New Testament. Jesus and His disciples were the Deliverance ministers and exorcists at that time. Not only that, but the Bible tells us of the Lord, "He said to them, "Go into all the world and preach the good news to all creation. Whoever believes and is baptized will be saved, but whoever does not believe will be condemned. And these signs will accompany those who believe: In my name they will drive out demons; they will speak in new tongues; they will pick up snakes with their hands; and when they drink deadly poison, it will not hurt them at all; they will place their hands on sick people, and they will get well." (Mark 16:16-18) There is no doubt that driving out demons is a valid Christian ministry for today that is needed, and that Jesus expects at least some of the church to practice this ministry.

Chapter Ten
A Timeline of Demons and Fallen Angels
From the Early Church to the Present Day, and
Summary of Modern Activities of Demons and Fallen Angels

~ 30 AD

Rev 12: 12,17, "For this reason, rejoice, O heavens and you who dwell in them. Woe to the earth and the sea, because the devil has come down to you, having great wrath, knowing that he has only a short time." So the dragon was enraged with the woman, and went off to make war with the rest of her children, who keep the commandments of God and hold to the testimony of Jesus."

For the last 2000 years, a war has been actively waging on earth between Satan, and the fallen angels and demons under Satan, against Jesus and Christians. Christians are those who "keep the commandments of God, and hold to the testimony of Jesus". The apostles and early Christians understood this was the situation, and spoke numerous times of the situation, and gave instruction for spiritual warfare, and how to best deal with the situation as Christians.

The fallen angels are also known as "glorious ones" in this passage from Peter (distinguished from Holy angels which are just called "angels"), wherein we see that many people did not (and still don't) understand the current situation:

2 Pet 2:10-12 "He is especially hard on those who follow their own evil, lustful desires and who despise authority. These people are proud and arrogant, daring even to scoff at the glorious ones without so much as trembling. But the angels, even though they are far greater in power and strength than these false teachers, never speak out disrespectfully against the glorious ones. These false teachers are like unthinking animals, creatures of instinct, who are born to be caught and killed. They laugh at the terrifying powers they know so little about, and they will be destroyed along with them."

The term "glorious ones" is meant in the sense of a "glow" or in modern terminology, "glory". This comes from the Greek "epaphrodito" or "upon aphrodite". Aphrodite is the Greek term for Venus, which is the "star of the morning", a term which is used of Satan in Isaiah 14. Thus "epaphrodito" means "Upon the star of the morning", as the fallen angels have counted themselves "in" with Satan, the "star of the morning".

That the "glorious ones" are fallen angels is confirmed in Jude:

Jude 1: 8-10 "Yet these false teachers, who claim authority from their dreams, live immoral lives, defy authority, and scoff at the power of the glorious ones. But even Michael, one of the mightiest of the angels, did not dare bring a blasphemous accusation against Satan, but simply said, "The Lord rebuke you." (This took place when Michael was arguing with Satan about Moses' body.) But these people blaspheme the things they do not understand. Like animals, they do whatever their instincts tell them, and they bring about their own destruction."

Here we see that the "glorious ones" are compared directly to Satan, a fallen angel, and the leader of the fallen angels.

A Biblical history of demons and fallen angels, based off of the Bible, becomes more difficult to write when the Bible ends. The New Testament was the last of the Holy Scriptures. So after the end of the New Testament, a history of demons and fallen angels must more be based off of facts established in the history books. At least it would seem entirely so, except for the book of The Revelation of John.

But before proceeding to Revelation there is something else I want to address. This is the concept of an "antichrist". An antichrist is a special type of false prophet, who exalts himself as some level or sort of Messiah, to be followed. Thus the term "anti-" "christ". Let us remember, "christ" means "the annointed" in Greek. The term "christ" was used in the Greek version of the Old Testament, the Septuagint, to translate the term "Messiah" from Hebrew into Greek. "Anti" means opposite, opposing, contrary, or against. So an antichrist is someone, anyone, who is an opposing anointed one, or someone anointed by Satan. An antichrist is someone who takes a leader/messianic-appearing role that is against Jesus Christ, and counterfeit to Jesus: who is the true Christ, the true Anointed One, and who is God's only begotten Son.

Antichrists are mentioned several times in the New Testament prior to the book of Revelation.

1 Jn 2:18-19 "Little children, it is the last time: and as ye have heard that antichrist shall come, even now are there many antichrists; whereby we know that it is the last time. They went out from us, but they did not really belong to us. For if they had belonged to us, they would have remained with

us; but their going showed that none of them belonged to us".

1 Jn 2:22 "Who is a liar but he that denieth that Jesus is the Christ? He is antichrist, that denieth the Father and the Son."

1 Jn 4:3 "And every spirit that confesseth not that Jesus Christ is come in the flesh is not of God: and this is that spirit of antichrist, whereof ye have heard that it should come; and even now already is it in the world."

2 Jn 1:7 "For many deceivers are entered into the world, who confess not that Jesus Christ is come in the flesh. This is a deceiver and an antichrist."

From these verses we can learn that there are multiple antichrists possible. Many were described as being present and operating in the time of the early church. There is not only one antichrist, but rather there are many antichrists.

However, there is one major antichrist mentioned outside of Revelation as well.

2 Thes 2:1-12, "Concerning the coming of our Lord Jesus Christ and our being gathered to him, we ask you, brothers, not to become easily unsettled or alarmed by some prophecy, report or letter supposed to have come from us, saying that the day of the Lord has already come. Don't let anyone deceive you in any way, for (that day will not come) until the rebellion occurs and the man of lawlessness is revealed, the man doomed to destruction. He will oppose and will exalt himself over everything that is called God or is worshiped, so that he sets himself up in God's temple, proclaiming himself to be God. Don't you remember that when I was with you I used to tell you these things? And now you know what is holding him back, so that he may be revealed at the proper time. For the secret power of lawlessness is already at work; but the one who now holds it back will continue to do so till he is taken out of the way. And then the lawless one will be revealed, whom the Lord Jesus will overthrow with the breath of his mouth and destroy by the splendor of his coming. The coming of the lawless one will be in accordance with the work of Satan displayed in all kinds of counterfeit miracles, signs and wonders, and in every sort of evil that deceives those who are perishing. They perish because they refused to love the truth and so be saved. For this reason God sends them a powerful delusion so that they will believe the lie and so that all will be condemned who have not believed the truth but have delighted in wickedness."

He is also called the "man of lawlessness". But by his description, it is clear that he is an antichrist, of major proportions. This likely also refers to the final antichrist mentioned, the false prophet, the major antichrist of the book of Revelation. "False prophet" is another term for antichrist, and literally is "pseudo prophet", a fake prophet.

In the book of Revelation, generally accepted as the book of the New Testament that was written last, we are given prophecy of the future. This book was intended to give us guidance from the time it was written, to the present day, and on until at least when Jesus returns.

There are many fascinating studies out there on the book of Revelation. (See Appendix for Resources) But a full study is not the point of this chapter or this book.

So far we have covered in this book what I would call a "direct attack" of people, by demons and fallen angels. A demonized person is under a "direct attack". A person experiencing a fallen angel apparition is under "direct attack", like Jesus during his temptation by Satan.

But with the beginning of the Christian church came a new form of attack- an attack from within the church, through people. This is the kind of attack comes through the "spirit of antichrist" (1 Jn 4:3) working through people who are antichrists.

Jesus warned of these false prophets in Matt 7:15-23 when He said,

"Watch out for false prophets. They come to you in sheep's clothing, but inwardly they are ferocious wolves. By their fruit you will recognize them. Do people pick grapes from thorn bushes, or figs from thistles? Likewise every good tree bears good fruit, but a bad tree bears bad fruit. A good tree cannot bear bad fruit, and a bad tree cannot bear good fruit. Every tree that does not bear good fruit is cut down and thrown into the fire. Thus, by their fruit you will recognize them. "Not everyone who says to me, 'Lord, Lord,' will enter the kingdom of heaven, but only he who does the will of my Father who is in heaven. Many will say to me on that day, 'Lord, Lord, did we not prophesy in your name, and in your name drive out demons and perform many miracles?' Then I will tell them plainly, 'I never knew you. Away from me, you evildoers!'"

Disguised like sheep (disguised as Christians), these antichrists and false prophets enter into the church, trying to do the work of the evil one, from within the church.

Not only that, but they have been around since during the time of the early church, and ever since the time of the early church. Judas who betrayed Jesus is a perfect example of a wolf in sheep's clothing, and so wolves have been present since the very earliest beginnings of the Christian church. While John (1 Jn 2:19) said that some false Christians would stay within the church for a while and then leave, thus making them apparent, Peter warned that many false teachers would remain within the church:

2 Pet 2:1-3 "But false prophets also arose among the people, just as there will also be false teachers among you, who will secretly introduce destructive heresies, even denying the Master who bought them, bringing swift destruction upon themselves. Many will follow their sensuality, and because of them the way of the truth will be maligned; and in their greed they will exploit you with false words; their judgment from long ago is not idle, and their destruction is not asleep."

Not only remaining in the church, these people, which I would term antichrists, would introduce destructive heresies into the church. These false teachers were present in those days, and have been present since then, with every new generation producing a fresh crop of tares among the wheat.

This is what I would call an "indirect" attack of Satan, made through people, through a spirit of antichrist, which comes from Satan.

Keeping that in mind, I want to examine some portions of the book of Revelation.

The first section that I feel I must cover for its historical significance is the letter to the churches. Perhaps you have heard of the concept of "church ages" being represented by each of the 7 letters in the beginning of the book of Revelation. Perhaps you have not heard of this. I personally loosely agree with this concept. I think that each of the letters do represent a "church age". In addition to that interpretation, I also think these letters are cyclic in their significance, warning of dangers that any church or fellowship can face today, or could have faced then, as the churches mentioned were literally facing those challenges at the time Revelation was written. Basically, I think the letters could be directed at any Christian from the time Revelation was written, to today, and on into the future.

The reason I believe this comes from my own study and prayer with God while I was trying to understand the book of Revelation, not long after I became Christian. What I believe God revealed to me was that there is a "key" to understanding some parts of the book of Revelation. That "key" is based on faith. That key is all the portions in which Jesus says "He who has an ear, let him hear.." which is repeated in each of the 7 letters to the churches. From the time the book of Revelation was written, to the present day, for the vast most part, all Christians have had ears and could hear. Which would mean that these sections were speaking to Christians then, to Christians who have lived in the last 2000 years, and to Christians today. We all have ears, and we all are to hear this message as applying to us. So while I believe each of these letters applied to literal churches at the time of the early church, I also believe they are dangers that each church in the last 2000 years could be faced with, and that the message has applied to all Christians from then to now. And also at the same time, I believe each of the churches is representative of a church age. Others have done much research on this, and I am their student. A paper I agree with on most points is referenced below. (One disagreement is on the pre-tribulation rapture of the church of Philadelphia, and the reading of "tereo se ek hora" in Rev 3:10, which I would translate as "guard you out of the hour". A second is that I would characterize the Laodicean church as "Ecumenical" rather than "Charismatic", and believe the letter better describes ecumenical churches in general- though of course some ecumenical churches are charismatic.) This is a fantastic piece of prophecy analysis work, in my opinion:

http://www.midnightcry.net/PDF/Seven%20Letters%20to%20Seven%20Churches.pdf

It's not very long, and I hope you will stop and read, it may help what I am going to get into next make more sense. It wasn't long after I concluded that the letters must be cyclic, that I found out that this idea has been around for quite some time, and each person believing this has a slightly different interpretation. And I took the fact that I learned this independently on my own, and then found many other Christians out there with the same view, as confirmation that yes, there probably indeed is something to all this "church age" teaching. And I wanted to cover a little on this teaching so as to lay some groundwork for the next concept I want to cover, the idea of cyclic major antichrists.

I have found there is another part of Revelation, besides the church letters, which is directed to potentially all Christians during the last 2000 years.

Rev 13:18 "This calls for wisdom. If anyone has insight, let him calculate the number of the beast, for it is man's number. His number is 666."

What this means is that if anyone has insight, during the last 2000 years, that person might try to calculate the number of the beast. If this calculation was successful, understanding might be had as to what was the beast, and more understanding could be gained as to the many symbolic visual pieces of the book of Revelation. This also implies that though the final antichrist might be the only one to fulfill some parts of his role described in Revelation, that other parts could be cyclic. This also implies that the beast and surrounding concepts might also be cyclic. Which means there have been several men, antichrists, whose names have represented the number of the beast, and some parts involving the beast and the antichrist are meant to be cyclic in their interpretation.

My conclusion from my own studies is that there has probably been at least 1 major antichrist in each church age (and perhaps several minor ones). God willing, in studying the church ages, and in knowing the man whose name calculates to 666, one could gain better understanding of the book of Revelation, history for the last 2000 years, and perhaps better understanding of what is foretold to come.

I don't have the calculations for the major antichrist of every age, but in this chapter I will be including in some possibilities of a few major antichrists, including how their name calculates to 666, in a way that corresponds with the "church ages". I will also include approximate dates for the church ages, just as a way to organize the last 2000 years in a Biblical historical manner, which I prefer over a worldlier historical manner.

In this way I hope to include, for the last 2000 years, both examples of the "indirect attacks" of people working for Satan, antichrists, upon the church from within, also those antichrists attacking from outside the church, and also examples of "direct attacks" by Satan, other fallen angels, and by demons. This is the best way I could think of to intelligently organize this information.

(Note: I would like to cover the period of time from shortly after Jesus to the present in much more detail, perhaps I will in a later book. There is too much here to give full detail in what is just meant to be a chapter. So for now there are just some highlights I want to point out, which are not at all exhaustive of this topic.)

The Church at Ephesus ~ 40 - 150 AD

Herod, antichrist

Nero 54-68, antichrist

Demons, Séances, ghosts, Incubus, Succubus

The Church at Smyrna ~ 100 - 312 AD

Diocletus 303, antichrist

Demons, Séances, ghosts, Incubus, Succubus

The Church at Pergamos ~ 300 - 600 AD

Constantine 312, antichrist

Demons, Séances, ghosts, Incubus, Succubus

Paganization of Christianity

The Church at Thyatira – Catholic ~ 600 AD – Tribulation

The pope(s) antichrist(s)

610 Mohammed is visited by a fallen angel, depicted incorrectly as Gabriel, who tells him he is chosen by God. In Muslim religious writings, the Hadith vol.9 Book 87 number 111 it is written, "But after a few days Waraqa died and the Divine Inspiration was also paused for a while and the Prophet became so sad as we have heard that he intended several times to throw himself from the tops of high mountains and every time he went up the top of a mountain in order to throw himself down, Gabriel would appear before him and say, "O Muhammad! You are indeed Allah's Apostle in truth" whereupon his heart would become quiet and he would calm down and would return home."

Demons, Gins, Fairies, Elves, Incubus, Succubus, Séances, ghosts

The Church at Sardis- Protestant ~ 1500 AD – Tribulation

Martin Luther, (antichrist?) establishes the Protestant clergy vs. laity system

Demons, Gins, Fairies, Elves, Incubus, Succubus, mermaids, Séances, ghosts

The Church at Philadelphia – Christian/Missionary ~ 1800 AD - Tribulation

Joseph Smith, antichrist, visited by an "angel of light", starts the Mormon cult which grows into a false religion of its own.

Evolution and Gap theory popularized

...Demons (though becoming out of vogue) Gins, Fairies, Elves, Incubus, Succubus, Séances, ghosts, psychic ESP, beginning of "New Age" movement

The Church at Laodicea – Ecumenical ~ 1900 AD – Tribulation

… Demons (very much out of vogue and have in many cases and places have been newly labeled as "mental illness" or "schizophrenia")

Sun Yung Moon, antichrist, founder of the Moonies and tied to the ecumenical World Council of Churches

Gins, Fairies, Elves, Incubus, Succubus, Alien abductions, flying saucers with Aliens, Séances, ghosts, psychic ESP

Evolution widely accepted and popular, and starting a panspermia trend/transformation

"New age" movement well established

Present Day Situation:

Summary of Modern Activities of Demons and Fallen Angels

Demons and Fallen Angels are responsible for a large number of supernatural and paranormal occurrences, and are behind many sinful activities, some of which are not detailed in specific in the Bible, but Are happening in present times.

All of the following supernatural things that demons or fallen angels are currently responsible for have been witnessed happening by myself, or are reliable 1st hand accounts from people I know. I have generalized a bit to help you better understand the broad scope of things demons and fallen angels can do. To clarify, an example of the extent of this generalization: I know someone who has seen a "mermaid", someone else who saw an "alien" and have seen some myself, someone else who saw a "gnome", but no one who has actually seen an "elf".

Satan, other fallen angels, and demons are responsible for:

1. People having "real-feeling" dreams and/or waking visions of the future, which may partially come true, which may seem to be warnings or may guide a person to do things, or may be totally neutral but unnerving.

People feeling they knew someone in a "past life", telepathic knowledge related to a "past life", a dream of a "past life", no matter how "real" it feels, even dreams of a "past life" which people assume must be memories because of how real the dreams feel, etc.

Also false "memories" of this life. A person can receive "visions" in the present which feel like they are real memories. A person feels like they are remembering something, when they actually are receiving a demonic vision in the present tense as they are "remembering" the event, a vision that feels like a memory but is not a real memory at all.. This can include "screensaver memories" found in the alien abduction and Milab phenomena.

2. Any telepathic, telekinetic, pyrokinetic, or psychic phenomena or powers that a person seems to have, from small to large occurrences (Human beings have no supernatural powers of their own at all.) This includes all magical powers, from using "earth" energy, "Spiritual" energy, "Chi" energy, reading auras or energy of people or things, also Karmic balancing, threefold Wiccan returning, or Taoist powers, etc.

3. People seeing "Apparitions". Often "Apparitions" seem to happen in a pocket of reality that is not in sync with the rest of the world. See previous 3 chapters for details on Mental, Physical, and Combination types of Apparitions.

For instance, a kid and his brother see a monster under a bed, and the kid tries to touch it, and it grabs his leg. He screams for his mother, who comes in, and the monster instantly lets go of his leg. His mother wants to know why he is screaming. The kid tries to explain what happened to his mother, and wants his brother to back him up- but the brother remembers nothing of seeing a monster, and claims the kid has just started screaming for no reason.

The kid experienced an "Apparition" of a fallen angel, which used it's powers to cause the kid to see and feel the monster under the bed, as well as to experience an "Apparition" of his own brother, thinking he was talking to and touching his real brother, but he was not. This "Apparition" was in a pocket of space-time out of sync with the rest of reality, but seamlessly spliced together with actual normal reality. To put it another way, the kid was "taken up in a moment of time" (Luke 4:5) and shown the monster, and a false image of his brother and the place where he was. From the brother's perspective, nothing happened- but from the kid's perspective it all really happened.

It is possible to get cuts or bruises while experiencing an Apparition, and to be given objects that you still have after the Apparition is over. To the person experiencing it, an Apparition seems to happen in a normal flow of time, in the real world, and is Completely Real to all of the bodily senses. Many of what is classified today as "Schizophrenic Hallucinations" are attributable to fallen angel "apparitions", of a particularly cruel sort customized to the attacked individual.

"Apparitions" of ghosts, including having ghosts interact with you or others, even if the ghost is a dead relative, friend, or dead pet. Even if other people have seen the same ghost, with you or not, it is still a fallen angel apparition-even if you see it in a house that has been known to be haunted for 100 years. Remember, Satan and other fallen angels have been here since the time of Adam, and are very old, a hundred year haunting is only a short time to them. Just as it is possible to be given objects during an apparition, which remain with a person afterwards, it is also Sometimes possible to videotape, audiotape, etc. things you see that are apparitions, and this includes the audiotapes and all types of pictures of ghosts.

"Apparitions" of strange glowing floating objects, sometimes shaped like orbs, netting, or any other kind of obviously paranormal object you might see, whether it appears to be alive, intelligent, or controlled somehow, or not. Just as it is possible to be given objects during an apparition, which remain with a person afterwards, it is also Sometimes possible to videotape, audiotape, etc. things you see that are apparitions, and this includes the pictures and videotapes of Orbs and similar things.

"Apparitions" of seeing an alien or a UFO, including an alien or a UFO interacting with you, including alien abductions. Just as it is possible to be given objects during an apparition, which remain with a person afterwards, it is also Sometimes possible to videotape, audiotape, etc. things you see that are apparitions, and this includes some of the taped footage of UFOs. As it is possible to get cuts or bruises while experiencing an Apparition, and to be given objects that you still have after the Apparition is over, and physical damage to the body can occur with this type of Apparition. Abduction scars that match known man-made stun guns which can be imitated perfectly, can be caused by a fallen angel during an Apparition. Radiation burns caused by a fallen angel Apparition of a UFO are also possible. Though I must note that not all UFOs are necessarily fallen angel Apparitions, nor are all injuries from such an encounter with a UFO necessarily caused by a fallen angel Apparition, if the UFO in question is not a case of fallen angelic Apparition.

"Apparitions" of a mermaid, fairy, unicorn leprechaun, gnome, nymph, elf, and any magical creature you can think of, etc.

"Apparitions" of human-appearing strangers that seem to come out of nowhere, and say something to you that makes you feel morally confused about something good you just did, and then soon disappear back into nowhere.

"Apparitions" of people you know, like your close friend- and you know this because your close friend later can't remember your conversation with them or things you did together.

"Apparitions" of people who look like people you know, but seem a little different. Like you see a friend from school somewhere, and they normally don't have glasses, but now they do, and they tell you they have always worn glasses. You assume you must just not have noticed before. Later you see them at school and ask them where their glasses went, as they no longer have them, and they look confused and say they've never had glasses.

"Apparitions" of strange weather that other people don't remember, who should be able to remember seeing it.

"Apparitions" of strange places, like a small strange village of trailers surrounded by cornfields, in the middle of nowhere off of country back roads, a village on no map, no one has heard of in the area, that you drive by and see but cannot find again. Any place that is out of place in time, called Timeshifts or Spacetime shifts, might be included in this, and just generally any strange place that appears and then disappears.

"Apparitions" of anything strange or impossible seeming, like a cartoon gremlin talking to you through your TV, seeing monsters under your bed, etc. Anything strange and disturbing that just doesn't seem real or possible.

"Apparitions" of Angels, God, the virgin Mary, even if they interact with you, and a person should be especially wary of anything they have encouraged one to do, as fallen angels are very likely behind this. Stigmata (cuts like Jesus had on his hands, feet, and side) might also appear on a person's body, caused by fallen angels. Anything that is not the Holy Spirit Must be immediately suspect to be a fallen angel- even if a beautiful angel which seems Holy appears before someone. Actually Jesus warned of false prophets and miraculous signs that would deceive even believers, which in many cases is what fallen angels have been doing lately (Matt 24:10-12, Mark 13:22-23) Mohammed received knowledge from a fallen angel that presented itself as a good and Holy angel, and Joseph Smith the founder of the Mormons had similar experiences.

4. An animal behaving in a strange manner, being more friendly with you than normal, like a squirrel dancing with you, or an owl talking to you

telepathically, or a spider or an insect acting strangely with you or communicating telepathically, or seeing animals or birds appear frequently that have some symbolic meaning to you. These might be apparitions caused by fallen angels but are far more likely caused by possessed animals with demons in them.

5. Feelings of deja vu, random feelings of disorientation, and feelings that you have lost time and are not sure where you have been. Feelings of "enlightenment", having a "revelation", having an "epiphany", etc. especially when a person then has a strong desire to go out and immediately do something, especially out of the routine, esp. without thinking or praying about it first or testing it against the Bible.

6. When someone seems to control the weather, like causing a rainstorm or tornado, even a hail storm- whether they "cast a spell" to "cause" this, make a wish, pray to spirits or gods, or "visualize" it happening and it does. Also, when any sort of "spells" seem to work for people, whether they are spoken ones, or elaborate ritualistic ones, or are attributed to "positive visualization".

7. A person hearing "nature", pagan gods, spirits, trees, the wind, thunder, the sun, the moon, the planets, etc. "talk" to them telepathically or give them "signs".

8. Remote viewing, bilocation, spirit traveling, astral planing, shapeshifting, making oneself "invisible", glamours, other Shamanistic practices, etc.

9. It is possible for demons to put thoughts in a person's head. People think in an "internal monologue" voice, which is their own. But, demons can perfectly imitate and mimic this "internal monologue" voice in a person's head, and make it seem to a person that they them self are coming up with thoughts, that are in fact not their own but are things that demons are "whispering in their ears", metaphorically speaking. Demons can also cause images of thoughts to appear in a person's mind, which a person may think that they have constructed them self, but have actually not. On a similar note demons can cause a person to have dreams, and causing people to have repetitive dreams of something or someone is a very effective but subtle way they use to encourage people to Sin.

10. It is important to note that when Christian people try to hold séances, play "light as a feather stiff as a board", tell ghost stories, use an ouiji board, tarot cards, a magic 8-ball, look at horoscopes, read occult books, talk to the dead, recite spells, etc. they are opening themselves up to have demons put thoughts in their heads that will try to make them lose faith in Jesus and

stray from Jesus, or cause supernatural things to occur that will make them lose belief in Jesus and stray from Jesus. A person can call them self a Christian, or seem to have good intentions, and still do these things (for example the TV show "Crossing Over" is all about helping people, but it in fact hurts them by leading them astray from Jesus).

11. Also "near death" experiences in which people almost die, or do die but are revived, and see a white light at the end of a tunnel, and angels calling to them are also suspect as being visions caused by fallen angels or demons. "Near-death" experiences that involve a person visiting or seeing Hell are definitely visions caused by fallen angels or demons, as the Lake of Fire is inaccessible today. Despite common misconceptions in both the world at large and the church, people do not presently go to Hell or the Lake of Fire when they die. The souls of all unsaved people are dormant until they are raised for judgment at the Second Resurrection, which has not occurred yet. As such no one goes to Hell or the Lake of Fire yet. Also, people cannot experience waking up at the Judgment in the future, and then come back to the present and be revived, as no one will experience waking up at the Judgment until after they are 100% permanently dead. In the same way I don't believe anyone can die, be revived a while later, and have seen Heaven either. The saved do not go to Heaven immediately after death, but also awake at either the First Resurrection of the Martyrs (to reign for 1000 years with Jesus on this earth after his physical return) or awake at the Second Resurrection for Judgment (Though they will be saved). So visions of Heaven are extremely likely to be caused by fallen angels as well. ((Heb 9:27 "Just as man is destined to die once, and after that to face judgment"))

12. A person seeing Jesus in the flesh. Jesus said that everyone would know it when he returned, and that people would claim he had returned, but to not be fooled.

"Then if anyone says to you, 'Behold, here is the Christ,' or 'There He is,' do not believe him. "For false christs and false prophets will arise and will show great signs and wonders, so as to mislead, if possible, even the elect. "Behold, I have told you in advance. "So if they say to you, 'Behold, He is in the wilderness,' do not go out, or, 'Behold, He is in the inner rooms,' do not believe them." For just as the lightning comes from the east and flashes even to the west, so will the coming of the Son of Man be." (Matt 24:23-27)

As such anyone who claims to have seen Jesus in the flesh has been deceived with an Apparition, like Rev. Sun Moon of the Moonies who claims he met

Jesus himself, and surely there are others, one being Kenneth Hagin.

Note: But to balance the picture in truth, the Bible does say that there are many gifts of the Holy spirit. The Bible also says that in the last days God would pour out his spirit on men and women, and the young men would see visions and the old men would dream dreams. For example, Paul had an experience in which he heard Jesus and saw a bright light that blinded him, and John among others had a detailed vision (like an Apparition) from a Holy angel which is recorded in the book of Revelation. So not all visions and dreams and prophecy is Satanic. But we are encouraged to test the spirits, and Must do so. It is imperative that we test all things like this against scripture and pray in the power of the Holy Spirit for discernment. We must not stifle the Holy Spirit, but must also do as we are told to do, and test to see if something is from God or not. Also, the Holy Spirit determines what gifts a person receives, and a gift for discernment or tongues, or whatever, is given by the Holy Spirit, and cannot be taught and passed on by one person to another person.

Ultimately, God can work in people's lives as he chooses, but all things must be tested against scripture. According to scripture, we need to exercise caution. We are warned to be on guard against miraculous signs and wonders, so as to deceive even the elect. The more showy something is, the more likely it seems to be of Satan. If it doesn't match scripture, then it surely is of Satan. The fruits of supernatural things need to also be examined.

Both Christians and non-Christians are at risk from deceptions from demons and fallen angels. Non-Christians are targeted to keep them from salvation and to encourage them to believe in other belief systems than Christianity, and Christians are targeted in an attempt to make them ineffectual as Christians. All of us humans are targeted out of hatred, because they do absolutely hate us.

All people, even Christians, who do not attribute Satanic activities to Satanic entities are in fact believing both in Christianity and in an undefined second belief structure system. There is no place for ghosts, fairies, etc. and human generated supernatural powers, in Christianity, nor a disbelief in the fallen angels and demons mentioned in the Bible.

Please see the chapter on Spiritual Warfare for more information on what to do to stop these things if you or someone you know is experiencing the things listed above or anything similar. Please also see the Resources section for ministries and people that are prepared to help you.

Chapter Eleven

The Case for Enoch by Guy Malone

(Originals located at http://www.alienresistance.org/book_of_enoch.htm and http://www.alienresistance.org/sons_of_seth.htm)

"At that time I beheld the Ancient of Days, while he sat upon the throne of his glory, while the book of the living was opened in his presence, and while all the powers which were above the heavens stood around and before him." - Book of Enoch 47:3 (Ethiopic, Artisan pub)

Since it's English translation in the 1800's from texts found in Ethiopia in 1768, The Book of Enoch (known today as 1st Enoch) has made quite a stir in academic circles. 1 Enoch has been authenticated as existing and in wide use before the church age (most scholars now date it at 200 BC). Multiple copies were discovered in 1948 in the Dead Sea Scrolls. This of course has caused many to wonder why it is not included in modern Bibles...

"Thou has seen what Azazyel has done, how he has taught every species of iniquity upon the earth... Samyaza also has taught sorcery... They have gone together to the daughters of men, have lain with them... The women likewise have brought forth giants..." Enoch 9:5-8

Parts of The Book of Enoch tell the story of wicked angels who abducted and mated with human women, resulting in the hybrid race known throughout secular and Biblical history as the Nephilim (giants, KJV).

While this account encompasses only the first four verses of Genesis 6 (but see also Genesis 3:15, 2 Peter 2:4-6, Jude 6-7), Enoch 1 relates this story in great detail. It lists the names of 18 "prefect" angels - of 200 - who committed this sin. According to the text, these angels also taught mankind the "making of swords and knives, shields and breastplates (metallurgy); ... magical medicine, dividing of roots (medicinal and hallucinogenic use); incantations, astrology, the seeing of the stars, the course of the moon, as well as the deception of man."

By Noah's time, "The earth also was corrupt (wasting - KJV notation) before God, and the earth was filled with violence... all flesh had corrupted his way upon the earth." (Gen 6:10-11) Afraid of the consequences, these angels appeal to Enoch to intercede with God on their behalf; God instead uses Enoch to deliver a message of judgment against them. Aside from the "taking of wives," God states that he would not forgive them for teaching mankind magical arts and warlike ways. As summarized by Pastor Chris Ward:

"According to the Book of Enoch (Not a Canonical Text), God judged the angels for producing the Nephilim. God decreed that the fallen angels (Watchers) were to be cast into Tartarus. The Nephilim were also judged and it was determined that their bodies were to return to the earth in peace but their souls were doomed to wander the earth forever (as) wandering spirits..." (Pastor Chris's Enoch web page, ww.logoschristian.org/enoch.htm which reprints this dialogue between God and Enoch, and his The Origin of Demons web page www.logoschristian.org/demon.htm)

The increasing acceptance and popularization of this important book among theologians helps cast light on the extra-terrestrial hypothesis (ETH) in general. Enoch is an ancient writing, which states that angels (not true space aliens, as stated by many UFO cults, and popular modern authors Erich Von Daniken and Zechariah Sitchin) visited ancient Earth and polluted mankind's DNA. While this case can easily be made solely from the canonized Bible (see Gen 2:1. 3:15, 6:1-4, Dan 2:43, Matt 24:37, Rom 1:21-25, 2 Cor 11:14-15, Eph 6:12, 2 Pet 2:4-6, Jude 1:6-7), Enoch is yet another witness against these incorrect interpretations of Earth's predelulvian era (i.e., before the flood of Genesis 6). The fact that they also gave mankind technology, which supposedly "advanced our race" (but which we actually used to destroy each other, and to incur God's judgment), lends itself to a more sinister understanding of today's UFO phenomenon...

Genesis 6 / Book of Enoch	Today / Any episode of the X-Files
Supernatural Beings identified as angels	Supernatural Beings identified as ET's
Took as wives "any whom they chose"	Abduction Phenomenon
Hybrid Race of Nephilim	Accounts of alien hybrids, cloning
Introduced Destructive Technology: Weapons of Warfare / Psychotropic Drugs / Astrology & Sorcery	Hitler's Foo Fighters / Roswell Crash / "Back-engineering" of Stealth Bombers, etc / Occult Arts, New Age Doctrines
Worshipped as Gods (Annanuki) /Nephilim hybrids were "heroes of old, men of renown..." Gen 6:4 - the factual basis for Greco-Roman deities	Zechariah Sitchin / UFO Cults / Immunity for Abduction Crimes /Called "Spirit Guides, Ascended Masters and/or "Space Brothers"

FAQ:

Q: What other evidences for Enoch's authenticity (as a sacred text) are there? Why isn't it in the Bible today? Jesus said that angels can't have sex, proving this book's falsehood...

A: The idea that Jesus said that angels cannot have sex is a very common objection to The Book of Enoch and the angelic understanding of Genesis 6 in general. However it is also a very common misinterpretation of what he actually said.

Matthew 22:29-30

"Jesus answered and said unto them, Ye do err, not knowing the scriptures, nor the power of God. For in the resurrection, they neither marry, nor are given in marriage, but are as the angels of God in heaven." (KJV)

"Jesus replied, "You are in error because you do not know the Scriptures or the power of God. At the resurrection people will neither marry nor be given in marriage; they will be like the angels in heaven." (NIV)

"But Jesus answered them, You are wrong, because you know neither the scriptures nor the power of God. For in the resurrection they neither marry nor are given in marriage, but are like angels in heaven." (RSV)

Looking carefully and without a preconceived notion, we see that Jesus said that the angels "in heaven" DO NOT marry (nor presumably - have sex, reproduce). He did not state that angels "in general" CAN NOT do so. An unmarried Christian who - like the angels of God in heaven - wishes to remain obedient to God's will, "does not" have sex, but not because he or she is physically incapable of doing so.

That angels cannot have sex would be a fair interpretation of this passage, if this were the only passage in scripture that came close to dealing with the topic. It is not however, and therefore any interpretation of this scripture will be in accord with all else that is written. Jude 6 and 2 Peter 2:4-6 clearly indicate that the sin of these angels was sexual in nature, affirming the hybrid understanding of Genesis 6.

When they "shape-shift," angels can appear like perfectly normal humans (Heb 13:2). We know from the Old Testament that they not only appear human, but that they can eat food as well (Genesis 18:6-8; 19:3. In fact, angels eat when in their "normal" state - Psalm 78:24-25 tells us that manna is the "food of angels"). There is no reason to assume that angels do not contain all the physical properties of a normal human being, when assuming human form. However, they are not human, which goes a long way towards understanding why their children were "superhuman" (known as the heroes of old, men of renown, legends, Titans, Giants... depending upon your Bible translation.)

While far-fetched or disturbing to some, Matthew 22:30 simply does not dogmatically infer that sexual reproduction is a physical impossibility for angelic beings. In fact, since Jesus specified the angels "in heaven," one would have to go beyond what is actually written (AND ignore what else IS written) to state that angels that ARE NOT in heaven - fallen - seeking to thwart God's purposes - CAN NOT have sex.

As Jesus said above, "Ye do err, not knowing the scriptures..." Taken as a whole, the entire body of scripture indicates otherwise.

Which brings up the question, WHY would they do so?

"...the sons of God saw that the daughters of men were beautiful..." Gen 6:2 NIV

Quite simply, "lust" would be the most obvious and scriptural answer.

Beyond that misunderstanding, there is no doubt today that The Book of Enoch was one of the most widely accepted and revered books of Jewish culture and doctrine in the century leading up to Jesus' birth.

It is usually noted first that New Testament author Jude directly quotes from 1 Enoch. "Behold he comes with ten thousands of his saints to execute judgment..." (1 Enoch 2, Jude 14-15). Additionally, "the citations of Enoch by the Testaments of the Twelve Patriarchs... show that at the close of the second century B.C., and during the first century B.C., this book was regarded in certain circles as inspired" (1).

Aside from Jude, Peter and Paul's affirmations of the angelic/hybrid interpretation, recognition of 1 Enoch "... is given amply in the Epistle of Barnabus, and in the third century by Clement and Irenaeus" (1). The Catholic Church's Origen - known as "the father of theology" - affirmed both the Book of Enoch and the fact that angels could and did co-habitate with the daughters of men. He even warned against possible angelic and/or Nephilim infiltration of the church itself. Oddly, while thousands of his writings are still considered by them as "sacred," this very issue got him labeled as a heretic when the faulty Sons of Seth "doctrine" was conceived! (2)

Additionally, the Coptic Orthodox Churches of Egypt (est'd appx 50-100

A.D.) still include Enoch as canonized text in the Ethiopic Old Testament (2). This fact alone should carry great weight for Western Christians when honestly studying the "case" for Enoch. Given their 1900+ year history, the fact that they were never "ruled" by Rome's theology, and that they currently number over 10 million - this is a very significant portion of The Body of Christ that has historically esteemed 1 Enoch as inspired doctrine.

Some today (who do not seem to believe in the inspiration of scripture) claim that most major themes of the New Testament were in fact "borrowed" from 1 Enoch. "It appears that Christianity later adopted some of its ideas and philosophies from this book, including the Final Judgment, the concept of demons, the Resurrection, and the coming of a Messiah and Messianic Kingdom" (3). No doubt, these themes are major parts of 1 Enoch, and appear there as complete theologies a full 200 years before any other NT writings.

Christian author Stephen Quayle writes, "Several centuries before and after the appearance of Jesus in Jerusalem, this book had become well known to the Jewish community, having a profound impact upon Jewish thought. The Book of Enoch gave the Jews their solar calendar, and also appears to have instilled the idea that the coming Messiah would be someone who had pre-existed as God (4)." Translator RH Charles also stated that "the influence of 1 Enoch on the New Testament has been greater than all of the other apocryphal and pseudepigraphical books put together" (3). The conclusions are somewhat inescapable given Enoch's dating and wide acceptance between 200 B.C. and 200 A.D. Either Christian authors, and especially the Nicene Council, did plagiarize their theology directly from Enoch, or the original version of Enoch was also inspired.

James H Charlesworth, director of Dead Sea Studies at Yale University, says in The Old Testament Pseudepigrapha & The New Testament (Trinity Press International),"I have no doubt that the Enoch groups deemed the Book of Enoch as fully inspired as any biblical book. I am also convinced that the group of Jews behind the Temple Scroll, which is surely pre-Qumranic, would have judged it to be quintessential Torah -- that is, equal to, and perhaps better than, Deuteronomy....Then we should perceive the Pseudepigrapha as they were apparently judged to be: God's revelation to humans(2 & 5)."

But perhaps the most telling argument for 1 Enoch's "inspiration" may well be that the Jewish understanding of the term "Son of Man" as a Messianic title comes - not truly from our Old Testament canon - but from the Book of Enoch! Ever wonder why Jesus refers to himself in the gospels as the "Son of Man" rather than the Son of God? (2) Of over 100 uses of the phrase "son of man" in the OT, it refers almost always to "normal" men (93 times specifically of Ezekiel, and certainly not as Messiah!), but is used only one time in the entire OT, in one of Daniel's heavenly visions, to refer to divinity. Despite the Old Testament's frequent lack of divine application of the phrase, 1 Enoch records several trips to heaven, using the title "Son of Man" unceasingly to refer to the pre-incarnate Christ. Of particular Messianic significance, Enoch describes the following scene (2):

The angels "glorify with all their power of praise; and He sustains them in all that act of thanksgiving while they laud, glorify and exalt the name of the Lord of Spirits forever and ever... Great was their joy. They blessed, glorified and exalted because the name of the Son of Man was revealed to them (1 Enoch 68:35-38)."

Both His disciples, and especially the Sanhedrin knew what Jesus was claiming - 84 times in the gospels! - when referring to Himself as the "Son of Man." This claim was considered an obvious blasphemy to the Pharisees & Sadducees, but it is eternal life to all who confess that Jesus of Nazareth was, and is, the Son of Man, The Messiah, God in the flesh, The Holy One of Israel, God's Christ - the Lord of All to whom every knee shall bow (Philippians 2:8-10).

Using "normal rules" of scriptural interpretation, we are never to draw firm doctrine from only one passage of scripture. Right? Daniel's single use of "Son of Man" (in a "night vision" at that - Dan 7:13), would not be sufficient to claim that the phrase is indeed Messianic, especially given the other 107 times it is not used in that way. 1 Enoch is the missing "second witness" needed (according to all other rules of interpretation) to understand the phrase's double meaning as an enduring Messianic title. It has been argued ever since Enoch's first English translation, that by using this title so familiar to the Jews, Jesus was actually affirming the truth of this book, that the prophet was taken on many trips to heaven before his "final" translation, and that He was the one whom Enoch saw there - the pre-existent Son of Man, whom Enoch prophesied would judge the souls of all men.

Interestingly, Daniel is ALSO the only OT use of the term "watcher" to ever refer to angels (Daniel 4:13, 17, 23 KJV). Strong's Concordance defines a watcher as a "guardian angel" (Strong's 5894). "The distinguishing character of the Watcher (opposed to other angels in the canon) appears to be that it spends much time among men, overseeing what they are doing. It is also interesting to note that both times one of these angels appeared to Daniel, he took pains to note that it was "an holy one," suggesting that some Watchers are not aligned with God while others are (4)." Found nowhere else in the OT canon but the book of Daniel, "watcher" is patently Enoch's term for these angels. Likewise, Daniel alone used Enoch's term "Son of Man" to refer to the pre-incarnate Christ, adding further intrigue to the case for 1 Enoch's inspiration, and an overall understanding of it's doctrinal acceptance among both Old and New Testament writers.

What we lose out on today by not examining 1 Enoch - even if only for its historical significance - is that it is perhaps actually more splendid than any other book in our canon in its exultation of Christ as King! It also gives clear, stern and oft-repeated warnings to the unsaved of swift destruction at the Coming of The Lord, but is also full of amazing promises of future glory for the elect! We are of course wise to stay clear of dangerous heresy, but... ask yourself if the below sounds like false doctrine? Keep in mind, this was written at least 200 years before Christ walked the earth, and perhaps before Noah's birth:

"Then shall the kings, the princes, and all who possess the earth, glorify Him who has dominion over all things, Him who was concealed; for from eternity the Son of Man was concealed, whom the Most High preserved in the presence of His power and revealed to the elect.

He shall sow the congregation of the saints, and of the elect; and all the elect shall stand before Him in that day. All the kings, the princes, the exalted, and those who rule over the earth shall fall down on their faces before Him, and shall worship Him. They shall fix their hopes on this Son of Man...

Then the sword of the Lord of Spirits shall be drunk from them (the lost); but the saints and the elect shall be safe in that day; nor the face of the sinners and the ungodly shall they thence-forth behold. The Lord of Spirits shall remain over them; And with this Son of Man shall they dwell, eat, lie down, and rise up for ever and ever..." Enoch 61:10-13

Literally Translated from the Ethiopic by Richard Laurence LL.D. Archbishop of Cashel Late Professor of Hebrew in the University of Oxford

"For more than a century, scholars and church officials debated as to whether or not certain gospels, epistles and apocalypses should be included. For instance, it was long debated which to include in the canon, the Book of

Revelation, or the Book of Enoch..."Liberty Magazine - December 7, 1935 (1)

Q: OK! OK! So why is it not in the Bible?

A: Uncertain as well as multiple authorship, and several slightly varying texts are among the main reasons cited for Enoch not "making it" into the generally recognized canon. In truth, the spiritual agenda(s) of the early Roman Church is most likely the ultimate reason however, and we will examine this agenda here as well. Let's begin with the first two though, before moving to the more incredulous, but quite valid "conspiracy theories."

"The Book of Enoch, like the book of Daniel, was originally written in Aramaic, and partly in Hebrew (1)." While there may have been Hebrew translations during the centuries B.C. (which early church leaders may or may not have had access to), today only the Ethiopic manuscripts exist, as well as some incomplete Greek and Latin translations, plus one Aramaic fragment from the Dead Sea Scrolls. By the time of Jesus' birth, "average" Jews were reading mainly the Greek Septuagint translation of their own Torah (completed 200 B.C.), as a result of their years of foreign captivity and the then current Roman occupation. To coin the vernacular, they had been assimilated. So unless an authentic Aramaic version appears miraculously today, there will never be any completely indisputable way to argue for a modern "canonization" of 1 Enoch, as the originals are lost, probably forever.

The honest problem facing the infant Roman Church of 390 A.D., when first assembling today's Bible, was that the existing copies of 1 Enoch varied, albeit in minor ways. "Unlike the (rest of the) Bible which was carefully copied and checked for errors by Jewish and Christian scribes throughout its history, The Book of Enoch is available in a number of ancient manuscripts that differ slightly from one another... and many errors have crept in... There is no way of knowing which versions are (exactly faithful to) the original and which are the errors. While this doesn't change its stories in any substantial manner, it does make it impossible to anchor beliefs or arguments on any given section... (4)."

Even to those who will rightfully argue that Enoch was unjustly banned, this alone is a legitimate reason to exclude it from the holy writ. When faced with the task of declaring what is and what is not the "inspired, infallible Word of God," erring on the side of caution and certainty must be the case every time! (Only those who do not believe in the divine inspiration, and modern integrity, of scripture will be dissatisfied with this reasoning.) So, while 1 Enoch is almost beyond doubt an "inspired" text, the translated copies available (presumably) in 390 A.D., and especially those we have today, could not with any certainty also be classified as "infallible."

Another less important but quite "legitimate" issue is that 1 Enoch is actually a collection of at least four different "books," possibly written by various authors over many centuries, and possibly not by the true Enoch of Genesis

The Artisan Publishers' introduction to The Book of Enoch says "there can be no shadow of doubt" that there is a diversity of authorship and perhaps even time periods represented across the span of 1 Enoch, but that there is also "nonetheless, uniformity." They attribute this to the very possible idea that as God raised up prophets (after Malachi...?), they published under the safety of a revered pseudonym, to avoid persecution and possible death at the hands of the religious powers-that-were, who wanted no "fresh words" from God (1). This could well be the case, but would make the book(s) of Enoch no less inspired of God if true. However, only the NT Book of Hebrews (written centuries closer to the Bible's assembly, with multiple matching manuscripts) has been accepted as canon with such uncertain authorship - without even a good solid guess agreed upon, that is.

Since "the real" Enoch of Genesis 5 was transported to heaven - permanently - it would be no stretch to imagine that it was also a normal experience during his lifetime. After all, the Bible says he walked with God for 300 years! (Genesis 5:22) The first 36 chapters (detailing the watchers' fall) are sometimes only reluctantly attributed to Enoch (given their pre-deluvian history), but there are varying theories regarding the rest of the book(s). For much of the 1800's, it was argued that the remaining chapters were actually the work of an early Christian scribe, but these claims were decisively put to rest with the discovery of the Dead Sea Scrolls, as were JT Milik's claims that chapters 37-71 were Christian.

Charlesworth says "The consensus communis is unparalleled in almost any other area of research; no specialist now argues that I Enoch 37-71 is (written by a first-century) Christian and (that it) postdates the first century... (2) and (5)." With this in mind, we must again face up to the very real dilemma of stating that that either the entire New Testament was "drawn" in a natural, secular way from 1 Enoch - with no supernatural inspiration - or that 1 Enoch and The New Testament are both from God.

It is also considered that possibly a single author assembled older prophets' inspired works around 200 B.C. and simply added Enoch's name to them all, to ensure widespread acceptance - "Hardly a practice that inspires confidence in the text (4)." But in reality, it is no secret academically that certain canonized OT books, as well as Mark's gospel, may have been originally written by another - or even multiple - inspired author(s) and later were also assembled under the inspiration of God by a single author, who put either his own, or the original author's name, to the work. For example, most agree that Moses actually wrote Job's story from other existing texts (or that he knew him personally), before he even wrote Genesis. Most of the Major Prophets and historical books contain clear breaks in the time period, and were finally assembled many years later - as the author "was carried along by the Holy Spirit (1 Peter 2:21)." Christians need to get over the idea that "inspiration" means the writer went into some mystical trance, while God "possessed them" and wrote the Bible. Inspiration simply means they were obedient to God's leading, and wrote what He said OR supernaturally revealed to them, or even that he guided their research, helping them discern truth from error, for the purpose of writing "an orderly account (Luke 1:3)." Here, Luke states that his gospel was an extended research project!

In that vein, I.D.E. Thomas has recently suggested one other possibility perhaps not considered in academic circles before the 1986 publication of The Omega Conspiracy. "Thomas suggests that the compiler may have written his book from texts originally written by Enoch himself. In such a case it would make perfect sense for the compiler to attach Enoch's name to the book for which he had provided the material (4) and (6)."

Even with all of this said, there is still no "clean" explanation for Enoch's 1000-year disappearance from even popular literature though. Despite the above reasons for not canonizing the book, it is painfully apparent that the church did in fact suppress The Book of Enoch. Only in studying both the goals and motives - positive and negative - of the Roman Church do the truest reason for Enoch's "fall from grace" become apparent.

(But despite the arguments presented here, please note that I have no intention of bashing the early Roman Catholic Church. Always remember, they have done the world an incredible service by assembling and preserving God's Word for the 1600+ years yet to follow. To make a distinction, the greatest sins and travesties they often stand accused - and guilty of - were not the work or intent of the earliest Church fathers, but of the corrupt political system that grew up in the centuries after the Roman system's formation. "It was not until hundreds of years later (5th - 7th centuries), that the first vestiges of this church government rose where there was a Roman bishop as the head of the Church, making it an official Roman

Church functioning similar to today's." (7))

Realistically however, there was also a "point" to the canon. The goal and even eternal function in assembling the earliest Bibles was NOT merely sorting out what was inspired of God and what was not. They also had the specific intent of promoting and preserving a solid doctrinal foundation for all believers in Christ. Like Paul, they had to passionately argue against Gnosticism - "the doctrine of salvation by knowledge (8)," or the idea that gaining "superior" and/or "hidden" knowledge ensures one some higher spiritual position - opposed to a simple obedient faith in Christ.

Arguing for 1 Enoch's "proper place" today, one (seemingly) Gnostic apologist states "Enoch had found and experienced God face-to-face, something which Gnostics strive for. The Church opposed Gnostics... Experiencing God was taboo... Putting a stamp of approval on such a wild tale (Enoch) would have too many people believing that they could experience God for themselves, instead of going into a church and being told what to believe... Those who experienced visions or personal insights became dangerous to the church. They could lead people astray by supporting independent thought and actions (3)." It's quite difficult to seriously consider this argument however, in light of the fact that a more common criticism of Catholicism is that they "worship," or at least perhaps TOO highly esteem, those who have had profound mystical experiences with God! For that matter, the Bible is NOTHING BUT a collection of "those who experienced visions or personal insights." It would quite a thin book if all such stories were left out!

The truth is that Gnostics "strive(d) for" experiencing God without knowing and submitting to Christ or His Body, the church. Even today, the wish to "experience God face-to-face" without Christ's mediation (1 Timothy 2:5) is not just an honest effort to avoid false religion (of which there is much), but to not submit to any spiritual authority at all - whether it be God's Church, God's Word or even God's Christ! It should always be kept in perspective that "the church" was not Rome's, or even man's idea. Jesus said "I will build my church, and the gates of hell will not prevail against it (Mt 16:18)." The early church rightly opposed Gnosticism, but beginning with Paul's letters, not with the Roman Church. Many who passionately promote (or just reprint and sell) 1 Enoch today do so not with the intention of promoting a deeper faith in God's inspired Word, but more with the intent of undermining the Bible's authority - and especially the church's. 1 Enoch's clear historical integrity but "lack of inclusion in the Bible" is often used to "springboard" arguments for other "favorite" heretical books, left out for all the right reasons. Modern Gnostics are often fond of several other "gospels" (such as Thomas and Mary, both of which have statements and theologies that clearly contradict the more reliable works by John, Matthew, et al, proving they were NOT inspired by God). In short (oops - too late for that!), the typical Gnostic and New Age arguments have nothing to do with why The Book of Enoch was not included in the Bible, or not preserved with other ancient works. (The true "reasons why" are actually more sinister...)

The forming church also had to publicly refute and stand against (from within!) the heresy of modalism, which in part suggests that Jesus Christ is a created being - eternal nonetheless, but inferior in substance to God the Father. The Council of Nicea was expressly interested in making sure that the doctrine of the Triune Godhead was clearly expressed by the canon, and especially that it would not be misunderstood by those who would read the Scriptures. Another "motive" was to refute "Pneumatomachians - who accepted the deity of Christ but said the Holy Spirit was an impersonal force... And so it was, and we are indebted today to a 4th century Luther that stood up to define the nature of Christ and God against a flood of falsehood (8)."

To be honest, in reading Enoch there seems to be in the multitude of heavenly trips a physical distinction sometimes made between The Father and the Pre-Incarnate Son. The phrases "Lord of Spirits" , "Ancient of Days," and "Son of Man" are used so often (perhaps interchangeably, perhaps not) that even a careful reading sometimes infers the (doctrinally acceptable - 1 Cor 15:24) separation of the eternal Godhead. On earth, "... all the fullness of the deity" was present in Jesus Christ, "the image of the invisible God." But 1 Enoch can at minimum cause confusion to the understanding of the Godhead - hard enough to grasp even today - in a way that other authors (Moses, Isaiah, Ezekiel, Paul and John) do not when speaking of their face-to-face encounters with God. (Did any gnostics still in the audience catch that phrase?) Even without the conflicting manuscripts or possible multiple authors coming into play (which careful examination of the rest of canon shows could have been worked out actually, if they so chose), I sincerely believe that if there was a legitimate, excusable motive for not including Enoch in the Bible, this was it.

This does not excuse why we had to wait 1000 years to re-discover this book however.

So finally, with the general integrity of the Holy Scriptures, and the legitimate reasons the early Roman Catholic Church may have rejected 1 Enoch covered respectfully (and in a way palatable for modern Christian academics), let's critically examine the real reasons behind the indisputable censure of 1 Enoch. There are many texts that - while not included as canon - have nonetheless retained their "position of honor" and even reverence among the (Western) historical Christian church. Among these are the Apocrypha (still included of course in modern Catholic Bibles - and, just FYI, even included in the original King James Bible), as well as The 12 Patriarchs, and writings too numerous to name by various "Church Fathers." All of these have remained in a relatively high-profile position throughout church history, more or less available for both scholars and laymen to draw from when studying the ancient origins of the Christian faith. Not so with Enoch.

Yes, ANY of the above are certainly "good enough" reasons to have disqualified Enoch from canonization. But only assuming you wanted to in the first place ...

With all of the evidence in, we have to own the fact that 1 Enoch was not merely "rejected for canonization." It was buried. Flat out suppressed. It was quite intentionally lost to history, with all copies destroyed or left to rot 10 stories deep under the Vatican. Enoch was not merely "left out of the Bible." It was dropped like a bad habit.

Okay, only for those who have come the distance, now let's talk dirt...

Point blank, Origen was right. Enoch was suppressed and labeled as heresy specifically to hide the truth of the fallen angels' past, present and future activity on earth.

Forget Roswell. Forget the X-Files. The most successful, enduring and damaging cover-up of "The Truth" about our planet's frequent visitors - has come from within The Church.

Part 2 - The Sons of Seth Theory - The Early Catholic Church's suppression of the truth of angelic abduction with special thanks to Pastor Chris Ward for his research of the ancient texts.

This article alleges the suppression of The Book of Enoch and the truth of angelic abductions by examining The Sons of Seth Theory, which was introduced approximately 400 A.D. Any resemblance found here to actual church leaders - living or dead - is purely a conspiracy theory.

As said in Part 1, the Church itself is responsible for perpetrating the most enduring and damaging cover-up in regard to abductions.

Beyond this, in accordance with prophecies made by Peter, Paul and Jesus Christ himself, they invented a completely false doctrine about the "proper interpretation" of Genesis 6. This heresy has robbed both the churched and unchurched from any hope of understanding the truth behind abductions. In short, Jews and early Christians knew full well that angels did, could and would abduct humans for the purposes of sex and hybridization, BUT these same texts also gave safeguards against such assault.

This rogue element of the early church (sort of an early Catholic Majestic 12, if you will) has left moderns at the mercy of a phenomenon they have no hope of understanding or defending themselves against. Today's society is doomed to repeat the errors of our ancient ancestors, by once again falling prey to the Watchers' sorceries and claims of divinity. Already, far too many are under the sway of UFO cults, claiming that they are led by "spirit-guides here to help humanity." Many more "normal" individuals in the world of scientific UFO research and supposedly the world's governments merely defer to their technology, by assuming the Watchers are a superior race from the stars. Citing Ezekiel 3:18 (while I'm making enemies anyway) allow me to also charge that the blood, the wrecked lives, and the eternal damnation of all souls who have fallen victim to either abductions or deceptive philosophies is on the hands of those who perpetrated - and today with knowledge maintain - these deceptive doctrines.

I realize these are astounding and damning claims, and I would not make them without offering sufficient proof. Because of the incorrect (but widely taught in seminaries) "Sons of Seth" interpretation of Genesis 6 introduced around 400 A.D., Christians start out at a disadvantage when studying the topic. For this reason, these arguments will be offered in a way meant to challenge and convince the Christian believer of these claims. Then, we'll look over other texts which received "the Enoch treatment." As made clear elsewhere on this site, I still maintain a belief in and respect for the integrity of scripture (the original languages that is) as God's inspired word. The problem here is that God's inspired word has been intentionally misrepresented by those entrusted to teach it.

<u>The Sons of Seth Heresy</u>

Beginning around 400 A.D., portions of the church began to take an unusual stand against the angelic interpretation of Genesis 6. Rather than teaching what the text clearly says (especially when examined in Hebrew, below), and what had been the Orthodox Jewish and early Christian view for all time previous, the idea was introduced that this passage "really" referred to the lineages of Cain and Seth, the surviving sons of Adam. They said it simply means that the "rebellious" lines of Cain were marrying the "faithful" descendants of Seth. The unfounded presumption of this theory is that ALL of Seth's descendants were godly, while ALL of Cain's were rebellious. While a sketchy pattern can be drawn from Genesis, it is really a ridiculous injustice to the concept of free will and of God's dealing with individuals to dogmatically hold to this position. It further implies that Sethites were somehow immune to the effects of the Fall itself.

Conspiracy aside, the angelic interpretation itself rather assaults the sensibilities of even those good men throughout the ages who would be tempted to apologetically shirk from believing and teaching God's word as inerrant truth. As J Timothy Unruh says "Modern Christians have often attempted to make this passage in Genesis more palatable intellectually by explaining the 'sons of God' as Sethites and the 'daughters of men' as Cainites, with their union representing the breaking down of the wall of separation between believers and unbelievers." (9) Ultimately, this position simply does not "hold water" under even casual study. (A brief but in-depth analysis of the Sons of Seth theory is online, posted by researcher and author Chuck Missler (11). Because of this, I will only touch on the relevant points continuing from Unruh's book, published earlier and available to be read online in it's entirety.)

Those who hold to the humanistic Sethite explanation have never been able to suggest a sufficient reason (or even a lame one actually) as to why the children of one "immoral" parent would be physical giants however, IF both parents were otherwise normal humans. While the angelic abduction scenario seems more like science fiction to today's intellectual Christian, the Sethite doctrine is actually easily revealed to be the fantasy!

The exact term "sons of God" (B'nai haElohim in Hebrew) used in Genesis 6:1-4, is used also in Job 1:6, 2:1 & 38:7 always referring to angels. Unfortunately, many competent Bible scholars of today still believe the "sons of God" are of human lineage. This is simply because it has been taught in seminaries for centuries, thanks to the deceptive and radically unsound doctrinal shift introduced by the church at this point in history.

Unruh continues, "The actual expression 'sons of God' occurs explicitly three other times (in Job, above)... and in each case the term refers indisputably to angelic beings.... There are as well implicit references to these sons of God in a number of other passages. There is no doubt in these passages the meaning applies exclusively to angels... A very similar term bar elohim is used in Daniel 3:25, and refers either to an angel or a theophany (ie, an appearance of God before the incarnation in Christ). The term 'sons of the mighty' (bene elim) is used in Psalm 29:1 and also Psalm 89:6, and again refers to angels. The sons of Elohim the mighty creator are confined to those creatures made directly by the Divine hand, and not born of other beings of their own order." (9) Any amount of honest research into this topic will turn up the same findings, that someone (or some being...) from within the 3rd - 5th century church did a great violence to the literal reading of the text in concocting the Sethite theory.

Dr. Arnold Fruchtenbaum, renowned Judaic scholar and one of the foremost authorities on the nation of Israel, agrees almost verbatim with this assessment, in his work Messianic Christology. While many who support the Sethite doctrine argue that the ENGLISH phrase son(s) of God is referred to in the Bible as simply meaning "believers" in general, there is a world of difference between the Old and New Testament use of this term. In the New Testament sense, the term is applied to those who have become "sons of God" through their faith in Christ, but by adoption (Romans 8 ; 1 John).

Fruchtenbaum writes "The term 'sons of God' is a general term which means 'to be brought into existence by God's creative act.' Because the term carries this meaning, it is used very selectively. Throughout the Old Testament the term 'sons of God' is always used of angels. But some want to make Gen 6:1-4 the one exception, and there is simply no warrant for making an exception here. In the New Testament the term 'sons of God' is expanded. Adam is called the son of God (Luke 3:38) because he was brought into existence by creation. Believers are called sons of God (John 1:12) because believers are considered to be a new creation (Galatians 6:15). But in Genesis, the text is dealing with a specific Hebrew expression, benei elohim, and, as it is used in the Hebrew Old Testament, it is a term that is always used of angels. The distinction in this passage then is not between Sethites and Cainites, but between humanity and angels." (10)

Fruchtenbaum, Unruh, Huie, Missler and other modern authors all offer similar academic works on these subjects, all citing the same Old & New Test passages to put forth sound and extensive rebuttals to many other objections frequently offered in defense of the Sethite interpretation, or other claims of some "human lineage." The point here though is that the Sethite theory introduced to (unleashed upon) the Christian mindset by the Church at this time clearly denies the truth of Scripture. As Missler rightly asserts "There is no basis for restricting the text to either subset of Adam's descendants... The entire view is contrived on a series of assumptions without Scriptural support...

"The "Sons of Elohim" saw the daughters of men that they were fair and took them wives of all that they chose. It appears that the women had little say in the matter. The domineering implication hardly suggests a godly approach to the union. Even the mention that they saw that they were attractive seems out of place if only normal biology was involved. And were the daughters of Seth so unattractive? ... If the lines of Seth were so faithful, why did they perish in the flood?" (11)

Implanting these false doctrines, which survive to this day, was a long battle which some determined force from within the Church finally accomplished, and Origen and other faithful men paid the ultimate price by being labeled heretics, exiled and/or even publicly burned to initiate and execute this great "cover up." (This tragic history is catalogued in E.C. Prophet's Fallen Angels & The Origins of Evil; Why Church Fathers Suppressed The Book of Enoch, but see also my online disclaimers to her work).

This pseudo-theology eventually succeeded in becoming the official church dogma however, surviving even to today's Bible institutions, despite the fact that the rest of the canon affirms the angelic interpretation many times over.

It is worth noting before moving on, that the Bible is far from the only ancient source that makes the argument that angels interbred with humans. The entire pantheon of Greco-Roman mythology is the same story retold, but romanticized by cultures who were deceived by these so-called "gods" who mated with human women to produce Hercules, etc. "The Book of Antiquities" (which you'll find in the study of almost any pastor you ask) by ancient historian Flavius Josephus also tells us that angelic hybridization produced the "Titans" of Greco-Roman culture, as shown from this research posted online by Bryan T. Huie (btw... that Greek word "Titanos," which was eventually translated from the Greek version of the Hebrew OT to give us "giant" in the King James Version, can also be translated "grey." Just some food for thought). Josephus writes:

"...they now showed by their actions a double degree of wickedness; whereby they made God to be their enemy, for many angels* of God accompanied with women and begat sons that proved unjust, and despisers of all that was good, on account of the confidence they had in their own strength; for the tradition is, that these men did what resembled the acts of those whom the Grecians called giants. But Noah was very uneasy at what they did..."

Continuing from Huie's webpage - * "This notion, that the fallen angels were, in some sense the fathers of the old giants, was the constant opinion of antiquity. As you can see, Josephus believed and recorded that "the sons of God" mentioned in Genesis 6 were fallen angels. As Whitson's footnote acknowledges, this belief was standard in the ancient world.

"Another well-known first century Jewish writer, Philo of Alexandria, shared Josephus' views on this topic. In his work "On the Giants," Philo wrote: "And when the angels of God saw the daughters of men that they were beautiful, they took unto themselves wives of all them whom they chose.' Those beings, whom other philosophers call demons, Moses usually calls angels..."(The Works of Philo, "De Gigantibus," translated by C.D. Yonge, p. 152)

"As shown above, the evidence that "the sons of God" mentioned in Genesis 6 are fallen angels is substantial. By their sexual immorality, these angels produced offspring, which were strong and violent. The concept of a race of giants which resulted from the union of gods and humans is virtually universal in the world's early civilizations." (12)

The "conspiracy" from within the Church quite literally changed the history of the world - both it's past, and it's future. Julius Africanus, St. Augustine and many others debunked and destroyed every document relating to the angelic invasion to successfully promote their "weather balloon / crash dummy" Sethite fallacy. Before long Christianity itself would eventually erode from being a dynamic, living, supernatural faith in a miracle working God to become merely "the new intellectualism," whose seat had moved from Athens to Rome.

The errors and ungodliness of the political elite who succeeded the 1st and 2nd century church's apostles, evangelists and martyrs are lamented elsewhere. But as this system began to promote the "mediation" of the priesthood (1 Tim 2:5), and as the doctrines of men (?) came to replace belief in the Word of God (Mark 6-8, 13), the then "Western world" spiraled downward into it's Dark Ages. The carefully chronicled histories of the ancients became known first as mythology, then finally as Saturday morning cartoons, and our race quite simply forgot about the truth.

But it's out there. In July 1947, about an hour outside of Roswell, New Mexico, the gods of old returned to find a basically God-fearing, Mom & apple pie loving kind of 1940's Americana culture - but one that had also just harnessed the most destructive force the world had ever seen, and who now held the undisputed title of "world champion superpower."

And thanks to the old church's now forgotten "cover-up" of the truth behind fiery chariots and abductions, we'd have NO CLUE as to what had just landed in our back yard...

But God did.

On the other side of the world, among a nearly forgotten people group that was - by destiny's clock - just seconds away from rejoining the fray of the mighty nations of the world, a goofy little kid chased his pet sheep into a cave. And on an otherwise normal hot summer's day in 1948, he walked out with the archeological find of the millennium.

A clay jar filled with some scrolls. Among them of course, were fragments from the book of Enoch.

As a matter of course, the Vatican paid top dollar for them.

"And I heard, but I understood not: then I said, Oh my Lord, what shall be the end of these things?

"And the angel said, Go thy way Daniel: for the words are closed up and sealed till the time of the end.

"Many shall be purified, and made white, and tried; but the wicked shall do wickedly; and none of the wicked shall understand; but the wise shall understand."

(End of the book of Daniel 12:8-10)

This article, and links for the notes and references made in this article, can be found online at www.alienresistance.org/book_of_enoch.htm

Key to notes:

(1) Artisan Publishers, The Book of Enoch (Ethiopic, Richard Laurence trans
(2) Chris Ward, D Min Return of the Watchers tape and/or his Enoch page
(3) The Book Tree, The Book of Enoch (Ethiopic, RH Charles trans, Preface by Paul Tice)

(4) Stephen Quayle, Aliens & Fallen Angels: The Sexual Corruption of the Human Race

(5) J.H. Charlesworth; The Old Testament Pseudepigrapha & The New Testament

(6) I.D.E. Thomas, The Omega Conspiracy

(7) "The Nicene Council," Let Us Reason ministries

(8) New Advent's Catholic Encyclopedia

(9) The Present Day UFO-Alien Abduction Phenomenon, by J Timothy Unruh

(10) Messianic Christology by Dr. Arnold G. Fruchtenbaum Ariel Ministries

(11) Mischievous Angels or Sethites, by Chuck Missler (appendix to Alien Encounters)

(12) Here A Little, There A Little website, by Bryan T Huie

Chapter Twelve
Timeline of Demons and Fallen Angels - Present to Future
Prophecy and Revelation (Part 1)

Any timeline concerning the future of demons and fallen angels is a matter of prophecy. The book of prophecy which covers this topic in specific is the book of the Revelation of John. Being a book of prophecy, correct interpretation of the book of Revelation without the guidance of the Holy Spirit in the gift of prophecy, would just be guesswork. What follows is the explanation of what I believe the Holy Spirit has led me to believe in my study of the book of Revelation, keeping study of the rest of the Bible, current events, and history in mind. Whether I am correct or incorrect, and no matter how correct or incorrect these ideas may strike you at first glance, I believe it is ultimately up to the God, Jesus, and the Holy Spirit to guide you and teach you in your understanding of these matters.

As the point is made, contained in 1 Cor 14, "Follow the way of love and eagerly desire spiritual gifts, especially the gift of prophecy... everyone who prophesies speaks to men for their strengthening, encouragement and comfort... he who prophesies edifies the church."

So to understand the book of Revelation, pray for the gift of prophecy.

In this it is best to keep in mind 1 Cor 13:2, "If I have the gift of prophecy and can fathom all mysteries and all knowledge, and if I have a faith that can move mountains, but have not love, I am nothing."

In this and of great importance is 1 John 4, the entire chapter should be read and heeded, and most pointedly,
"Dear friends, do not believe every spirit, but test the spirits to see whether they are from God, because many false prophets have gone out into the world. This is how you can recognize the Spirit of God: Every spirit that acknowledges that Jesus Christ has come in the flesh is from God, but every spirit that does not acknowledge Jesus is not from God. This is the spirit of the antichrist, which you have heard is coming and even now is already in the world."

The gift of discernment of spirits should also be prayed for earnestly. "Oh God my Father, Jesus my Lord, please do not let me be deceived!"

That being said, here are my views:

Before the fall of Babylon (also called the "prostitute") the forces of Satan will gather all the rulers of the world together for a battle. Three demons that look like frogs will gather the kings of the whole world together for a battle against Jesus. These demons will gather the kings of the world together for this battle against Jesus before Jesus has returned, showing the demons are anticipating Jesus' soon return.

Rev 16:12-21 "The sixth angel poured out his bowl on the great river Euphrates, and its water was dried up to prepare the way for the kings from the East. Then I saw three evil spirits that looked like frogs; they came out of the mouth of the dragon, out of the mouth of the beast and out of the mouth of the false prophet. They are spirits of demons performing miraculous signs, and they go out to the kings of the whole world, to gather them for the battle on the great day of God Almighty."
(Jesus says) "Behold, I come like a thief! Blessed is he who stays awake and keeps his clothes with him, so that he may not go naked and be shamefully exposed."
"Then they gathered the kings together to the place that in Hebrew is called Armageddon. The seventh angel poured out his bowl into the air, and out of the temple came a loud voice from the throne, saying, ?It is done!? Then there came flashes of lightning, rumblings, peals of thunder and a severe earthquake. No earthquake like it has ever occurred since man has been on earth, so tremendous was the quake. The great city split into three parts, and the cities of the nations collapsed. God remembered Babylon the Great and gave her the cup filled with the wine of the fury of his wrath. Every island fled away and the mountains could not be found. From the sky huge hailstones of about a hundred pounds each fell upon men. And they cursed God on account of the plague of hail, because the plague was so terrible."

After the fall of Babylon, Jesus will come again. It is right before this time that Satan will be deceptively leading all the kings of the world to fight against Jesus. Right around the time of this gathering for the battle of Armageddon is when the Rapture will take place. Before the battle the Rapture will occur.

[This is after the 6th bowl of the seventh trumpet, and right before or at the time of the 7th and final bowl of the seventh trumpet. Rev 11:15-19 is describing the same time period as Rev chapters 15 and 16. Notice how they both end with the same great hailstorm and earthquake. These sections run parallel. The 7 bowls are the 7 plagues, and these plagues take place after the 7th and final trumpet, in the time between when the 7th trumpet sounds and the time when Jesus returns. The 7th and final trumpet sounds, and then the 7 plagues come, and then Jesus returns. Revelation reveals it is after the 6th plague and before or at the time of the 7th plague of the seventh trumpet that the Rapture will occur. This is what is also told in,

1 Cor 15:52 "In a moment, in the twinkling of an eye, at the last trump: for the trumpet shall sound, and the dead shall be raised incorruptible, and we shall be changed."

"At the last trump" is "en eschatos salpigx" in Greek. (Strong's (1722)(2078)(4536)) Although "en" is translated as "at" 113 times in the NT KJV, "en" is translated as "in" 1902 times, "with" 140 times and "among" 117 times. "Eschatos" means last, and the word itself implies that there has been something before the last. Thus the "last trumpet" must imply that there has been at least one prior trumpet, or "first trumpet" in contrast to the "last trumpet". These trumpets are clearly seen in the book of Revelation, and we know the "last trumpet" referenced to in 1 Cor 15 is the same 7th and last trumpet as in Rev 11: 15-19. However, the parallel ending of Rev 11:15-19 (terrible hailstorm and earthquake) and Rev 15 and 16 shows that these are describing the same time period. As such "en eschatos salpigx" should be translated with the more common meaning of "en". It should read "In the last trump" or even "among the last trump" because it is In the last trumpet section of the book of Revelation that the Rapture is clearly pointed out by Jesus (Rev 15:16), with his warning: Jesus says "Behold, I come like a thief! Blessed is he who stays awake and keeps his clothes with him, so that he may not go naked and be shamefully exposed." This falls in between the 6th and 7th bowl of the 7th and last trumpet.]

Babylon will fall before Jesus returns. I think Babylon will fall at the time of the Rapture, or shortly afterwards. The remaining people will already have been gathered prepared for the battle of Armageddon, by the three evil spirits that look like frogs. All the people fighting Jesus will be defeated and die as Jesus returns and the battle of Armageddon ensues. In Jesus' victory, the "beast" and "False Prophet" (or the final "Antichrist") will be thrown alive into the "lake of fire" (or Hell).

Rev 19:11-21 "I saw heaven standing open and there before me was a white horse, whose rider is called Faithful and True. With justice he judges and makes war. His eyes are like blazing fire, and on his head are many crowns. He has a name written on him that no one knows but he himself. He is dressed in a robe dipped in blood, and his name is the Word of God. The armies of heaven were following him, riding on white horses and dressed in fine linen, white and clean. Out of his mouth comes a sharp sword with which to strike down the nations. He will rule them with an iron scepter. He treads the winepress of the fury of the wrath of God Almighty. On his robe and on his thigh he has this name written: KING OF KINGS AND LORD OF LORDS.

And I saw an angel standing in the sun, who cried in a loud voice to all the birds flying in midair, ?Come, gather together for the great supper of God, so that you may eat the flesh of kings, generals, and mighty men, of horses and their riders, and the flesh of all people, free and slave, small and great.? Then I saw the beast and the kings of the earth and their armies gathered together to make war against the rider on the horse and his army. But the beast was captured, and with him the false prophet who had performed the miraculous signs on his behalf. With these signs he had deluded those who had received the mark of the beast and worshiped his image. The two of them were thrown alive into the fiery lake of burning sulfur. The rest of them were killed with the sword that came out of the mouth of the rider on the horse, and all the birds gorged themselves on their flesh."

Satan will be cast into the Abyss, and locked there for 1000 years.

Rev 20:1-3 "And I saw an angel coming down out of heaven, having the key to the Abyss and holding in his hand a great chain. He seized the dragon, that ancient serpent, who is the devil, or Satan, and bound him for a thousand years. He threw him into the Abyss, and locked and sealed it over him, to keep him from deceiving the nations anymore until the thousand years were ended. After that, he must be set free for a short time."

This Abyss is the same place that other fallen angels, that once sired the Nephilim, are currently bound.

Jesus will reign as The King on Earth during this 1000 years, with all the martyrs not only of the Tribulation, but of the ages before the Tribulation reigning with Him as priests of God and of Christ.

Rev 20:4-6 "I saw thrones on which were seated those who had been given authority to judge. And I saw the souls of those who had been beheaded because of their testimony for Jesus and because of the word of God. They had not worshiped the beast or his image and had not received his mark on their foreheads or their hands. They came to life and reigned with Christ a thousand years. (The rest of the dead did not come to life until the thousand years were ended.) This is the first resurrection. Blessed and holy are those who have part in the first resurrection. The second death has no power over them, but they will be priests of God and of Christ and will reign with him for a thousand years."

Then Satan will be let out again and will deceive many people again, once again deceptively leading armies to fight against Jesus, and his people. This means there will be people left who are the descendants of those who did not fight and die in the battle of Armageddon. These people are who the resurrected martyrs will be priests to, and these are the people Satan will deceive and lead to battle. All of these people of Satan's army will die, and Satan will be thrown into the lake of fire (or Hell) where he will remain forever.

Rev 20:7-10 "When the thousand years are over, Satan will be released from his prison and will go out to deceive the nations in the four corners of the earth 'Gog and Magog' to gather them for battle. In number they are like the sand on the seashore. They marched across the breadth of the earth and surrounded the camp of God's people, the city he loves. But fire came down from heaven and devoured them. And the devil, who deceived them, was thrown into the lake of burning sulfur, where the beast and the false prophet had been thrown. They will be tormented day and night for ever and ever."

Isa 14:15-17 "Nevertheless you will be thrust down to Sheol, To the recesses of the pit. Those who see you will gaze at you, They will ponder over you, saying, 'Is this the man who made the earth tremble, Who shook kingdoms, Who made the world like a wilderness And overthrew its cities, Who did not allow his prisoners to go home?'

Eze 28:18-19 "So I brought fire from within you, and it consumed you. I let it burn you to ashes on the ground in the sight of all who were watching. All who knew you are appalled at your fate. You have come to a terrible end, and you are no more."

At some point, perhaps either when the Beast is thrown into the lake of fire, or when Satan is later thrown into the lake of fire, the other fallen angels working with Satan will also be thrown into the lake of fire. As far as I can tell, the Bible is unspecified as to when this will occur.

Mat 25:41 "Then he will say to those on his left, 'Depart from me, you who are cursed, into the eternal fire prepared for the devil and his angels."

There is some argument to be made that a judgment of these angels will occur, involving Christians in a judging role, before they are thrown into the lake of fire.

1 Cor 6:2-4 "Do you not know that the saints will judge the world? And if you are to judge the world, are you not competent to judge trivial cases? Do you not know that we will judge angels? How much more the things of this life! Therefore, if you have disputes about such matters, appoint as judges even men of little account in the church!"

All of the dead will rise again. Jesus will judge everyone at Judgment day, and will reward those who were saved by their belief in him according to what they have done, and will sentence those who were not saved because of their unbelief in him according to what they have done. And all people who did not have belief in him will join Satan in the lake of fire (or Hell).

Rev 20:11-15 "Then I saw a great white throne and him who was seated on it. Earth and sky fled from his presence, and there was no place for them. And I saw the dead, great and small, standing before the throne, and books were opened. Another book was opened, which is the book of life. The dead were judged according to what they had done as recorded in the books. The sea gave up the dead that were in it, and death and Hades gave up the dead that were in them, and each person was judged according to what he had done. Then death and Hades were thrown into the lake of fire. The lake of fire is the second death. If anyone's name was not found written in the book of life, he was thrown into the lake of fire. "

Then all the people who follow Jesus, whose names are written in His book of life, will live with God and Jesus. God will be their God, and Jesus will be their God, and they will be His children. They will live with Him in the beautiful Holy City, and there will nevermore be death, mourning, crying, or pain for them. They will be God's children, and Jesus' children, and live in peace with Him forever.

Rev 21:18 "Then I saw a new heaven and a new earth, for the first heaven and the first earth had passed away, and there was no longer any sea. I saw the Holy City, the new Jerusalem, coming down out of heaven from God, prepared as a bride beautifully dressed for her husband. And I heard a loud voice from the throne saying, "Now the dwelling of God is with men, and he will live with them. They will be his people, and God himself will be with them and be their God. He will wipe every tear from their eyes. There will be no more death or mourning or crying or pain, for the old order of things has passed away."

He who was seated on the throne said, "I am making everything new!" Then he said, "Write this down, for these words are trustworthy and true."

He said to me: "It is done. I am the Alpha and the Omega, the Beginning and the End. To him who is thirsty I will give to drink without cost from the spring of the water of life. He who overcomes will inherit all this, and I will be his God and he will be my son. But the cowardly, the unbelieving, the vile, the murderers, the sexually immoral, those who practice magic arts, the idolaters and all liars — their place will be in the fiery lake of burning sulfur. This is the second death."

Rev 22:20 "He who testifies to these things says, "Yes, I am coming soon." Amen. Come, Lord Jesus."

This brings us pretty much to the end of the book of Revelation, it is a book with a blessing, "And behold, I am coming quickly. Blessed is he who heeds the words of the prophecy of this book." (Rev 22:7) I encourage you to read the rest, heed the prophecy, and receive this blessing.

Some of the following material in this chapter will cover parts of the book of Revelation with the assumption that you the reader have read the book at least once, and thus have some familiarity with the material contained in the book of Revelation.

Having come to end of the book of Revelation, there is still much to be discussed, and many unanswered questions.

What is Mystery Babylon? Who are the 3 evil spirits that look like frogs? What are the locust things that come out of the Abyss? Who is the beast out of the Abyss, called "Apollyon" or "Abaddon"? Who is the antichrist? How do you calculate the number of the beast, which is 666? How do I heed the words of prophecy of this book? And numerous more questions...

I'm going to try to cover what answers I have to these questions. I don't have all the answers, but I believe God has showed me some things. Some of these questions and their answers relate more directly to fallen angels and demons than others, but to some extent all of they all do, as they help us better be aware of what Satan and his minions are doing today, and will be doing in the future.

First off, much of what needs to be heeded in this book is to be found in the first chapters, dealing with the churches. I believe these correspond to church ages, and to modern church types. These are covered a bit in my Time of Jesus to the Present Timeline chapter. (Much of this is researched from here though I disagree some and have changed Laodicean accordingly. [1])

The four main types of churches today are the Catholic (Thyatira), Protestant/Reformation (Sardis), Christian fundamentalist/missionary/charismatic (Philadelphia), Ecumenical (Laodicea). There is a warning appropriate to each church in the letters of Revelation. Each letter can also arguably apply to every Christian and church on a local warning level. Heed the instructions and warnings of these letters.

Another way to heed the book of Revelation is to not take the mark of the beast. Many people speculate this will be a microchip or something similar, which will be either in the forehead or right hand. Whatever the mark is, it will be required to buy or sell anything. Most people will accept it as a normal and ok thing, and find it acceptable. Whatever you do- do not take the mark of the beast! Die or be imprisoned, but do not take the mark of the beast! It would be better to die than to take the mark of the beast!

Rev 14:9-13 "A third angel followed them and said in a loud voice: "If anyone worships the beast and his image and receives his mark on the forehead or on the hand, he, too, will drink of the wine of God's fury, which has been poured full strength into the cup of his wrath. He will be tormented with burning sulfur in the presence of the holy angels and of the Lamb. And the smoke of their torment rises for ever and ever. There is no rest day or night for those who worship the beast and his image, or for anyone who receives the mark of his name." This calls for patient endurance on the part of the saints who obey God's commandments and remain faithful to Jesus." Then I heard a voice from heaven say, "Write: Blessed are the dead who die in the Lord from now on."

"Yes," says the Spirit, "they will rest from their labor, for their deeds will follow them."

The mark of the beast will be the number of a man's name, his number which is 666, or the name of the beast.

Rev 13:16-18 "He also forced everyone, small and great, rich and poor, free and slave, to receive a mark on his right hand or on his forehead, so that no one could buy or sell unless he had the mark, which is the name of the beast or the number of his name. This calls for wisdom. If anyone has insight, let him calculate the number of the beast, for it is man's number. His number is 666."

"If anyone has insight let him calculate" means that this portion of Revelation is cyclic, and has been possible for many people over the last 2000 (plus) years to calculate the number of the beast. So how does one calculate this number of the man's name to 666? A man's name is in letters, and 666 is in numbers. So calculating must involve some sort of alpha-numerical code or equivalency.

The first antichrist was perhaps Herod, mentioned in the New Testament. Actually 3 Herods are mentioned in the New Testament. The first tried to have Jesus killed at his birth, the second let Jesus be crucified, accepted worship as "god", and died of worms, and the third spoke to Paul while Paul was imprisoned.

In Hebrew, Herod was often spelled HORODOS. In the Hebrew alpha-numerical code, O is equal 6. So Herod's name would read h6r6d6s.

Caesar Nero (Neron Kaeser in the Roman) ("nrwn qsr" in Aramaic) I have read equals to 666 in Aramaic. Nero was known for early Christian persecution, 54-68 AD.

I have also read that the name of Diocles Augustus equals 666. He is also called Diocletus, and is another Roman emperor known for persecuting Christians early 300 AD.

The title of the Roman Catholic Pope, V I C A R I U S F I L I I D E I, is equal to 666 in Roman numerals. This title means "Vicar of the Son of God".

The name of Martin Luther in Hebrew also equals to 666. This was apparently calculated by Petro Bongo, canon of Bergam, in "Objections Regarding the Pope". The Roman Catholic church has also apparently suggested that "Loutherana", another spelling of Luther, equals 666.

And so that's what I've found on antichrists past. [2]

But if it is true that anyone can calculate the number of the beast, which is 666, then this must also hold true today. When I first became a Christian I started looking at the book of Revelation, trying to figure out what it meant.

198

After much thought and prayer, and some research, I think God showed me something on the current antichrist.

What is modern alpha-numerical code in use today? In English, it may seem that a=1, b=2, etc. But this is not the alpha-numerical code in English that we use in everyday life. Who ever uses that code. No, the code we use in everyday life is a bit different.

It's 1800MYPIZZA and 1800CALLNOW. The modern alpha-numerical code in English today is the telephone keypad. So take a look, and what does your keypad say?

It says 6= M, N, O. What, or who, corresponds to those letters? What can a person even spell with those letters? And the answer I reached was M-O-O-N, of which the 3 letters in the name each equal 666. M, N, and O each are a 6, equaling 666. There is little doubt, after some research, that Sun Myung Moon is an antichrist. And I took this alpha-numerical calculation of 666 as confirmation that he is one of the major antichrists of this age. It is also interesting that Moon changed his birth name in 1953. His name was Mun Yong Myong. But Yong means "dragon" and he changed it specifically so as to not cause Christians alarm. Even more interesting is that if one uses his first name he was born with, Mun, and his new middle name Myung, combined with Moon or Myong as his last name... his initials are MMM, once again equaling 666.

Moon is best known as the founder of the Unification church. Moon owns the Washington Post Newspaper, and allegedly has ties with some "big" Christians with well known names, such as Jerry Falwell and Tim Lahaye. Moon has also been said to have influence, through his followers, over the World Council of Churches. I can find little to prove this, however in a memorandum from the Church of Greece's dated about 2005, it reads, "Thus, for example, the allegation that "one of the five chairmen of the W.C.C. collaborates closely with the Unification Church of the Korean pseudo-messiah Moon" has never been denied." [3]

There is no doubt Moon has many ecumenical religious front- organizations, and the Christian ecumenical movement is his pet project that he works on when not proclaiming himself as a "messiah". (These allegedly include the Council of National Policy, the Coalition for Religious Freedom, American Freedom Coalition, Concerned Women of America, Women's Federation for World Peace, Family Federation for World Peace, and others. [4]

Moon says Jesus himself appeared to him when he was 15 years old, and gave him a mission. As Satan himself appears as an angel of light, so did a fallen angel, likely Satan, appear to Moon, claiming to be Jesus.

Some people might also find it interesting that using the telephone keypad alpha-numerical code, "A World Council of Churches" equals 111. Multiply that by 6, and you have 666. But of course, that isn't a man. It is astounding how many churches are members of the world council of churches, many people probably attend such a church and don't even realize it. [5]

In any case, I think Moon is one modern day antichrist of major importance, which I believe the M-O-N, 666, Revelation-based calculation from the telephone keypad affirms.
Moving on to another question: Who are the 3 evil spirits that look like frogs?
We are going to spend some time on this question, because oddly enough, there is a huge amount of information that can be gleaned from the answer to this question. In fact, this is one of the most important prophecy-related questions that I think a Christian can ask about the book of Revelation.

Let's look at what the book of Revelation says in detail:
Rev 16:13-21"Then I saw three evil spirits that looked like frogs; they came out of the mouth of the dragon, out of the mouth of the beast and out of the mouth of the false prophet. They are spirits of demons performing miraculous signs, and they go out to the kings of the whole world, to gather them for the battle on the great day of God Almighty. "Behold, I come like a thief! Blessed is he who stays awake and keeps his clothes with him, so that he may not go naked and be shamefully exposed." Then they gathered the kings together to the place that in Hebrew is called Armageddon.
The seventh angel poured out his bowl into the air, and out of the temple came a loud voice from the throne, saying, "It is done!" Then there came flashes of lightning, rumblings, peals of thunder and a severe earthquake. No earthquake like it has ever occurred since man has been on earth, so

tremendous was the quake. The great city split into three parts, and the cities of the nations collapsed. God remembered Babylon the Great and gave her the cup filled with the wine of the fury of his wrath. Every island fled away and the mountains could not be found. From the sky huge hailstones of about a hundred pounds each fell upon men. And they cursed God on account of the plague of hail, because the plague was so terrible.

(2 chapters on the details of Babylon's destruction follow, there is praise to God, and it is said that the time of the wedding of the Lamb has come, and then...)

Rev 19:11 "I saw heaven standing open and there before me was a white horse, whose rider is called Faithful and True. With justice he judges and makes war. His eyes are like blazing fire, and on his head are many crowns. He has a name written on him that no one knows but he himself. He is dressed in a robe dipped in blood, and his name is the Word of God. The armies of heaven were following him, riding on white horses and dressed in fine linen, white and clean. Out of his mouth comes a sharp sword with which to strike down the nations. "He will rule them with an iron scepter." He treads the winepress of the fury of the wrath of God Almighty. On his robe and on his thigh he has this name written: KING OF KINGS AND LORD OF LORDS. And I saw an angel standing in the sun, who cried in a loud voice to all the birds flying in midair, "Come, gather together for the great supper of God, so that you may eat the flesh of kings, generals, and mighty men, of horses and their riders, and the flesh of all people, free and slave, small and great." Then I saw the beast and the kings of the earth and their armies gathered together to make war against the rider on the horse and his army. But the beast was captured, and with him the false prophet who had performed the miraculous signs on his behalf. With these signs he had deluded those who had received the mark of the beast and worshiped his image. The two of them were thrown alive into the fiery lake of burning sulfur. The rest of them were killed with the sword that came out of the mouth of the rider on the horse, and all the birds gorged themselves on their flesh."

What we see happening here is that these evil spirits gather all these people together to war against Jesus before he returns. These people that are preparing to war against Jesus are not Christians. Also, they are preparing to war against Him before He returns. How do they know Jesus is about to return? If they are being gathered together to war, it must mean they think they will have someone to fight- yet Jesus hasn't returned yet. And do these people know it is Jesus they are preparing to war against? No matter what they think of Jesus, they are not Christians, and their view of Jesus must be negative.

Let's review some facts about evil spirits, or demons. Demons don't have bodies, and they cannot materialize or apparate physically. Bodies and apparitions are things that indicate fallen angels. Yet here demons are said to look like frogs. People can't see demons, so how could a demon look like a frog? In order for a demon to be seen, it would have to be in the body of some person or animal. In this case, the animal that they are described to look like is a frog.

So let's say these 3 demons were inside and controlling 3 frogs. How likely do you think it is that people would follow 3 frogs to gather for war? Would an army of humans let themselves be led by 3 frogs? There is nothing to indicate that these frogs could talk, but perhaps these frogs would be able to convince people they could communicate telepathically, and that they could do (deceptive) signs and wonders, through other non-bodied demons and fallen angels working with them under the dragon. That could make sense- except that people just don't seem likely to let themselves be led by 3 frogs, no matter the circumstances. It sounds as convincing as a fairy tale.

But note that John doesn't say the three evil spirits "are 3 frogs", he says they "looked like frogs". So assuming they are not frogs, what else might these demons be inside of that looks like a frog?

Let's say that John was shown in his Revelation vision an image of something he had never seen before. Let's say he saw a body that was of no known animal that he was familiar with, and obviously to him was not a man either. It makes sense that if John didn't know what this creature was, and had never seen anything like it, that he would describe it as "looking like" something he was familiar with. John chose a frog.

But just because John had never seen the image of this creature before doesn't mean we never have. Closer to Jesus' return in linear time than John, and closer to the Tribulation, it stands to reason that we may have become familiar with this image, even though John was not.

Is there any creature today that is a familiar image to us, that John would have never seen before? Some creature that if we had to describe as looking like an animal, we would choose to say it looks like a frog? Is there perhaps something we call by another name, because we have been taught to for whatever reason, but if we had never seen or heard of it before, and we had to describe it, we would say it looks like a frog?

Although I was not the first to come up with this idea, and I'm not sure who was, I did think of this on my own a few years ago while studying the book of Revelation. I propose that the culturally common image of a "gray alien" looks much like a frog. There are many similarities that I would like to point out to you.

1. Frogs and grays both have large eyes, and similar facial features.

One webpage says of gray aliens, "They are normally between 3 1/2 to 4 feet tall with large heads and black "wrap around" eyes. They have limited facial features, slit mouth and no nose to speak of." [6] Frogs also have what I would describe as large heads with black "wrap around" eyes. Frogs also have a slit mouth, and no nose to speak of, just a couple of holes. Another report of "gray aliens" describes them as thus, " Their face is dominated by large black eyes, without pupils. They have two nostrils, slit-like mouths and small ears lacking earlobes." [7] A frog has a slit like mouth, and two nostrils, and their ears also lack lobes.

2. Frogs and gray aliens have similar hand and finger structure. Of gray aliens, "Reports of the fingers vary from 3 to 4, long, webbed". [8] The sketch below is of an alien hand. [9] From Wikipedia on Gray aliens, "Hand is generally described with four fingers and no thumb with slight webbing between fingers. Two fingers appear longer than the others. Sometimes fingernails are reported."
This sketch of an alien hand is compared to a picture of a frog's webbed feet, and a diagram of human verses frog skeletal hand structure. Both the hands and feet of most frogs are webbed.

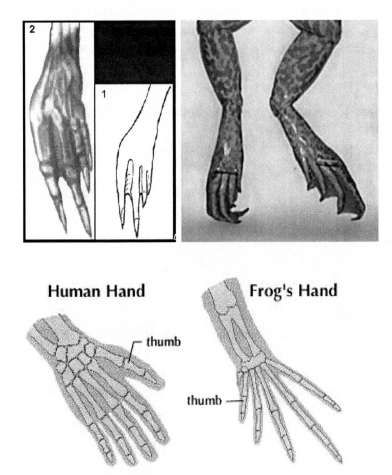

In "Space Travelers and the Genesis of the Human Form", by Joan D'Arc, we find the following, "The arms of the alien gray are frail and spindly, and there is a "bend" where the elbow should be. The fingers are long and thin, and generally with rounded pads or bulbs at the end, while some are reported as being tapered at the end. There are usually 4 fingers and a thumb, but sometimes 3 fingers and a thumb are noted." Frogs also are known for having rounded pads or bulbs on their fingertips. Frog fingers are typically long and thin, and webbed. Below a frog is compared to a close-up of the fingers of a Hollywood depiction of a "gray alien" from "Close Encounters of the Third Kind". Notice the long fingers.

3. Both ray aliens and frogs have no distinguishable external genitalia. With both gray aliens and frogs, it is very difficult to distinguish what gender they are, because there is no external genitalia. Wikipedia says of Grays, "Other reports have them appearing to be naked. In most cases, clothed Greys have no determinable gender and naked Greys have no visible external genitals." Frogs also have no visible external genitalia. Of gray aliens, "No external reproductive genital, possible reproduction by a cloning method." [10]

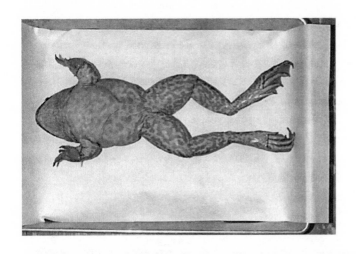

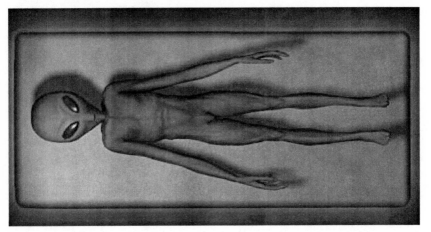

4. Frogs and gray aliens both have no hair. "Frogs have no hair." [11] Wikipedia says of gray aliens, "Head generally described as hairless, sometimes a slight fuzz. Bodies are hairless."

And so there are 4 reasons why I think John might have likened the creature he saw in the vision of Revelation, if it was a gray alien, as looking like a frog. Additionally, I do want to add a couple equally strange similarities:

5. Both frogs and gray aliens absorb through their skin. From Wikipedia, "Greys reportedly absorb food as well as excrete waste through the skin, which makes them emit a foul odor." Of frogs, Wikipedia says, "The physiology of frogs is generally like that of other amphibians (and differs

from other terrestrial vertebrates) because oxygen can pass through their highly permeable skin. This unique feature allows frogs to "breathe" largely through their skin."

6. Both frogs and gray aliens reproduce through external reproductive means. Grays are said to reproduce their own kind by cloning, which is an external non-mammalian reproductive method which would take place in a lab, and growth would occur in an artificial womb environment. Frogs also reproduce externally, the male and female components issuing out of the body and fertilizing, then growing in an external environment like a pond.

I personally do believe that what John saw, which he described as "3 evil spirits that looked like frogs", was 3 demons in the bodies of 3 gray aliens. Though it is nothing conclusive, it is also interesting that in an English alphabet Gematria code (A=6, B=12, C=18, etc.) that "Gray aliens" and "Alien Grays" both equal "666".

We will cover more on gray aliens in the next chapter.

References:
[1]http://www.midnightcry.net/PDF/Seven%20Letters%20to%20Seven%20 Churches.pdf
[2] These calculations were drawn from Dr. Sam Storms page http://www.enjoyinggodministries.com/article/42-june-6-2006-some-observations-on-the-number-of-the-beast-666 . Also from http://www.666myth.com/666_Ancients.html , by Titus Nguiagain, PhD.
[3] (Ekklesia, no. 14 (Jan. 10, 1990), pg. 511a)
http://uncutmountain.com/uncut/docs/Memorandum_on_the_WCC_Athen s_Conference.pdf
[4] Much info found here http://www.rense.com/general20/unholy.htm and some confirmed here
http://www.rickross.com/reference/unif/Unif12.html
[5] A list can be found here: http://www.oikoumene.org/en/member-churches/global-bodies-and-mission-communions/wcc.html

[6] http://www.burlingtonnews.net/greys.html

[7] http://www.hyper.net/ufo/occupants.html

[8] http://www.crowdedskies.com/grey_alien.htm

[9] From "Drawing based on alleged alien hand as supplied by Leonard Stringfield (1) and Interpreted by Artist Al Reed (2,3). From Stringfield's UFO Crash/Retrievals: Amassing the Evidence, Status Report III".

[10] The alien picture and quote are from http://www.crowdedskies.com/grey_alien.htm

[11]http://www.worldbook.com/wb/worldbook/cybercamp/html/walkfr og.html

Chapter Thirteen

Timeline of Demons and Fallen Angels - Present to Future
Prophecy and Revelation (Part 2)

In the last chapter, I presented reasons why I think and believe that the "3 evil spirits that looked like frogs" from Revelation 16, are 3 gray aliens. If it is the case that what John saw in Revelation was 3 demons in the bodies of 3 gray aliens, what does it mean prophetically? And how would this work?

Among all the visible paranormal activities that are going on today, including ghosts, fairies, Bigfoot, orbs, and many others, it is the Alien phenomenon which stands out as unique. Out of all the activities of demons and fallen angels today, it is the alien phenomenon that is mentioned in the book of Revelation, showing great Biblical prophetic significance.

The events in the book of Revelation will truly come to pass, and as such it is important for Christians in the future to remain alert and try to be aware of what is going on in the world around them, as the prophecy is taking place. Christians today also need to be aware of what is going on around them and taking place in the world, as the events of today are preparatory for the events of tomorrow.

I would bet that you the reader has seen the image of a "gray alien" before. This image is common in today's culture. "Gray aliens" are featured in movies, television shows, books, and on advertisements in print. Worldwide, there are self-accounts of people being "abducted" by these creatures. The phenomenon is closely tied to people claiming to have seen UFOs, Unidentified Flying Objects, which are said to be hard to identify because they look or move in a way which seems impossible by known modern human technology. In short, people who are educated as to modern technology don't know of any aircraft that humans have which can do the things these UFOs do.

These "gray aliens" are commonly associated with these UFOs, because they sometimes have been seen by people with or on these UFOs, in flight or sometimes on the ground. People who have had an "abduction" experience, called "abductees", often claim that they have been taken aboard a UFO, or have woken up inside what appeared to be a spaceship as they could see stars or planets through a window in the ship. Likely you the reader have heard of or seen something in a movie or on TV, or in a book, which portrays something like this happening, as many entertainment pieces have now been based off of the accounts of these "abductees".

In this paranormal or supernatural phenomenon, indeed the accounts of abductees is all the data we have to draw from in determining what has been taking place. Here is a summary drawn from books and videos I've studied on the subject:

Many abductees reported being forcibly sexually molested during these abductions, and forced to undergo painful procedures that seem somewhat medical in nature. There are accounts of children, even of preschool age, being abducted, and attacked in these ways. Abductees often report feeling paralyzed during these experiences. Many abductees report that their sperm or ova have been painfully removed from their body. Some abductees even report being pregnant, and the child being removed from their uterus. Some abductees report seeing strange hybrid babies and children, which look like a cross between a human and a gray alien. The "gray aliens" tell the abductees that these are their own children. Abductees sometimes have scars, cuts or bruises after the abductions are over.

Some things about "gray aliens" are even more alarming, in a spiritual sense. One is that many abductees report that the "gray aliens" tell them they are special and have been chosen for a mission of some sort. Often these missions either involve playing a special role during a coming time of crises, or in spreading the news to other people that the "gray aliens" are here to help. "Gray aliens" tell the abductees that they are here to help mankind, they claim knowledge of cataclysmic events to come in the future from which we will need their help. "Gray aliens" claim they are from another solar system or another planet, usually one or another in the Orion Nebula [1], and some reports that say they are from another dimension or time have also been made. The most incredible thing is that the "gray aliens" also claim to have taken part in the evolution of mankind, and also claim they created mankind. Some say they altered the DNA of primates to produce humans, others say they planted life here on Earth and prior which there was no life on Earth. In both cases the "gray aliens" talk of the theory of evolution as if it were a fact. (This idea of life on Earth having evolved from life planted here from somewhere else is known as "panspermia" or "exogenesis".) The "gray aliens" say they have been here repeatedly throughout mankind's past, citing polytheistic mythologies, and OT visions of prophets of the Lord God, as recording some of their earlier activities. Some "gray aliens" have even claimed that Jesus Himself was a "hybrid alien" fathered by them. [2]

The gray aliens also say they are more spiritually advanced than us, and claim they can help us in spiritual growth. Most of the time this growth involves psychic powers, telepathy, telekinesis, and ways in which to see the future. The "gray aliens" describe themselves as spiritually more advanced, having paranormal or supernatural powers, and oftentimes the result is that their abduction victims come to view them in a way as being like "gods", whom they look to for guidance, and take a worshipful attitude towards. The "gray aliens" have so convinced some of the abduction victims of their story that they are here to help, that the abductees willingly choose to take on a role of service to the "gray aliens", despite the sometimes painful abductions and violations that they have suffered at the hands of the "gray aliens".

Many people have made a study of UFOs and aliens in a serious and even academic manner. In summary, they seem to generally conclude that there is some tie between aliens, UFOs, and many world governments. As far as civilians have been able to research these things, the evidence they have points to many world governments as having some level of knowledge of aliens and UFOs. They say this is a knowledge that is kept "Top Secret", and tied to the military branches of government.

Regarding the US government, there is much speculation that in the USA the elected government officials, such as the members of Congress and the President, do not have a high enough security access to even be allowed to know the details of this "Top Secret" information. Of posed is the question of just how much influence the American people have over the running of their own government, if the people they elect to run things are not allowed this "Top Secret" information. Researchers speculate that if this is the case, it would seem that a "Shadow Government" organization of some sort, with authoritative power, is pulling many of the strings of the elected government which lacks that authoritative power. Other people suggest that some elected officials do have knowledge of this "Top Secret" information, but belong to secret cultish societies, of a satanic nature, and as such refuse to share this information they have on UFOs and aliens, due to allegiance to these secret societies and oaths of secrecy that they have taken. There is much speculation on why the US government in particular does not share its knowledge or involvement with UFOs and aliens.

However, what is not speculative in any way is that the US government and military do have knowledge of UFOs. There is real and indisputable evidence, gathered under the Freedom of Information Act, that the military does have awareness and knowledge about UFOs. Probably the most startling case I have read is that in the 1960s, UFOs hovered near a nuclear missile silo, and somehow turned off the facility and the nuclear missiles. (Individuals involved in the event, no longer in military service, have indeed gone on record and spoken publicly in conference settings about what they witnessed during this event. [3]) I think it is clear that with an event like that happening, the government and military have then and since taken the subject of UFOs and aliens seriously, yet the information they have has not been made public. There is really no other conclusion that makes any sense, in light of the reality of this event, which surely would have been taken as a serious potential threat. [4]

Because of the secrecy of this "Shadow Government," there is little hard evidence to go on, but from what evidence there is, the researchers in this field seem to conclude that the US government has either received teaching on technology from the "gray aliens", or have been given some technology by them in order to learn about it hand-on. One way or the other, some UFOs today are claimed to be "Top Secret" military aircraft, with abilities that suggest antigravity propulsion of some kind. There seems to be reason to think the military acquired this technology from "gray aliens" rather than that they developed it through purely normal scientific research and experimental methodology. Indeed, the earliest records of UFOs in modern times are from the 1890s. [5] This was long before anyone could have considered UFOs to have even possibly been man-made. It therefore makes sense that if some UFOs today are "Top Secret" man-made aircraft, that the technology might likely have been acquired from whoever had this technology in the 1890s; the "gray aliens".

So while some UFOs people have seen are thought to be driven by aliens, today others are thought to be man-made (with alien guidance) and driven by human pilots, and are of a "Top Secret" military nature. Though much of what I've read has been centered on a US "Shadow Government", the same activities could be taking place among other world governments or world "shadow governments".

If this is the case, then it would seem that there are people in some sort of government over the government, a "shadow government", which may have had some contact with the "gray aliens" themselves. It is unknown if the shadow government is working with them in a planned way. It would seem reasonable that the "shadow government", if in contact with the "gray aliens", would be told the same kinds of things that the "abductees" have been told. It is unknown if the shadow government believes the claims of the "gray aliens", that they are from another planet, that they are spiritually advanced, that they are here to help us. All we really know, is that compared to the hard evidence that the US government knew some UFOs disarmed their nuclear missiles, the response of the government has been to deny the reality of UFOs to the public. This makes no sense, and clearly indicates the government and military has a secret, a secret response to UFOs- which they will not share with the public. And there is some evidence to think that this secret is not just of a response to a potential threat, but by now is also a secret involvement with the "gray aliens". There is reason to think, with all seriousness, that the US has a shadow government, which not only has knowledge of the reality of UFOs and aliens, but also is involved with them in a cooperative sense. The same might be concluded of other world governments. (I apologize for my USA-centricism, but I do live there and much of the research I've studied has been USA-centric.)

In light of this information on the current world situation, let's look again at the key verses in the book of Revelation.

Rev 16:12-16 "The sixth angel poured out his bowl on the great river Euphrates, and its water was dried up to prepare the way for the kings from the East. Then I saw three evil spirits that looked like frogs; they came out of the mouth of the dragon, out of the mouth of the beast and out of the mouth of the false prophet. They are spirits of demons performing miraculous signs, and they go out to the kings of the whole world, to gather them for the battle on the great day of God Almighty."

(Jesus says) "Behold, I come like a thief! Blessed is he who stays awake and keeps his clothes with him, so that he may not go naked and be shamefully exposed.

Then they gathered the kings together to the place that in Hebrew is called Armageddon."

These scriptures may indicate that 3 gray aliens will someday gather the kings of the entire world together before Jesus returns, for the great battle of Armageddon. Not only that, but these gray aliens will gather the kings for the battle before Jesus has returned, in preparation for His return.

How could present information on UFOs and "gray aliens" be extrapolated from in order for this foretold event to take place? We are at point A, which I have described above. We know what point B is, as it is described in Revelation. So how would things have to go in the unfolding of events, in order for the world to move from point A to point B?

As you are likely aware, today the theory of evolution is taught in schools as a fact. Though I do not believe in the validity of this theory whatsoever, some people do, even Christians do who believe in "guided evolution". Whether you don't believe in evolution, or you believe in guided evolution, I think any Christian could arrive at the same conclusion on this matter involving "gray aliens". We were created by the Lord God, and even if that creation did theoretically involve guided evolution, it was a process guided by the Lord God. We were not created by "gray aliens", nor was our "evolution guided" by gray aliens. The Lord God alone is our creator, even in the theoretical context of guided evolution.

Today evolution is taught as fact. The idea that life that evolved on Earth came from life that evolved somewhere else, called panspermia or exogenesis, is becoming a more popular concept in recent years. As much as believing in evolution is a matter of faith... or as much as believing in guided evolution verses random-chance evolution is a matter of faith for some people, panspermia is also a matter of faith. What if someday people were told by reliable sources, such as the government or mainstream media, that "gray aliens" were real and from another planet in another solar system? What if someday people were told by reliable sources that the "gray aliens" had said they guided the evolution of mankind, or were the ones who originally brought life to the Earth from another place? If this were the case, many people would believe it. Many people would take on faith that "gray aliens" were the closest thing we had to "creators" within the concept of the theory of evolution. Instead of even the idea that the Lord God guided the evolution of man, the statement of the "gray aliens" would challenge that they were the ones who guided our evolution. This is what these "gray aliens" are already telling abductees in present times, and some abductees view them as "gods". What if the "gray aliens" revealed their presence to the entire world, and told the entire world they put life on earth, and guided its evolution? Much of the world would believe them, and come to view them as the "creators", the "gods", of humanity. And this is one reason why people might follow them to war at the battle of Armageddon. These events I've described would be one way to get from the present point A to the future Revelation point B.

If people believed the lies of these "gray aliens", they would follow them to battle, especially if they believed the grays were our friends or protectors. The "gray aliens" might tell people that a warring alien race was coming to invade or destroy the Earth, and that they would be here soon, so all the people must prepare for battle. They might even name Jesus, and say He is another alien that they don't get along with, coming to destroy the earth or try to take over, so everyone needs to defend themselves and the planet Earth from Him. Whatever the "gray aliens" would tell people, they convince them to gather for battle before Jesus has returned, so they have prepared the people for war by telling the people that something is arriving that they, the whole earth, must fight against for some reason. Somehow, to these lost people, the "gray aliens" will have them convinced that they are gathering to fight a bad guy who is coming, rather than telling them the Savior of the world, Jesus Christ, is returning. It is possible, as we know that Satan quotes the Bible, that the book of Revelation itself might be twisted. The book of Revelation might be twisted in such a way that the "gray aliens" teach it is a tale of the future- but of an evil alien overlord's plans to conquer earth in the future. Who knows what evil things they might say about the Lord Jesus, and how they might twist things. People, especially those without the Truth, will read into things what they want to see, and what their prejudices cause them to expect to see, it happens all the time. Without the light of Truth, who is the Lord Jesus Christ, people cannot see, and walk in darkness. Even if they see events unfolding before their eyes, foretold thousands of years ago, by The Son of God Jesus the Christ, the Savior of the World, they still may not see them clearly. The Lord God help them, that they may repent, and call on the name of Jesus, and be saved.

Back to the 3 evil spirits that look like frogs, the "gray aliens" of modern times. There is something else that will have to take place between the present and the time of Revelation. There is something else which would have to change.

As I have described in earlier chapters on physics, it is entirely possible that alien abductions today could be perpetrated by fallen angels. They are capable of causing people visions, of causing apparitions, that would entirely explain alien abductions. They also could appear as "gray aliens" to speak to people within the government, and then leave. A fallen angel can so manipulate people that one fallen angel could apparate as several "aliens", and as several UFOs, all at once. That is no doubt the current case. Current alien abductions and encounters are without a doubt caused by fallen angels, apparating as aliens. Whatever UFOs that people encounter that are not man-made, also are caused by fallen angel apparitions. And fallen angels could deceive those in the government, or the shadow government, just as well as they could an abductee, a civilian in isolation.

In fact, that fallen angels are responsible for modern "gray alien" and alien encounters has been proven from a Christian perspective.

Several Christian researchers have found that "alien abductions" will stop cold in the name of Jesus Christ. The most notable among these are Joe Jordan, a MUFON researcher and Christian counselor, who has worked with over 350 "abductees", and with permission, has made public online over 80 documented cases, of the name of Jesus stopping abductions. You can read and listen to these testimonies on his website, CE4Research.com. Pastor Chris Ward a deliverance/exorcism minister who found the same thing with those he was counseling for deliverance, and Guy Malone, a former abductee since childhood who shares his testimony that he has been set free from abductions happening in his life, by the name and power of Jesus Christ. (See Resources in Appendix for more information.)

An abductee will not only have that particular abduction stop cold in the name of Jesus Christ, but also abductees that trust in Jesus to help them and call on him, also have abductions terminated as a life pattern.

It makes total sense that these "alien" encounters are caused by fallen angels, that the "aliens" are fallen angels, when you understand that the aliens and the ship will just disappear before the abductee, and they will find themselves back where they started, when they call on Jesus for help. This is a spiritual warfare matter. This Christian research proves that these are fallen angels (and in some cases demons also), and this research proves these are not "aliens". Praise the Lord Jesus Christ that these abductions will stop in His name! (And I do, because I am one of those people who has experienced "alien" abduction attacks, and Jesus has set me free from the fallen angels doing that to me anymore. Praise Jesus!!!!)

And so as Christians, we know that today these experiences are being caused by fallen angels, with sometimes demons helping.

But what does the book of Revelation say will be the case in the future?

Rev 16:12-16 "The sixth angel poured out his bowl on the great river Euphrates, and its water was dried up to prepare the way for the kings from the East. Then I saw three evil spirits that looked like frogs; they came out of the mouth of the dragon, out of the mouth of the beast and out of the mouth of the false prophet. They are spirits of demons performing miraculous signs, and they go out to the kings of the whole world, to gather them for the battle on the great day of God Almighty."

(Jesus says) "Behold, I come like a thief! Blessed is he who stays awake and keeps his clothes with him, so that he may not go naked and be shamefully exposed."

"Then they gathered the kings together to the place that in Hebrew is called Armageddon."

What we read here is that these are spirits of DEMONS. "They are spirits of demons". Not fallen angels. Today physical aspects of abductions are being caused by fallen angels. Demons don't have the bodily power to apparate like fallen angels do. Fallen angels today are the ones appearing as "gray aliens". But in the future, we read that it is DEMONS that look like "gray aliens" who will gather the kings of the world for war. So once again, we are at point A, and in Revelation we see point B. How would things change so that we would get from point A (fallen angels apparating as "gray aliens") to point B (demons somehow appearing in the form of "gray aliens")?

Reviewing what we know about demons, demons are disembodied spirits of dead Nephilim. They don't have bodies, and can't apparate like fallen angels do. Therefore, if a demon was to appear in the form of a "gray alien", what would have to happen? The demon would have to be inside and controlling the body of something that looked like a "gray alien".

We know that in truth, there are no "gray aliens". The bodies of "gray aliens" that abductees see are actually just fallen angels. So what body could a demon get inside of that looks like a "gray alien", since no such body truly exists?

What things are there that have bodies that demons could get inside of? The only thing we know of that have bodies that demons can get inside of and control are humans, and animals. Neither humans nor any animals look exactly like a gray alien. I have a theory on the answer to this, which I will get to in a minute, but first I want to discuss a third possibility.

Some abductees claim they have seen "hybrid" children, as I mentioned earlier. And some people might be inclined to say, "a hybrid human/gray alien looks like a gray alien" and say that perhaps 3 hybrids are what is referenced to in the book of Revelation. So let's review some information on fallen angel and human interbreeding.

Fallen angels and human women have interbred before, and the result was the giant Nephilim, who were about 30 feet in height. They in turn mated with human women and produced slightly smaller giants. All of those whose paternal line traced back to fallen angels were spiritually demons, and when their giant bodies died, they became disembodied evil spirits, and are on the earth as demons to this day. The giants whose paternal line traced back to humans were spiritually human, and when they died their souls went to the grave, and they will be resurrected on judgment day like all other humans.

All of the fallen angels who sired the Nephilim were imprisoned by God in the Abyss until the time of judgment. And God flooded the entire world, and killed everyone and all animals, except for Noah, his family, and the animals on the ark. God destroyed the world by water because of this horrible perverse interbreeding of fallen angels and humans. Some fallen angel DNA survived through the human women on the ark, producing more human giants after the flood. When those giants gathered into tribes and began to multiply, God had the Israelites kill off those entire tribes. And this was because of the curse on them from being descendents of the Nephilim descendents, a curse which their imprisoned fallen angel ancestors had placed upon them. (All this is covered in detail in several earlier chapters of this book.)

There are several points I would like to make. The first is that the Nephilim were giants, and generally looked like giant men. I think it is safe to guess that the fallen angels did the best job they could to have normal offspring with human women. It seems unlikely that enormous cannibalistic giants was their goal. Yet that is what they got. Why couldn't they control this? Because God is the one who creates, and God is the one who forms each life in it's mother's womb. While some people argue that fallen angels could produce "gray alien" looking offspring with human women today if they wanted, based on the fact that God has control over this, it seems unlikely. What seems far more likely is that fallen angels would get the same result in modern times that some of them got is pre-flood times: human looking giants. I would like to point out that Gen 6:4 is important for showing that hybridization is not taking place in present times, rather than the opposite that some Christians suggest. This is because it is a matter of God-breathed scripture that fallen angel (including one appearing as an "alien") and human interbreeding, produces Nephilim, who look like giant men, and there are no Nephilim, or human-looking comparable giants in existence today (at least 30 ft. in height).

Also, God has said that each thing will reproduce after its kind. A fallen angel in pre-flood times surely would have had to try to match DNA of human-kind VERY closely in order to get any resulting offspring whatsoever. Otherwise it would be like trying to cross a dog and a cat- they are 2 different kinds, and you can't cross them to get a hybrid. In the same way, if a fallen angel apparated as a "gray alien" with DNA that would match its external appearance as much as possible- it would be an entirely different kind than mankind. As such, the result would be no offspring at all. It simply wouldn't work, no more than breeding a mouse and an elephant. Even humans and chimpanzees can't interbreed, and their DNA is at least 95% similar. Even when animals of the same kind are interbred, if they are too dissimilar in variation, the offspring that results is sterile.

Some people might argue that modern technology might make some difference, and make this feat possible. My response to that is that the power and abilities that God created angels as inherently having in their bodies are far superior to any technology we have today, and any technology we ever will have. There is nothing that science or tools or technology could give fallen angels that is beyond what they are inherently already able to do. See the earlier physics chapters for more details.

Another reason modern interbreeding seems unlikely, is that any fallen angel who attempted to breed with a human today would surely be thrown in the Abyss, just like the fallen angel fathers of the Nephilim. They would be taken out of the picture, and be chained in the prison of the Abyss. It is hard to prove this point, but it does seem to make sense to me. One could argue that during the tribulation, the world would be about to be destroyed by fire anyway, and as such a fallen angel would risk the punishment of the Abyss. Though this is arguable, I still doubt that God would allow such a thing to happen, as it is the Lord God who forms us all in the womb, and gives the breath of life. I do not think the Lord God would allow this to happen, or go along with this.

As for the hybrids that abductees are seeing, I think they can be explained by 2 powers fallen angels have. The first is the ability of fallen angels to cause illness in the body, and affect the body. This is demonstrated in the book of Job, and would explain why the women's bodies seem pregnant. They are not truly pregnant (at least not ever with a hybrid) but the fallen angels affect their bodies so that they feel pregnant and their body behaves as pregnant. Twice I have had my body tell me I was pregnant, when I was not. Once time I had a false pregnancy last 8 weeks, before a doctor found there was no baby and perhaps never had been, if there was, it had died within the first week and been reabsorbed and was not findable on an ultrasound, and shortly after I miscarried... nothing. Sometimes the body can think it is pregnant when it is not. False pregnancies can and do happen more often than people think. Besides as a result of natural flukes and illness, I think fallen angels can cause false pregnancies like this without a real living baby being involved. As for the hybrid babies and children that abductees see- they are apparitions caused by the fallen angels, and it is just another deception. See earlier chapter on powers of Fallen angels for more detail on these powers.

Ultimately though, my conclusions I base on the scriptures. And moving on to relevant Bible verses, some Christians say that when it comes to hybrids that these verses apply:

Mat 24:36-42 "But of that day and hour no one knows, not even the angels of heaven, nor the Son, but the Father alone. "For the coming of the Son of Man will be just like the days of Noah. "For as in those days which were before the flood they were eating and drinking, they were marrying and giving in marriage, until the day that Noah entered the ark, and they did not understand until the flood came and took them all away; so shall the coming of the Son of Man be. "Then there shall be two men in the field; one will be taken, and one will be left. "Two women will be grinding at the mill; one will be taken, and one will be left. "Therefore be on the alert, for you do not know which day your Lord is coming.

People argue that these verses apply because of the phrases "just like the days of Noah" and "they were marrying and giving in marriage". People say this indicates that just as in the pre-flood world, fallen angels and humans will be married and interbreeding when Jesus returns. And I do not doubt that Jesus was referencing to the perverse sin of fallen angels and humans marrying and interbreeding when He said "marrying and giving in marriage". I believe the people Jesus was speaking to at that time were more familiar with the details of Genesis 6 and certain portions of First Enoch than many Christians are today. A such it makes sense that Jesus would reference somewhat casually to these interbreeding events in this way.

However, the point of this passage seems to clearly be that people will be continuing in their sin right up until judgment, unaware that judgment is at hand- just like the people in Noah's time. I do not see here a prophetic significance that clearly indicates modern or future hybrids. The point of the passage is that Jesus' return will be like the flood- unexpected. And also that people will be carrying on in daily life, and in their sin, right up until judgment is upon them. The point of the passage is to be on alert for Jesus' return- and the point of the passage is not to indicate modern day hybrids.

Although I do want to point out a similarity between the end times when Jesus returns, and the days preceding the flood. In both cases, fallen angels were trying to effect the world in such a way so as that no one could be saved. Before the flood, the Nephilim and their paternal descendents were trying to outbreed humanity, so that eventually every person born would have a demon spirit, and would not have a human spirit which could be redeemed by Jesus and saved. In the end times, Satan will be taking a different approach. Anyone who is Christian will be killed or die for being Christian, and the world will ruled in such a way that likely no more people will come to Christ and be saved. In a world where (almost) all the Christians are dead, and everyone worships the beast, it would be a difficult time for any more lost people to come to be saved by Jesus. And so in both cases, the result is that no one else would be saved- and partially for this, judgment of the world comes soon after.

There is a verse in Bible prophecy which actually does seem to try to convey a message about this hybrid subject, and is fitting in that it seems to apply to the end times, and the last kingdom of men, the kingdom of the antichrist that exists, immediately before Jesus returns. I first saw this verse used in a way to make a surface attempt to prove there would be hybrids, by some that claim this verse is applicable. But after taking a look at the Hebrew and Greek, I came to the exact opposite conclusion: this verse clearly says there will be no hybrids.

So here are 3 different translations of this verse, two from the Hebrew, and one from the Greek Septuagint.

Let's take a close look at Daniel 2:43

"And whereas thou sawest iron mixed(6151) with miry clay, they shall mingle(6151) themselves with the seed of men: but they shall not cleave(1693) one to another, even as iron is not mixed(6151) with clay." Hebrew, KJV

"And in that you saw the iron mixed(6151) with common clay, they will combine(6151) with one another in the seed of men; but they will not adhere(1693) to one another, even as iron does not combine(6151) with pottery." Hebrew, NASB

"Whereas thou sawest the iron mixed(4874) with earthenware, they shall be mingled(4874) with the seed of men: but they shall not cleave(4347) together, as the iron does not mix itself with earthenware." Greek, Septuagint

The Hebrew (6151) "mingle, mix, combine" is only used here in the OT (except in Dan 2:41 as "iron mixed with clay" again), but (6151) is closely related to (6148) which means "to traffic as in barter, to give or be security as a kind of exchange" (Strong's). It also means "have fellowship with or share in". (BDB)

In the Greek, "mixed, mingled" are the same word (4874) in the Greek phrasing which is means to "associate with or have company with".

In the Hebrew: "cleave, adhere" (1693) is used only here, but is related to the more usual word (1692) which is very similar, and is used in Genesis as "cleave unto his wife".

In the Greek: cleave (4347) "pros-kollao", is used several times in the New Testament.

Eph 5:31 "For this cause shall a man leave his father and mother, and shall be joined(4347) unto his wife, and they two shall be one flesh."

Matt 19:5 "And said, For this cause shall a man leave father and mother, and shall cleave(4347) to his wife: and they twain shall be one flesh?"

Mark 10:7 "For this cause shall a man leave his father and mother, and cleave(4347) to his wife"

Because this "cleaving" of man and wife might seem ambiguous as to whether sex is implied, or some more purely spiritual joining, I want to point out that the root and usual form is join (2853) "kollao", which means "to glue, join, or fasten firmly together, to cleave". Here are some Greek usages for (2853) "kollao" in the NT:

1 Cor 6:15-16 "Know ye not that your bodies are the members of Christ? shall I then take the members of Christ, and make [them] the members of an harlot? God forbid. What? know ye not that he which is joined(2853) to an harlot is one body? for two, saith he, shall be one flesh."

So "cleaving"(4347 proskollao) is equal to "joining"(2853 kollao) which means to have sex. Cleaving means sex, which may not be limited to just intercourse.

So lets just clarify and re-examine this verse in the Hebrew and the Greek, based on these words more detailed meanings.

"And whereas thou sawest iron mixed(6151) with miry clay, they shall "traffic as in barter, give or be security as a kind of exchange, have fellowship with or share in"(6151) themselves with the seed of men: but they shall not "cleave or join sexually" (1693) one to another, even as iron is not mixed(6151) with clay." Hebrew, KJV

"Whereas thou sawest the iron mixed(4874) with earthenware, they shall "associate with or have company"(4874) with the seed of men: but they shall not "cleave or join sexually"(4347) together, as the iron does not mix itself with earthenware." Greek, Septuagint

Let's just assume Dan 2:43 really is talking about fallen angels in the first place, as other Christians have proposed in trying to prove the existence of hybrids. I think what Daniel really says here by "mingling" is that there will be traffic, association, fellowship, and company with fallen angels (the terms traffic, exchange, security, have the implication of mistreatment, and a violation of rights like people are objects to be trafficked in). The idea here is that the fallen angels traffic in the seed of men, but don't join sexually with the seed of men. But what is meant by the phrase "seed of men"? That phrase can mean "the children of men".

I've heard of many abduction accounts in which people have sex with aliens, besides all the accounts of sexual molestation. That being the case, how can Dan 2:43 mean that fallen angels will mingle themselves with humans, but not cleave sexually? As cleaving here means a sexual joining, then the scripture would contradict reality if the scripture was claiming that fallen angels won't have sex with people- because they do. There are many accounts of aliens, though not typically the grays, having sex with people. And there are also many accounts of "gray aliens" sexually molesting people. As fallen angels can apparate in many forms, all these accounts are attributable to them. As such sex is taking place, and the scripture would contradict reality if "seed of men" referred to humans in general.

But I don't think that is what the verse is saying. I think the verse is referring not to fallen angels mingling/trafficking with humans themselves, but rather, that the fallen angels are mingling/trafficking with the reproductive "seed" of men. Let's look at the verse again:

"And whereas thou sawest iron mixed with miry clay, they shall mingle themselves with the seed (2234) of men: but they shall not cleave one to another, even as iron is not mixed with clay." KJV

I think the word "seed" here is supposed to have an unusual meaning. As evidence for this, the word for "seed" (2234) above in Hebrew is only used here in the entire Old Testament. This is almost like God wanted the word to stick out because it required a closer look. This word is most closely related to the word "seed" (2233) which many times is used to refer simply to plant seeds, the actual reproductive genetic material of the plant. It is also used to refer to descendents. However, I think the plant seed definition fits closer to the prophetic meaning which God meant here. In this sense, I think that "seed of men" refers not to people, but to the genetic reproductive material of men and women, namely eggs and sperm.

As such, what Dan 2:43 is really saying is that fallen angels will traffic/mingle with the "seed of men" in a more "reproductive component" sense (eggs/sperm), but that the fallen angels themselves will NOT join sexually to the "seed of men".

As such Dan 2:43 means that fallen angels will "traffic as in barter" in human genetic material, but the fallen angels will not join to it. This interpretation makes the scripture not completely contradict reality, and prophetically shows there are no modern day hybrids, nor will there be.

So as ironic as it is, the main verse that some Christians have been using to show that there would be hybrids in the end times, I think actually would prove that there will be no hybrids, assuming this verse is even applicable. When actually studied in the Hebrew and Greek with more than a cursory glance, this verse contains a lot of information illustrating the present situation of abductions taking place. (Actually these verses could be applied in retrospect to gins, fairies, incubus/succubus accounts of earlier times as well.)

In any case, the interpretation of the verse needs to be applied consistently. Fallen angels have sex with people, the abduction accounts are firm and consistent, so this verse cannot be saying otherwise. The only other explanation is that Fallen angels are trafficking in as to barter, but not sexually joining with there productive material of humans. That interpretation fits both modern abductions accounts, and the Hebrew and Greek of Dan 2:43.

So the only option that matches reality, case accounts, etc, is that "seed of men" must be referring to genetic material (eggs/sperm) and that fallen angels mingle (traffic) in eggs/sperm, but don't cleave/join/glue/adhere to the eggs and sperm or simply put, there is no joining of the fallen angels with human eggs/sperm and therefore no interbreeding or hybridization. That's the only consistent reading of this verse that I see which doesn't contradict reality.

And so I hope that I have now covered why there are no hybrids, and won't be hybrids. Getting back to the earlier question, as there are no hybrids and won't be hybrids, the demons that look like "gray aliens" will not be hybrids:

This really only leaves 2 options. The first is humans, and the second is animals. Humans don't look like frogs, but some animals do (such as a frog). Revelation mentions demons, and looking like a frog, but doesn't say these are human bodies inhabited by demons. Theoretically, a human could put on a frog mask, or have plastic surgery, and look like a frog. But I don't think that is what Revelation is describing.

My personal theory on this is that these demons will take control of the bodies of animals. These animals will look like gray aliens. They will be genetically engineered animals that look like gray aliens. As God gave dominion over the animals to man, I believe that men will genetically engineer these animals that look like gray aliens. I do not believe that fallen angels have the dominion over animals to make these creatures on their own, but that rather they must deceive men into using modern technology to genetically engineer these animals. They would be sterile monsters, abominations, being incapable of reproduction. It could be that through surgery genetalia might be removed, or through diseases like encephalitis that their heads might become enlarged. I really don't know how a person would make a sterile animal that looks like a gray alien. Now do I know who would make these, or where. Perhaps a rich Satanist in a secret private lab somewhere. I really don't know.

However I would guess that the person or people making such an animal would be deceived into thinking they were not creating this animal, but rather that they were doing something else. I don't know what exactly, but it is horrendous to think of what people could be deceived into doing if they were under the guidance of fallen angels. Perhaps in a highly compartmentalized fashion, where each person only did a small piece of the puzzle, and so really had no idea what the overall goal was. And although I think that if this theory is true, that fallen angels already know how to accomplish this feat, I also believe that they must get humans to make this thing themselves, surely through deception. And so that is what would be going on somehow, to get from point A to point B.

And what would be the result? If there was a "gray alien animal" that was fully controlled by a demon, it could behave intelligently. But the most important thing about it is that if a Christian walked up to it and said "The Lord Rebuke You", the demon might leave, but the body would stay put. The demon might leave the animal, but the "gray alien animal" body would not disappear. This is a great and huge contrast to a fallen angel who is apparating in the form of a "gray alien", who would disappear when rebuked in spiritual warfare. A fallen angel would disappear, but the body of a demon-possessed animal would not disappear. It might fall to the ground, or act like a dumb animal would, but it's body would not disappear.

Another result would be that people would believe that "gray aliens" are real extra-terrestrials from another planet. As some people say, they won't believe in aliens until they see a cold dead body of one. Unlike with a fallen angel, a remaining dead body would be possible with a demon-controlled genetically engineered animal that looks like a gray alien. These the kings of the earth would potentially follow to the battle.

Moving on to another question, what are the locust things that come out of the Abyss? The best guess I have is that they are the fallen angel fathers of the Nephilim, who are only allowed to come out looking in a certain way, and only allowed to inflict certain harm on people. In such they are limited in how they can apparate, and God restricts their powers, and the resulting torment they cause is of their own destructive and evil inclinations. In the entire Bible, the fallen angels who sired the Nephilim are the only entities that are told to be in the Abyss (also called Tartaros).

Rev 9:1-11 "The fifth angel sounded his trumpet, and I saw a star that had fallen from the sky to the earth. The star was given the key to the shaft of the Abyss. When he opened the Abyss, smoke rose from it like the smoke from a gigantic furnace. The sun and sky were darkened by the smoke from the Abyss. And out of the smoke locusts came down upon the earth and were given power like that of scorpions of the earth. They were told not to harm the grass of the earth or any plant or tree, but only those people who did not have the seal of God on their foreheads. They were not given power to kill them, but only to torture them for five months. And the agony they suffered was like that of the sting of a scorpion when it strikes a man. During those days men will seek death, but will not find it; they will long to die, but death will elude them.

The locusts looked like horses prepared for battle. On their heads they wore something like crowns of gold, and their faces resembled human faces. Their hair was like women's hair, and their teeth were like lions' teeth. They had breastplates like breastplates of iron, and the sound of their wings was like the thundering of many horses and chariots rushing into battle. They had tails and stings like scorpions, and in their tails they had power to torment people for five months. They had as king over them the angel of the Abyss, whose name in Hebrew is Abaddon, and in Greek, Apollyon."

What we also see here is that a "star that had fallen... was given the key to the shaft of the Abyss", likely a fallen angel (though not Satan as he is "the dragon" not a "star" in Revelation's imagery) opens up the Abyss. This indicates to me that the Abyss will not be opened prior to this time, is not open today, and that humans will not open it, and humans do not have the power to open up the Abyss.

Related to this, I have read an article by Brian Huie which states that there is some reason to think that the "Beast out of the sea" is the king of the fallen angels currently imprisoned in the Abyss. I have also seen an article by Neville Stevens along these lines. [6]

If this is the case, that fallen angel called ABADDON or APOLLYON may easily fit himself into this "real extra-terrestrial" deception. Who is APOLLYON or ABADDON? I would tend to think he is a fallen angel, one of the fathers of the Nephilim, probably their leader. First Enoch calls the leader of the imprisoned fallen angels by the name "Semjaza". That is likely who the "beast out of the sea" truly is. Which is an entirely different matter from who he will claim to be. Fallen angels are known to be liars and deceivers. It is entirely possible that he will claim to be Apollo the Greek sun "god". Or he might claim to be Ceaser. All that we can truly know is what we read in the Bible, including,

Rev 17:8 "The beast, which you saw, once was, now is not, and will come up out of the Abyss and go to his destruction. The inhabitants of the earth whose names have not been written in the book of life from the creation of the world will be astonished when they see the beast, because he once was, now is not, and yet will come."

Whoever he claims to be, it will be astonishing to the non-Christian world. It may be a "god" of myth, or a dead world king or leader. Whoever it is was in existence before the Book of Revelation was written, and I would think likely is mentioned in the history books somewhere in some context.

Rev 17:8-11

"The beast, which you saw, once was, now is not, and will come up out of the Abyss and go to his destruction. The inhabitants of the earth whose names have not been written in the book of life from the creation of the world will be astonished when they see the beast, because he once was, now is not, and yet will come.

 This calls for a mind with wisdom. The seven heads are seven hills on which the woman sits. They are also seven kings. Five have fallen, one is, the other has not yet come; but when he does come, he must remain for a little while. The beast who once was, and now is not, is an eighth king. He belongs to the seven and is going to his destruction."

From this we can glean additional information on the identity of this fallen angel, the beast from the sea or Abyss. Because this fallen angel was, and is not at the time of the writing of Revelation, it would make sense that he is of the 5 kings that had fallen as of the time of the writing of Revelation. Some people say these kings can be determined from additional scripture in Daniel, and suggest that these 5 kings are the 5 kingdoms of Assyria, Babylon, Media, Persia, and Greece. [x] Other people suggest the 5 kingdoms were Egypt, Assyria, Babylon, Medio-Persia, and Greece. [y] Personally I would favor this latter interpretation. So for example, perhaps this fallen angel will say he is Nebuchadnezzar or Alexander the Great. When one includes Egypt, the possibility that this fallen angel could claim to be a deceased Egyptian pharaoh, come back to life, or claim to be an Egyptian "god" of legend. Some people claim there is an uncanny similarity between the legends of the Egyptian "god" Horus, and what the Bible teaches about Jesus. [z] There are many Egyptian "gods" or pharaohs that might be likely possibilities for who this fallen angel could claim to be, and would work in this context. Most Egyptian "gods" are considered to be based off of stories of men who were very early rulers of Egypt, and each pharaoh was considered to be a "god-man" or incarnation of one of the Egyptian "gods".

We also read in Rev 3:3-4,

"One of the heads of the beast seemed to have had a fatal wound, but the fatal wound had been healed. The whole world was astonished and followed the beast. Men worshiped the dragon because he had given authority to the beast, and they also worshiped the beast and asked, "Who is like the beast? Who can make war against him?"

This is the attitude that the world will soon come to have towards the beast, which Christians should understand and look out for.

As to another question, What is Mystery Babylon? My best answer on this is that the United States of America is Mystery Babylon today, and still will be in the end times. There is much to be learned about Babylonian symbology in American Architecture. For instance, the United States has the largest idol to Ishtar, the main Babylonian goddess, in the entire world. [7] Most people call it the statue of Liberty. The United states also has the largest Asherah Pole, a tribute to the same Babylonian goddess who was also called Ishtar. It is also associated with Baal. We call it the Washington Monument. [8] And each of these sits inside of one great city, the Bosh-Wash Megalopolis. Not only this, but the verses in Revelation on Mystery Babylon seem to most accurately fit the USA out of every nation on the planet. The wealth, the influence, the power of the United States seems best of any nation to fit the description of Mystery Babylon. [9]

Personally, I find the most conclusive evidence in the verse,

Rev 18:23 "and the light of a lamp will not shine in you any longer; and the voice of the bridegroom and bride will not be heard in you any longer; for your merchants were the great men of the earth, because all the nations were deceived by your sorcery."

The word here for "sorcery" is "pharmakeia" which means "medicine, drugs, spells, poisoning". This is closely related to the modern word for "pharmacy" and "pharmaceuticals". The United States is the largest inventor, manufacturer, and seller of medicine and drugs in the world. It is my personal belief that these are the sorceries referred to here in Revelation. In particular, I think psychiatric drugs are the worst of these sorceries.

Without a doubt the most horrible thing about these drugs is how Satan deceives people with them. People will be experiencing fallen angel apparitions, which get labeled as schizophrenic hallucinations, and they will take an antipsychotic, and the attacks will lessen or stop. Why? Not because the drug did something to help them, but rather because Satan called off the attack, in order to make it seem like the drug worked, so that the person will believe that the drug works, and that their problem isn't spiritual. The same thing happens with demons oppressing people into depression, and other problems, the person takes a drug and they feel better because Satan calls off the attack. And as a result the person is drugged, and cant think as clearly because they are on these drugs, and is blinded from the spiritual attack they are under. These man-designed drugs for the most part, when they seem to work, only seem to help aid people in belief in evolution, and in mankind's ability to heal itself. Spiritual warfare issues become ignored and labeled as medication-needing mental health conditions. The pharmaceutical/medical industry in the spread of these drugs is one of the most everyday horrible lies. It just promotes the false hope and belief that mankind will ever be able to heal all disease, or stop death, and be self-sufficient. We are not self-sufficient, nor will we ever be. We need a savior, we need the savior, we need Jesus the Christ.

References:

[1] http://anotherotherkin.tripod.com/UFO/aliens.htm#GREYS

[2] http://www.luciferianliberationfront.org/deceive.html

[3] http://www.nicap.org/babylon/missile_incidents.htm

[4] http://www.cufon.org/cufon/malmstrom/malm1.htm
http://www.ufoevidence.org/Cases/CaseSubarticle.asp?ID=1019

[5] http://cbs11tv.com/watercooler/ufo.ufo.sightings.2.649573.html

[6] at http://users.aristotle.net/~bhuie/abaddon.htm and
http://www.zionministry.com/bst_dan.html

[x]
http://www.lastdaysmystery.info/beast_which_has_the_seven_heads_and_ten_horns.htm

[y] http://thepre-wrathtribune.blogspot.com/2007/12/beast-empireseven-heads-part-5.html

[z] http://www.religioustolerance.org/chr_jcpa5.htm and
http://en.wikipedia.org/wiki/Horus

[7] http://www.freemasonrywatch.org/statue_of_liberty.html

[8] http://salvationrevelation.com/washington-monument-the-shaft-of-baal/

[9] http://yahushua.net/babylon/babylon.htm

Chapter Fourteen

Gifts of the Holy Spirit, Testing the Spirits, and Spiritual Warfare

Before we get to spiritual warfare, I thought it would be helpful to cover gifts of the Holy Spirit. Once you know that you are dealing with a demon or fallen angel then spiritual warfare methods would be applicable. However, I have found in my experiences and research that sometimes the hardest step is to identify that you in fact having an experience or encounter with a demon or fallen angel.

Hopefully the summary of modern day activities of demons and fallen angels in an earlier chapter would help you the reader to identify some things easily. But demons and fallen angels are liars, and very intelligent liars.

In an earlier chapter I covered the concept of an "antichrist", and we are told that the "spirit of the antichrist" now does exist. Not only that, but we are told that many people are deceivers and antichrists.

1 Jn 4:3 "And every spirit that confesseth not that Jesus Christ is come in the flesh is not of God: and this is that spirit of antichrist, whereof ye have heard that it should come; and even now already is it in the world."

2 Jn 1:7 "For many deceivers are entered into the world, who confess not that Jesus Christ is come in the flesh. This is a deceiver and an antichrist."

Now a person who is an antichrist is someone who has believed, trusted and followed a spirit of antichrist, and not Jesus the Christ, and who does not confess that "Jesus the Christ is come in the flesh". Just like there are many antichrists, there are also many spirits of antichrist. These deceptive spirits of antichrist are literally demons and fallen angels that work for Satan. So "spirit of antichrist" is another term for a demon or fallen angel.

Antichrists are also called "false prophets". "False prophets" practice false prophecy. "False prophecy" is of course in contrast to "prophecy", real and true and from God prophecy.

Before going into details about prophecy, one fact about prophecy is that it is a gift of the Holy Spirit.

There are many gifts of the Holy Spirit that are listed in the Bible, specifically in the New Testament. These are true gifts from the Holy Spirit, given to Christians. The important point I want to make right now is that just like a spirit of antichrist (demons and fallen angels) do counterfeit the gift of the Holy Spirit of "prophecy", with a gift of "false prophecy" (from themselves, demons and fallen angels)... Demons and fallen angels do also try to counterfeit many if not all of the other gifts of the Holy Spirit.

Fallen angels and demons (who are antichrist spirits) will and do counterfeit the gifts of the Holy Spirit. For every "true gift of the Holy Spirit", there is potentially also a "false gift of the antichrist" which is what occurs when demons and fallen angels try to counterfeit a gift of the Holy Spirit.

This is one reason why the Bible teaches emphatically,

1 Jn 4:1-3 "Beloved, do not believe every spirit, but test the spirits to see whether they are from God; because many false prophets have gone out into the world. By this you know the Spirit of God: every spirit that confesses that Jesus Christ has come in the flesh is from God; and every spirit that does not confess Jesus is not from God; and this is the spirit of the antichrist, of which you have heard that it is coming, and now it is already in the world."

As Christians, the responsibility that the Bible teaches is placed on us is for us to test the spirits. The Bible teaches us that a spirit of the antichrist will not confess that Jesus the Christ has come in the flesh, and that a spirit from God will confess that Jesus the Christ has come in the flesh. We also read,

1 Cor 12:1-3 "Now about spiritual gifts, brothers, I do not want you to be ignorant. You know that when you were pagans, somehow or other you were influenced and led astray to mute idols. Therefore I tell you that no one who is speaking by the Spirit of God says, "Jesus be cursed," and no one can say, "Jesus is Lord," except by the Holy Spirit."

And from this we are given an obvious clarification that a spirit that curses Jesus is not from God, and that no one can say, "Jesus is Lord" but by the Holy Spirit. A spirit that curses Jesus would seem an obvious and easy to recognize counterfeit, by which you would know that spirit has failed your test of that spirit. Knowing a spirit has passed the other test isn't as easy and obvious.

It is tantamount in importance, when you are dealing with a spirit, that you understand what "Jesus the Christ has come in the flesh" means. Otherwise you cannot discern, by questioning a spirit, if they are confessing Him as such or not.

You must know who Jesus the Christ is, and who He is not.

These may seem basic to you, but there are a lot of people out there that trust too willingly. As the children's song says, "Be careful little heart who you trust." You must be on your guard. Another Highly important thing to keep in mind is that Jesus is the "Word" of God. The Bible is also the "Word of God". Jesus said:

Matt 5:17 "Do not think that I came to abolish the Law or the Prophets; I did not come to abolish, but to fulfill."

What does this mean? It means that the Holy Spirit of Jesus, and any true spirit from God (like a Holy angel) is never going to teach, do or say, or try to get you to teach, do or say ANYTHING that is contrary to the Bible. People say, "The best defense is a good offense". Something that is absolutely invaluable in "testing the spirits" to tell if they are of God or of Satan, is to know what the Bible teaches. To know the entire Bible, you need to read the entire Bible. Once you have read something in the Bible, the Holy Spirit will help you retain and remember it.

Heb 10:14-17 "For by one offering He has perfected for all time those who are sanctified. And the Holy Spirit also bears witness to us; for after saying, "THIS IS THE COVENANT THAT I WILL MAKE WITH THEM AFTER THOSE DAYS, SAYS THE LORD: I WILL PUT MY LAWS UPON THEIR HEART, AND UPON THEIR MIND I WILL WRITE THEM," He then says, "AND THEIR SINS AND THEIR LAWLESS DEEDS I WILL REMEMBER NO MORE."

Jn 14:26 "But the Counselor, the Holy Spirit, whom the Father will send in my name, will teach you all things and will remind you of everything I have said to you."

The Holy Spirit will remind us of what is taught in the Bible, and teach us all things. God will put His laws on your heart and write His laws on your mind. It just makes it so much easier for us if we actually read the Bible. It is time well spent. You do not need to actually memorize the Bible to learn and be reminded by the Holy Spirit of what you have read, for Jesus told us the Holy Spirit will remind us of all that He has said. Reading the Bible, especially the whole Bible, is invaluable in "testing the spirits".

In other cases, in which the spirit cannot be questioned, but rather a dream, or a vision, is happening: If at all possible while this is ongoing, rebuke in the name and authority of the lord Jesus Christ. Say, "The Lord Jesus Christ rebuke you." Also, take a minute, and begin to pray in the name of Jesus Christ that God would remove any false vision or dream from you. If the vision or dream, etc. is from God, it will remain, but if it is not from God, then it will stop. And it is God who has said in His Word that we need to test the spirits, and I believe when we do this, God is pleased, and it is much safer for us to stay guarded against deceptions. God isn't going to mind if you take the time to do what He has already told you to do - to test the spirits!

Now that we've covered some basics about testing the spirits, I want to go into both the gifts of the Holy Spirit, and also cover some counterfeit false gifts from a spirit of the antichrist (demons and fallen angels).

What are the gifts of the Holy Spirit? Some key verses tell us what they are, and some about what they are like, and why they are given:

Rom 12:6-8 "We have different gifts, according to the grace given us. If a man's gift is prophesying, let him use it in proportion to his faith. If it is serving, let him serve; if it is teaching, let him teach; if it is encouraging, let him encourage; if it is contributing to the needs of others, let him give generously; if it is leadership, let him govern diligently; if it is showing mercy, let him do it cheerfully."

Eph 4:11-16 "And He gave some as apostles, and some as prophets, and some as evangelists, and some as pastors and teachers, for the equipping of the saints for the work of service, to the building up of the body of Christ; until we all attain to the unity of the faith, and of the knowledge of the Son of God, to a mature man, to the measure of the stature which belongs to the fullness of Christ. As a result, we are no longer to be children, tossed here and there by waves, and carried about by every wind of doctrine, by the trickery of men, by craftiness in deceitful scheming; but speaking the truth in love, we are to grow up in all aspects into Him, who is the head, even Christ, from whom the whole body, being fitted and held together by that which every joint supplies, according to the proper working of each individual part, causes the growth of the body for the building up of itself in love."

1 Cor 12:4-12 "There are different kinds of gifts, but the same Spirit. There are different kinds of service, but the same Lord. There are different kinds of working, but the same God works all of them in all men. Now to each one the manifestation of the Spirit is given for the common good. To one there is given through the Spirit the message of wisdom, to another the message of knowledge by means of the same Spirit, to another faith by the same Spirit, to another gifts of healing by that one Spirit, to another miraculous powers, to another prophecy, to another distinguishing between spirits, to another speaking in different kinds of tongues, and to still another the interpretation

of tongues. All these are the work of one and the same Spirit, and he gives them to each one, just as he determines. The body is a unit, though it is made up of many parts; and though all its parts are many, they form one body. So it is with Christ."

1 Cor 12:28-13:3 "And in the church God has appointed first of all apostles, second prophets, third teachers, then workers of miracles, also those having gifts of healing, those able to help others, those with gifts of administration, and those speaking in different kinds of tongues. Are all apostles? Are all prophets? Are all teachers? Do all work miracles? Do all have gifts of healing? Do all speak in tongues? Do all interpret? But eagerly desire the greater gifts. And now I will show you the most excellent way. If I speak in the tongues of men and of angels, but have not love, I am only a resounding gong or a clanging cymbal. If I have the gift of prophecy and can fathom all mysteries and all knowledge, and if I have a faith that can move mountains, but have not love, I am nothing. If I give all I possess to the poor and surrender my body to the flames, but have not love, I gain nothing."

1 Cor 14:1-6 "Follow the way of love and eagerly desire spiritual gifts, especially the gift of prophecy. For anyone who speaks in a tongue does not speak to men but to God. Indeed, no one understands him; he utters mysteries with his spirit. But everyone who prophesies speaks to men for their strengthening, encouragement and comfort. He who speaks in a tongue edifies himself, but he who prophesies edifies the church. I would like every one of you to speak in tongues, but I would rather have you prophesy. He who prophesies is greater than one who speaks in tongues, unless he interprets, so that the church may be edified. Now, brothers, if I come to you and speak in tongues, what good will I be to you, unless I bring you some revelation or knowledge or prophecy or word of instruction?"

1 Cor 14:12-33 "So it is with you. Since you are eager to have spiritual gifts, try to excel in gifts that build up the church. For this reason anyone who speaks in a tongue should pray that he may interpret what he says. For if I pray in a tongue, my spirit prays, but my mind is unfruitful. So what shall I do? I will pray with my spirit, but I will also pray with my mind; I will sing with my spirit, but I will also sing with my mind. If you are praising God with your spirit, how can one who finds himself among those who do not understand say "Amen" to your thanksgiving, since he does not know what you are saying? You may be giving thanks well enough, but the other man is not edified. I thank God that I speak in tongues more than all of you. But in the church I would rather speak five intelligible words to instruct others than

ten thousand words in a tongue. Brothers, stop thinking like children. In regard to evil be infants, but in your thinking be adults. In the Law it is written: "Through men of strange tongues and through the lips of foreigners I will speak to this people, but even then they will not listen to me," says the Lord. Tongues, then, are a sign, not for believers but for unbelievers; prophecy, however, is for believers, not for unbelievers. So if the whole church comes together and everyone speaks in tongues, and some who do not understand or some unbelievers come in, will they not say that you are out of your mind? But if an unbeliever or someone who does not understand comes in while everybody is prophesying, he will be convinced by all that he is a sinner and will be judged by all, and the secrets of his heart will be laid bare. So he will fall down and worship God, exclaiming, "God is really among you!" What then shall we say, brothers? When you come together, everyone has a hymn, or a word of instruction, a revelation, a tongue or an interpretation. All of these must be done for the strengthening of the church. If anyone speaks in a tongue, two--or at the most three--should speak, one at a time, and someone must interpret. If there is no interpreter, the speaker should keep quiet in the church and speak to himself and God. Two or three prophets should speak, and the others should weigh carefully what is said. And if a revelation comes to someone who is sitting down, the first speaker should stop. For you can all prophesy in turn so that everyone may be instructed and encouraged. The spirits of prophets are subject to the control of prophets. For God is not a God of disorder but of peace, as in all the congregations of the saints."

1 Cor 7:7-8 "Yet I wish that all men were even as I myself am. However, each man has his own gift from God, one in this manner, and another in that. But I say to the unmarried and to widows that it is good for them if they remain even as I." "Gift of celibacy"

Eph 3:6-8 "to be specific, that the Gentiles are fellow heirs and fellow members of the body, and fellow partakers of the promise in Christ Jesus through the gospel, of which I was made a minister, according to the gift of God's grace which was given to me according to the working of His power. To me, the very least of all saints, this grace was given, to preach to the Gentiles the unfathomable riches of Christ" (apostleship/evangelist)

So what are the gifts of the Holy Spirit? Here's a list, in Biblical order (or as close as I could figure it):: Apostleship, prophecy, teaching, pasturing, evangelism, miracles, healing, faith, distinguishing between spirits or discerning of spirits, message of wisdom, message of knowledge, serving, encouraging/exhortation, contributing to the needs of others or giving, showing mercy, leadership or governing, celibacy, interpretation of tongues, speaking in different kinds of tongues.

As I count them, there are 19 gifts of the Holy Spirit. Some people have more than one gift, but every Christian has at least one gift. The Holy Spirit chooses what gift to give a Christian, and the person themselves does not get to choose their gift. People can of course ask for a particular gift, but sometimes they will not be given that gift. The important thing to remember is that each gift is important and needed and special and is a gift and a blessing from God.

Gifts of the Holy Spirit are used to build up and help the church, both inside, and in its growth, and accomplishing the great commission of spreading the gospel of Jesus the Christ.

In distinguishing between true gifts of the Holy Spirit and false gifts of the spirit of antichrist (demons and fallen angels), there are some things to keep in mind. One thing is that a supernatural "gift" which is apart from the Christian church, and apart from Jesus Christ, and brings glory to some other person or being besides Jesus the Christ and God the Father, is a gift to be considered a false gift. A gift which leads one to get involved with magic, worshipping angels, the occult, cults, witchcraft, practices of divination, etc. is not a gift of the Holy Spirit.

In this I want to point out that the body is designed to function together as a whole- we really do need each other. We all need teachers, we all need discerners of spirits, and apostles, and givers, and speaker in tongues, and interpreters for those speakers, and truly we all do need each other.

For example, one gift is prophecy. There is a lot of varying opinion about what prophecy includes. Some things include visions and dreams, of the present, past, or future. Some people say the gift of prophecy in the New Testament is different than the gift in the Old Testament. Some people say that true prophecy does not today include messages of repentance or else there will be destruction (like with Jonah). Some people say prophecy today is only used to convict people of their sin by touching them with miraculous knowledge about themselves, or knowing just what to say to them to help them feel conviction that leads to repentance. In addition to the earlier verses pertaining to prophecy, we also read:

Act 2:17-18 " 'AND IT SHALL BE IN THE LAST DAYS,' God says, 'THAT I WILL POUR FORTH OF MY SPIRIT UPON ALL MANKIND; AND YOUR

SONS AND YOUR DAUGHTERS SHALL PROPHESY, AND YOUR YOUNG MEN SHALL SEE VISIONS, AND YOUR OLD MEN SHALL DREAM DREAMS; EVEN UPON MY BONDSLAVES, BOTH MEN AND WOMEN, I WILL IN THOSE DAYS POUR FORTH OF MY SPIRIT And they shall prophesy."

Num 12:6 "He said, "Hear now My words: If there is a prophet among you, I, the LORD, shall make Myself known to him in a vision. I shall speak with him in a dream."

Amos 3:7 "Surely the Sovereign LORD does nothing without revealing his plan to his servants the prophets."

The word "prophecy" as used in the Bible must be defined by what the Bible teaches about it. We cannot just make up our own definition of the word "prophecy" based on what we would like it to be.

Prophecy is of the past, present, or future. Prophecy does take the forms of dreams and visions. It is a matter of getting a message from God, and I personally will not limit how it looks when it happens. What I will say is that the content of the message, compared to the Bible, must be examined in testing the spirits to tell if a prophecy is from God or not, and in having this gift the confirmation of the Holy Spirit is also vitally important.

There are other Biblical standards for prophecy:

Deut 18:20-22 "But the prophet who shall speak a word presumptuously in My name which I have not commanded him to speak, or which he shall speak in the name of other gods, that prophet shall die.' "And you may say in your heart, 'How shall we know the word which the LORD has not spoken?' "When a prophet speaks in the name of the LORD, if the thing does not come about or come true, that is the thing which the LORD has not spoken. The prophet has spoken it presumptuously; you shall not be afraid of him."

Deut 13:1-5 "If a prophet or a dreamer of dreams arises among you and gives you a sign or a wonder, and the sign or the wonder comes true, concerning which he spoke to you, saying, 'Let us go after other gods (whom you have not known) and let us serve them,' you shall not listen to the words of that prophet or that dreamer of dreams; for the LORD your God is testing you to find out if you love the LORD your God with all your heart and with all your soul. "You shall follow the LORD your God and fear Him; and you shall keep His commandments, listen to His voice, serve Him, and cling to Him. "But that prophet or that dreamer of dreams shall be put to death, because he has counseled rebellion against the LORD your God who brought you from the land of Egypt and redeemed you from the house of slavery, to seduce you from the way in which the LORD your God commanded you to walk. So you shall purge the evil from among you."

1 Sam 3:19-20 "Thus Samuel grew and the LORD was with him and let none of his words fail. And all Israel from Dan even to Beersheba knew that Samuel was confirmed as a prophet of the LORD."

The message of future things from a true prophet, with the true gift of prophecy, will come to pass as the prophet foretold. The words of a true prophet with a true gift of prophecy will not fail. A true prophet of God with a true gift of prophecy will not encourage the worship or service of other gods, period. We learn that even a false prophet can potentially have a sign or wonder that comes true, but that prophet will be known to be false by the fact that he encourages the worship or service of other gods- not the Lord God or Jesus the Christ. Indeed, some people miss that the Bible teaches this, and only qualify that the message of the prophet will come true… but sometimes demons and fallen angels can give (albeit limited) information about the future and give false prophecy. Though many times the message of a false prophet about the future will only come to pass partially, or vaguely. Messages from God will come to pass as God said, in every detail that God gave, and if there is a repentance condition then that will be fulfilled consistently also, as God said in His message.

False prophecy will also sometimes take a tormenting form, in which a person is pushed to do things that violate the Ten Commandments, or other directions given in scripture, and this is a way to determine false prophecy- by it pushing a person to violate clear Biblical laws of what is sin. God is consistent, and He will not ask or push His people to sin.

So as the Bible teaches, with prophecy, 1 Cor 14:29 "And let two or three prophets speak, and let the others pass judgment."

The term here "pass judgment" in the Greek is "diakrino" (1252), to discern, separate, make a distinction, try, or decide. This is from the same root word as "diakrisis"(1253) which is used in 1 Cor 12:10 in the gift of "discerning of spirits". So we are actually told in the Bible that after someone prophesies, that others are to discern regarding the prophecy.

So we as Christians must test the spirits. The better we know the Bible, and what the Bible says about testing the spirits, the more we pray for discernment, and the closer we draw to the Lord Jesus, the better we will be at testing the spirits.

So if a person is having an interaction or attack from a demon or fallen angel, whether it assumes the form of a spirit of antichrist in particular, or not, there are spiritual warfare methods that will help. And the first step is identifying that you are dealing with a demon or fallen angel, in whatever manner or form they take.

"Spiritual Warfare" is called such because truly we are all in the middle of a spiritual war.

Rev 12: 12,17 "For this reason, rejoice, O heavens and you who dwell in them. Woe to the earth and the sea, because the devil has come down to you, having great wrath, knowing that he has only a short time." So the dragon was enraged with the woman, and went off to make war with the rest of her children, who keep the commandments of God and hold to the testimony of Jesus."

For the last 2000 years, a war has been actively waging on earth between Satan, and the fallen angels and demons under Satan, against Jesus and Christians. Christians are those who "keep the commandments of God, and hold to the testimony of Jesus". The apostles and early Christians understood this was the situation, and spoke numerous times of the situation, and gave instruction for spiritual warfare, and how to best deal with the situation as Christians.

The fallen angels are also known as "glorious ones" in this following passage from Peter (distinguished from Holy angels which are just called "angels"), wherein we see that many people did not (and still don't) understand the current situation:

2 Pet 2:10-12 "He is especially hard on those who follow their own evil, lustful desires and who despise authority. These people are proud and arrogant, daring even to scoff at the glorious ones without so much as trembling. But the angels, even though they are far greater in power and strength than these false teachers, never speak out disrespectfully against the glorious ones. These false teachers are like unthinking animals, creatures of instinct, who are born to be caught and killed. They laugh at the terrifying powers they know so little about, and they will be destroyed along with them."

The term "glorious ones" is meant in the sense of a "glow" or in modern terminology, "glory". This comes from the Greek "epaphrodito" or "upon aphrodite". Aphrodite is the Greek term for Venus, which is the "star of the morning", a term which is used of Satan in Isaiah 14. Thus "epaphrodito" means "Upon the star of the morning", as the fallen angels have counted themselves "in" with Satan, the "star of the morning".

That the "glorious ones" are fallen angels is confirmed in Jude:
Jude 1: 8-10 "Yet these false teachers, who claim authority from their dreams, live immoral lives, defy authority, and scoff at the power of the glorious ones. But even Michael, one of the mightiest of the angels, did not dare bring a blasphemous accusation against Satan, but simply said, "The Lord rebuke you." (This took place when Michael was arguing with Satan about Moses' body.) But these people blaspheme the things they do not understand. Like animals, they do whatever their instincts tell them, and they bring about their own destruction."

Here we see that the "glorious ones" are compared directly to Satan, a fallen angel, and the leader of the fallen angels.

We are cautioned, as Christians, to not be like those who will be destroyed. We are not to laugh at the "terrifying powers" that be, the "glorious ones", the fallen angels. We are not to speak out disrespectfully against them. The key word there is "disrespectfully". But everywhere there is darkness we are to expose it with light, which often requires the action of speaking out.

It is pointed out that we should not "scoff at the power of the glorious ones". We also should not "blaspheme the things we do not understand", which could be applied generally.

What is blasphemy? Here's some hopefully helpful definitions from the dictionary: "the crime of assuming to oneself the rights or qualities of God", "from Gk. blasphemia "profane, speech, slander," from blasphemein "to speak evil of." Second element is pheme "utterance"".

What is to blaspheme? Definitions: "utter obscenities or profanities", "speak of in an irreverent or impious manner". What is blasphemous? Definition: from Thayer's we get, "speaking evil, slanderous, reproachful, railing, abusive".
Probably the most helpful definition is "the crime of assuming to oneself the rights or qualities of God".

I would also like to point out something Paul said: Gal 1:8 "But even if we, or an angel from heaven, should preach to you a gospel contrary to what we have preached to you, let him be accursed!"

One thing that I notice is that Michael thought it was the Lord's place to rebuke Satan, not his place. Paul said, "let him be accursed" but did not say, "I curse him". Michael, a powerful archangel said "The Lord rebuke you." Not "I rebuke you." That is an example to us. We are able to cast out demons in Jesus' name, as the Gospels describe. This is similar, and I think the point here is to, in realism and humility, realize we are powerless apart from Jesus and God's protection of us, and on our own weaker than these fallen angels present on the Earth, and we should be apprehensive of those facts, and act and speak accordingly.

Our power comes from Jesus the Christ, and from God the Father, and not from ourselves. We see above when dealing with fallen angels (Satan in this example) that even the Holy archangel Michael (a powerful angel) did not say, "I rebuke you" but rather said "The Lord rebuke you." Michael realistically understood that the Lord God is the one with the power, and the Lord, Jesus the Christ is also referenced here, and Michael called on the Lord, requested and asked that the Lord rebuke the fallen angel. Michael understood it was not his place or "right" to rebuke Satan, but rather that it was God's place and "right" to rebuke Satan. Looking at the definition of blaspheme above, this makes a lot of sense. It is something Christians may slightly do in their choice of wording, in ignorance, but it is blasphemous as a Christian to assume you have the right and place to rebuke fallen angels yourself apart from being under the given authority of Lord Jesus the Christ and the Lord God the Father.

We are to follow this example, whether it comes to demons or fallen angels. As this passage illustrates, there is a wrong way to do this:

Acts 19:11-16 "God was performing extraordinary miracles by the hands of Paul, so that handkerchiefs or aprons were even carried from his body to the sick, and the diseases left them and the evil spirits went out. But also some of the Jewish exorcists, who went from place to place, attempted to name over those who had the evil spirits the name of the Lord Jesus, saying, "I adjure you by Jesus whom Paul preaches." Seven sons of one Sceva, a Jewish chief priest, were doing this. And the evil spirit answered and said to them, "I recognize Jesus, and I know about Paul, but who are you?" And the man, in whom was the evil spirit, leaped on them and subdued all of them and overpowered them, so that they fled out of that house naked and wounded."

We are not to have a spirit of fear, but at the same time we need to be apprehensive of who really has power over fallen angels and demons: it is not us, but the Lord Jesus Christ, and us only through Him. Jesus has given us authority as his disciples, but we need to use it correctly, as given authority, in His name.

Luke 10:17-20 "And the seventy returned with joy, saying, "Lord, even the demons are subject to us in Your name." And He said to them, "I was watching Satan fall from heaven like lightning. "Behold, I have given you authority to tread upon serpents and scorpions, and over all the power of the enemy, and nothing shall injure you. "Nevertheless do not rejoice in this, that the spirits are subject to you, but rejoice that your names are recorded in heaven."

As such, when it comes to dealing with the enemy spirits of Satan in this spiritual war that is waging all around us, I think it best to follow Jesus' example and instructions.

But we need to keep in mind that when Jesus rebuked demons and Satan, that Jesus was the Son of God. All of our power over the enemy comes through Jesus. While Jesus said, "Come out of that person", we are doing so under the authority Jesus has given us, and under His authority, and under the name of Jesus.

Now I am not a deliverance minister, though I have practiced what is called "self-deliverance" in Jesus' name and under His authority. Praise the Lord Jesus! But I am not an expert on deliverance ministry. Please see the Resources section for more information from Christians who do practice deliverance ministry and are much more experienced than I am. Yet I do know that they teach as I state above, and this I found worked for me, that we only have authority over the enemy when we are under the Lord Jesus, under His blood, and under His name, and what part we can do we do successfully only under the authority and in the name of the Lord Jesus Christ.

There are many examples of Jesus casting out demons throughout the gospels. Jesus also told his followers to cast out demons. The point I am making is also shown in Mark 9:16-29:

"And He asked them, "What are you discussing with them?" And one of the crowd answered Him, "Teacher, I brought You my son, possessed with a spirit which makes him mute; and whenever it seizes him, it dashes him to the ground and he foams at the mouth, and grinds his teeth, and stiffens out. And I told Your disciples to cast it out, and they could not do it." And He answered^ them and said^, "O unbelieving generation, how long shall I be with you? How long shall I put up with you? Bring him to Me!" And they brought the boy to Him. And when he saw Him, immediately the spirit threw him into a convulsion, and falling to the ground, he began rolling about and foaming at the mouth. And He asked his father, "How long has this been happening to him?" And he said, "From childhood. "And it has often thrown him both into the fire and into the water to destroy him. But if You can do anything, take pity on us and help us!" And Jesus said to him, "'If You can!' All things are possible to him who believes." Immediately the boy's father cried out and began saying, "I do believe; help my unbelief." And when Jesus saw that a crowd was rapidly gathering, He rebuked the unclean spirit, saying to it, "You deaf and dumb spirit, I command you, come out of him and do not enter him again." And after crying out and throwing him into terrible convulsions, it came out; and the boy became so much like a corpse that most of them said, "He is dead!" But Jesus took him by the hand and raised him; and he got up. And when He had come into the house, His disciples began questioning Him privately, "Why could we not cast it out?" And He said to them, "This kind cannot come out by anything but prayer."

What this shows us is that some evil spirits can only come out with prayer. (This is also something to keep in mind as applicable for some "self-deliverance situations".) In other words, we must ask the Lord God and the Lord Jesus to make the evil spirit come out, and not enter in again. By saying "The Lord Jesus Christ rebuke you" a person can pray to the Lord Jesus as they say it, pray out loud, and be asking Jesus to make the evil spirit come out and stay out, as they address the evil spirit in Jesus' name. Though some deliverances require much prayer beforehand and during the deliverance than that. Calling out to Jesus, "Jesus!" also is prayer to Jesus.

We read how the apostle Paul would cast out a demon; the correct way to do this is seen in Paul's choice of words: Acts 16:18 "And she continued doing this for many days. But Paul was greatly annoyed, and turned and said to the spirit, "I command you in the name of Jesus Christ to come out of her!" And it came out at that very moment."

Where Jesus said, "I command you to come out", we must recognize we are under Jesus' authority and say "I command you in the name of Jesus Christ to come out." Where Jesus could say, "I rebuke you", we would say "The Lord Jesus rebuke you."

Speaking of addressing demons, I find it important to note that Jesus himself did not have much dialog with demons that he was casting out of people.

Jesus asked demons their name: Mark 5:9 "And He was asking him, "What is your name?" And he said to Him, "My name is Legion; for we are many."

Jesus told demons to be quiet: Mark 1:25 "And Jesus rebuked him, saying, "Be quiet, and come out of him!"

And most importantly Jesus told demons to come out. As seen above with Paul, the early church closely followed the example that Jesus set. Jesus said,

Mark 16:17-18 "And these signs will accompany those who have believed: in My name they will cast out demons, they will speak with new tongues; they will pick up serpents, and if they drink any deadly poison, it shall not hurt them; they will lay hands on the sick, and they will recover."

I think there is something noteworthy here, in that we are to cast out demons in Jesus name, but that does not mean we should have lengthy conversations with them or listen to them or take heed of things they say.

When it comes to fallen angels in specific, in addition to the methods above, we are told that Jesus resisted Satan with scripture, and told him to get away.

Matt 4:1-11 "Then Jesus was led up by the Spirit into the wilderness to be tempted by the devil. And after He had fasted forty days and forty nights, He then became hungry. And the tempter came and said to Him, "If You are the Son of God, command that these stones become bread." But He answered and said, "It is written, 'MAN SHALL NOT LIVE ON BREAD ALONE, BUT ON EVERY WORD THAT PROCEEDS OUT OF THE MOUTH OF GOD.'" Then the devil took^ Him into the holy city; and he had Him stand on the pinnacle of the temple, and said^ to Him, "If You are the Son of God throw Yourself down; for it is written, 'HE WILL GIVE HIS ANGELS CHARGE CONCERNING YOU'; and 'ON their HANDS THEY WILL BEAR YOU UP, LEST YOU STRIKE YOUR FOOT AGAINST A STONE.'" Jesus said to him, "On the other hand, it is written, 'YOU SHALL NOT PUT THE LORD YOUR GOD TO THE TEST.'" Again, the devil took^ Him to a very high mountain, and showed^ Him all the kingdoms of the world, and their glory; and he said to Him, "All these things will I give You, if You fall down and worship me." Then Jesus said^ to him, "Be gone, Satan! For it is written, 'YOU SHALL WORSHIP THE LORD YOUR GOD, AND SERVE HIM ONLY.'" Then the devil left^ Him; and behold, angels came and began to minister to Him."

We are told in James 4:7 "Submit therefore to God. Resist the devil and he will flee from you." This applies not only to "the" devil, Satan, but also to the other fallen angels. In Luke 10 Jesus said he has given to his disciples "authority… over all the power of the enemy", and this includes demons and fallen angels.

Indeed, we are in a spiritual war, and these are the basic things Christians need to know about spiritual warfare. We in this battle we are told to put on the full armor of God.

Eph 6:10-20 "Finally, be strong in the Lord, and in the strength of His might. Put on the full armor of God, that you may be able to stand firm against the schemes of the devil. For our struggle is not against flesh and blood, but against the rulers, against the powers, against the world forces of this darkness, against the spiritual forces of wickedness in the heavenly places. Therefore, take up the full armor of God, that you may be able to resist in the evil day, and having done everything, to stand firm. Stand firm therefore, HAVING GIRDED YOUR LOINS WITH TRUTH, and HAVING PUT ON THE BREASTPLATE OF RIGHTEOUSNESS, and having shod YOUR FEET WITH THE PREPARATION OF THE GOSPEL OF PEACE; in addition to all, taking up the shield of faith with which you will be able to extinguish all the flaming missiles of the evil one. And take THE HELMET OF SALVATION, and the sword of the Spirit, which is the word of God. With all prayer and petition pray at all times in the Spirit, and with this in view, be on the alert with all perseverance and petition for all the saints, and pray on my behalf, that utterance may be given to me in the opening of my mouth, to make known with boldness the mystery of the gospel, for which I am an ambassador in chains; that in proclaiming it I may speak boldly, as I ought to speak."

The Bible teaches about spiritual warfare. We do not have to go anywhere to be on the front lines, and we do not need to provoke to start the violence of this war, for Satan has gone off to make war against us. The violence is all around us, and we are on the front lines in one way or form or another. This war is present. This war is raging on around us, and against each of us, all the time. And our effectiveness as Christians in reaching the lost, as the church, is in many ways dependent on our effectiveness in becoming spiritual warriors whom practice Biblical spiritual warfare under the Warrior who is our Savior and King, Jesus the Christ.

Please see the resources section for more educational information and testimonies to study on this topic, that is so essential for the church, of spiritual warfare and deliverance ministry.

Appendix - Resources:

<u>Books</u>

The Holy Bible, by God the Father, God's Son Jesus the Christ, and the Holy Spirit hardcopy available free at FreeBibles.net or read free online at biblegateway.com, free concordances and studies at searchgodsword.org and blueletterbible.org

Come Sail Away, UFO Phenomenon and the Bible, Guy Malone seekye1.com

Case Files of an Internet Exorcist, by Pastor Chris Ward at www.logoschristian.org/exorcist/

Unholy Communion: The Unwanted Piece of the UFO Puzzle, by Joe Jordan and Dave Ruffino at www.ce4research.com

Blood on the Doorpost by Bill & Sharon Schnoebelen at Withoneaccord.org

Pigs in the Parlor, by Frank Hammond,
Deliverance Workers Manual, by Frank Marzullo

SPIRITUAL WARFARE : Defeating the forces of darkness,
by Dr. Preston Bailey Jr.

Betrayed by Her Guardian Angel, Demonic Spirits and You,
by Stacie Spielman http://www.articlesandbooks.com

Alien Intrusion UFOs and the Evolution Connection, by creationist Gary Bates of Creation Ministries International at www.alienintrusion.com

UFO cults and the New Millenium, by William Alnor, Phd.

The Facade, by Michael S Heiser at www.facadethebook.com/

Also StopAlienAbduction.com and the World Alien Resistance Network

<u>Websites</u>

http://www.alienresistance.com... Combined work of Guy Malone, Pastor Chris Ward, and Joe Jordan

http://www.ce4research.com.. Joe Jordan

http://www.logoschristian.org... Pastor Chris Ward

AncientOfDays.net. – DVDs, Ancient of Days Biblical Ufology Conferences

http://www.michaelsheiser.com.... Michael Heiser, Phd.

http://www.mt.net/~watcher/ufos.html... David and Brenda Flynn http://www.stevequayle.com/index1.html.... Steve Quayle

http://www.withoneaccord.org... Bill and Sharon Schnoebelen

www.drdino.com... Kent & Eric Hovind of Creation Science Evangelism

http://www.creation.com... Website of Creation Ministries International

my websites www.paradoxbrown.com, walkintruth.net

Videos

On UFOs, "aliens", and spiritual warfare: www.ChristianSymposium.com

http://www.ancientofdays.net... DVDs of the Ancient of Days Biblical Ufology Conferences, best in Secular and Christian researchers

http://www.UFOs101.com... Introductory DVD to UFO/alien topic

http://www.alienresistance.org... DVDs of Pastor Chris Ward, Joe Jordan, and Guy Malone, and others (On these 3 sites, DVDs are available on a name-your-own-price donations basis)

View some free online at http://www.myspace.com/ufosbible

myspace.com/ufosthehiddentruth, myspace.com/deep_mindquest, .myspace.com/newagevsthetruth; interesting webpages by Deep Mindquest

On creationism, free online downloads of Hovind lectures:
drdino.com/downloads.php,
also see http://www.creation.com for lots of info

Counseling/Deliverance

Joe Jordan of CE4 Research - www.ce4research.com

Alien Resistance Counselors - AlienResistance.com

Bill & Sharon Schnoebelen - www.withoneaccord.org

Logos Christian Fellowship Deliverance Team - www.logoschristian.org

Mitsi Burton of The Way of Jesus Christ Ministries - JesusTheDeliverer.org

Other: www.freestickers.net... for free anti-alien stickers

NOTE: I typically do not necessarily completely 100% agree with the majority of the resources listed above on every single point they present. No one is perfect but Jesus the Christ, and we all do tend to get a few things wrong. But I include them because they are generally good resources that do contain a lot of good educational and informational material and/or are potentially helpful and beneficial to those that need help.

About the Author/Testimony

Hello reader,

My writing name is Paradox Brown.

Sparing you many of the details of my life, I'll just cover the points pertinent to this book, and it's writing.

When I was a child I had fallen angel apparition experiences including a "ghost" and an "alien". The "alien" I saw when I was 5, in my parents bedroom, in the daytime. There was nothing dreamlike about these experiences. The "ghost" thing I saw when I was 6, and I had recently gained a belief in Christianity. I prayed to God to make it go away, and when I opened my eyes, it was gone.

There were some rather sharp turns in the following years. By the age of 9, I had become an atheist. At the age of 15 I had many fallen angel apparition experiences. These started happening when I started dating a polytheist, from a long line of polytheists, and met a friend of his who was also a polytheist and practiced sorcery. You may remember from Chapter 8 that I contend that angels (Holy or fallen) can create entire "holodeck"-like vision experiences, which we experience as real. While I do see this in the Bible, my reason for being able to see this so easily Biblically – whereas others may not - is that I know so from personal experience. My apparition experiences included a complete replica of a school I was attending, and replicas of many real human people who were my friends - only some of the replicas were slightly different than the real people. There was nothing dreamlike about these experiences, and they felt entirely real.

Generally, these fallen angel apparitions were intelligently designed to attack my sanity, and to push me to arrive at the conclusion that I was somehow switching back and forth between two almost identical parallel universes. Being rather into science fiction, this was an idea I was familiar with. I had become a sort of Taoist and pantheist by then. I believed in an infinite number of different parallel universes, and believed that in a way, I was god, and everything else, living or nonliving, was also god. I also believed in evolution, and that all the different parallel universes were alive and evolving into a meta-macrocosmic utopia. My mind had become rather broken, and it wasn't until I was in my 20th year that God started to heal me of this brokenness. Thank God!

When I was 19 years old, I decided to meditate one day. And I believed that all religions were true somehow or somewhere. And I decided that day to randomly focus on Jesus, and I remembered how I had felt as a little child, when I believed in Jesus Christ. And I tried to imagine the faith and peace in knowing I was safe in Jesus Christ. And I focused on believing in Jesus, that He was real, and true. And I fell asleep with a deep sense of peace.

While I was sleeping, I had a dream. Or rather, a dream was given to me. In the dream I was shown that I would be in a car wreck, with a sibling, in a gray car, with seatbelts that hooked onto the doors, and I was shown the location of this wreck, midway between two cities I knew, and that I would break my ankle. But my sibling and I would not die. In the dream I cried out, "Oh Please God!?" and God saved us. And I was also shown that the man I was in a relationship with at the time would not come see me at the hospital after the car wreck.

And when I woke up I immediately told this entire dream to that man, and how it didn't feel like a normal dream. And I said something to him about how I felt that he and I should repent and become Christians, though I didn't understand it or why I was saying it. Neither of us did, and I soon forgot about the whole thing.

Just about a year later all of things I saw in the dream came to pass. One odd thing was that the car I was in I did not own when I had the dream, and had never seen before, but had later acquired under strange circumstances. To the smallest detail, this dream came true. I cried out "Oh Please God!?" right before we hit the first time, and the Lord God saved us both from dying in that car wreck. Praise the Lord God and the Lord Jesus Christ! Even the police on the scene said it was a miracle that we didn't die, let alone that we both climbed out of the car and walked away. (And that was when I realized I had the broken ankle.) I came to remember this dream later, and the man who was with me when I had it verified to me, that yes, I had truly had this dream and told him about it. And he and I were both in shock about it, and what it meant.

During that time, I was in the middle of a process of remembering many things I had forgotten, about my experiences when I was 15, and some things from when I was younger. Though I was making some progress, I had not turned to Jesus Christ. And I was in a very, very, very dark and confused place. God had started healing my mind, and it was already mostly whole again, in my memories of what had happened to me, but until I turned to

Him I remained very confused.

A local prayer group that met at a Starbucks (Thank you again!) started praying for me to be saved. And shortly after, I was laying in bed one day, and realized there was a voice in my head, which wasn't me. So I asked it's name. And it replied, to my astonishment because I thought surely I was imagining things, "Mashaal". Well, I immediately had the revelation that it was a demon, and got very frightened that I was going to Hell. And I prayed to Jesus for Him to come into my heart and be my Lord and Savior. And I prayed for God to make the demon go away. And immediately there was this warm feeling of peace, and my head got all quiet... I realized then that my mind had been full of this static white background noise for a while, and it was suddenly gone- I had gotten so used to it that I didn't even realize it was there until it was gone. And I thanked God and Jesus for making it leave. But all the while I was questioning if this was really happening. Soon after, I rushed down to the computer and looked up the word "Mashaal". I think in Hindu, in some language, it means "torches"... which fits with one of the names for Satan, the "torchbearer". That was all I could find on it.

I soon called a local pastor I didn't know which I found in the phone book, the local First Baptist church, and told him what had happened. And he told me that the angels in heaven were rejoicing that I had asked Jesus to save me, that Jesus had saved me, and that now I belonged to Jesus and was saved. He told me the Holy angels were having a big party just because I had been saved, and I was in wonderment.

From that point on I started reading the Bible, setting myself to read the whole book. I also started going to church every week. And I began asking God, and God began teaching me, about my own life and what had happened to me, all the things I did not understand. I wanted to understand all these things that had happened to me, which I didn't understand, these paranormal or supernatural things. I came to realize immediately Satan had somehow caused the experiences when I was 15. And I came to understand that the "alien" I saw as a child was also from Satan. Over the next few years I came to understand the differences between fallen angels and demons better, and even that there was a difference between the two was the first big step. I stopped believing there were any parallel universes, and came to realize the experiences that had fractured my mind at 15 were attacks by Satanic entities. I called them demons then, now I would call them fallen angels. Also, during this time, my entire morality changed, as Jesus changed me.

I also stopped believing in evolution within a period of about 2 weeks, when God gave me another dream. A Holy angel of the Lord God appeared to me in the dream, and showed me the book of Genesis, played out like a movie, all the way to about Abraham. The point of the dream was "The book of Genesis is true." The Holy angel of the Lord asked me if I understood these things I had seen… and at the time I did not want him to leave but to stay, and so I hesitated and thought of lying and saying I had not understood something. But before I could say a thing, the angel looked at me with eyes that were blazing like fire in how they felt (though not visually on fire) as he looked at me… and I realized he could read my mind, and was in my mind, in a dream, and I said, "Yes." Then there seemed to be some communication between the Holy Angel and I think God the Holy Spirit, that I would not remember the details of the dream. Then I felt horribly sorry that I had hesitated, and was very scared, and was very distressed. And then I felt Jesus was there, and this supernatural feeling of peace and love that I could physically feel (in that place between asleep and awake) enveloped me, and I knew everything was ok. And when I was totally calm and not distressed anymore, and totally at peace and knowing He loved me, and wasn't scared of Him leaving but He knew I was ok with it, then the feeling calmed. And then I woke up, and I was very much at peace and happy. I still don't remember the details of the dream, but within 2 weeks I went from being an evolutionist to being a young earth creationist, just from reading through Genesis and knowing "The book of Genesis is true."

It wasn't long after this that I started trying to read and understand the book of Revelation. (I was starting to get the idea that I might have the gift of prophecy and I figured Revelation was prophecy, so I guess I was drawn to reading and studying it.) I asked and received a strong confirmation from the Holy Spirit that the "alien" I saw as a kid fit into the Bible at the "3 evil spirit like frogs… spirits of demons" verse in Revelation. And I subsequently have put a lot of time into trying to understand this, and the book of Revelation in general.

Over the next several years many things in my life changed…turned upside-down really. When a person becomes Christian, his or her life doesn't just become perfect… but there is a newfound strength in God and Jesus, strength from God and Jesus, that makes everything better than it ever was before. When I fall, the Lord is there to help me with the pain and to pick me up again. Thank the Lord and Bless the Lord!

One thing that happened was I eventually came to remember a few "alien abduction" experiences, which had happened recently, after I had become Christian. I realized these things were ongoing, and remembered the painful incident with some "grays". I got in contact with the folks at Alien Resistance, a Christian ministry specifically dealing with spiritual warfare, especially of "alien abductions." I looked at their writings and talked to some of them. The next time fallen angels tried to abduct me, and I could tell something was starting to happen, I followed the spiritual warfare methods I had come to know from the people at Alien Resistance, and I called out for Jesus Christ to rebuke the evil which was starting to attack me. And it left. By the power and authority and name of Jesus the Christ it left! I haven't been "abducted by aliens" since. Praise the Lord!

I had felt for a few years that I had some things to say on this spiritual warfare topic, having what I thought were some original thoughts on the subject. And I started writing this, my first book, to tell my ideas and what insight I believe God has given me. I feel it is important for Christians to better understand these topics. And having children, for their sake, and for the sake of all children, I think the Christian church needs to be better informed and prepared on these spiritual warfare issues. I don't want to see what happened to me as a child happen to any more children, and this book is my effort to help God change that. My most important prayer remains that God will bring my children to choose salvation in the Lord Jesus Christ, and that they will become Christian, and be saved. But second to this, I also pray He will break any curses that could potentially be passed on to them, and that He will keep them safe and protect them from demons and fallen angels, and the havoc they can wreak in a life.

And so I try to continue my growth as a Christian, and I don't know where all God is going to lead me, but I am thankful for God's blessings and that God has done so much to help me in so many ways, change me, heal me, teach me, and put some wonderful people into my life.

In the service of the Lord Jesus the Christ,

Paradox Brown

LaVergne, TN USA
10 May 2010
182204LV00009B/59/P